THE HOUSE
OF SECRETS

The Hidden World of the Mikveh

VARDA POLAK-SAHM

*Translated from the Hebrew
by Anne Hartstein Pace*

BEACON PRESS
Boston

Beacon Press
25 Beacon Street
Boston, Massachusetts 02108-2892
www.beacon.org

Beacon Press books
are published under the auspices of
the Unitarian Universalist Association of Congregations.

12 11 10 09   8 7 6 5 4 3 2 1

This book is printed on acid-free paper that meets the uncoated paper
ANSI/NISO specifications for permanence as revised in 1992.

Translated from the Hebrew by Anne Hartstein Pace

Text design and composition by Wilsted & Taylor Publishing Services

Library of Congress Cataloging-in-Publication Data
Polak-Sahm, Varda.
    [Bet ha-setarim. English]
    The house of secrets : the hidden world of the mikveh / Varda Polak-
Sahm ; translated from the Hebrew by Anne Hartstein Pace.
        p. cm.
    Includes bibliographical references and index.
    ISBN-13: 978-0-8070-7742-9 (hardcover : alk. paper)
    1. Mikveh. 2. Jewish women—Religious life. 3. Purity, Ritual—Judaism.
I. Title.
    BM703.P6513 2009
    296.7'5—dc22   2008053967

To my daughter,
Elinor Tzlil,
with much love

Author's Note

In Judaism, a *mikveh* is a bath designed for the purpose of ritual immersion. The word "mikveh," as used in the Hebrew Bible, literally means a "collection"—generally, a collection of water.

This book is based on ten years of research in various mikvehs in Israel. The dialogue that appears in these pages comes from conversations I had with women in the central mikveh portrayed—both women who worked there and women who came to the mikveh for immersions and ceremonies. Most of these conversations I tape-recorded directly. In several instances, conversations were recorded by the women outside my presence, for the sake of privacy.

To protect the identities of the interviewees, their names have been changed and identifying features of some locations have been altered.

Contents

Prologue

"You have to be a virgin when you get married, otherwise, when you enter the waters of the mikveh, these bubbles will come out of that hole in your body—you see it? *Nu*, come on, stop giggling . . . there, under where the pee-pee comes out? —and they'll make this *ploop ploop ploop* sound and everyone will know that you're not a virgin and it's a terrible disgrace! And God will punish you for it too, with a terrible punishment!" So my two childhood playmates, Big Aliza and Little Aliza, had sternly warned me one afternoon as we huddled together in the corner of the enclosed balcony of my family's apartment. We were squatting, our heads tucked deep between our legs, our hands clutching small round mirrors in brightly colored plastic frames as we strained to catch a glimpse of our girlish private parts, which as yet had no need for the blanket that the Creator had covered Adam and Eve's nakedness with when, mouths full of forbidden fruit, they were suddenly mortified to find themselves in that condition. Thereafter, God imparted a veil of hair to human genitalia maturing to a ripe and fruitful state, forever embedding the sinners' iniquity in the body's memory.

I was led to the mikveh on the eve of my first wedding, in August 1973, by a small procession of women: my mother, two aunts, two close girlfriends, and the groom's sister and mother.

I was not a virgin. Worse, I was in the early stages of pregnancy. No one had told me what sound a twelve-week-old fetus might make in the waters of the mikveh.

We traveled on foot. I climbed the steep route that rose

directly from my house, which sat at the bottom of a narrow road, to the gates of the mikveh. The path was straight and sharp, like the white arrow on a one-way street sign, warning that should one turn tail and run in the opposite direction, punishment would follow. And punishment in this case would be meted out to the rebellious female not by a traffic cop, but by the All-Knowing One who sits on high.

Now the all-knowing voices of my little friends from long ago rose to a terrifying crescendo in my mind. Here it was—the awful, dreaded moment had arrived—and just as the two of them had described, the waters of the mikveh would give away the secret of my body, which had had sexual relations in love but in sin, without a proper Jewish wedding ceremony. Even more frightening, the waters might betray the sound of my precious baby, the fruit of my sincere desire and pure love for a man; they might reveal to one and all, too soon, the existence of the tiny precious soul inside me, which was peacefully reveling in the warmth of my womb, safe from harm, afloat in protective amniotic fluid. *Ploop ploop ploop,* the Alizas' girlish voices pounded in my ears. *Ploop ploop ploop,* they chirped in a teasing duet.

Stop!! I pleaded silently, my eyes shut tight as my knees wobbled and my body broke out in a sweat. But the Alizas ignored me. Their giggly voices only became more shrill and insistent.

"Enough!" I yelled out loud. "Enough!!"

"Huh? What 'enough'? You have to get undressed!" my mother scolded me in her soft baritone.

I closed my mouth, and when I opened my eyes I found myself kneeling by the edge of an enormous round pool like in an ancient Roman bath, with naked women ascending and descending into the water like the angels on Jacob's ladder. I wrapped my arms around my waist, holding the long white bathrobe I wore tightly against my sides.

"Take off the robe already. Look, no one else here is making any fuss. What do you have that they don't? Just what treasure do you think you're hiding?"

I have a child inside me, Mother, I said to myself as I kept my expression blank.

"What are you being so shy for? People will think you have some defect. Come on, take off the robe," urged my mother, pulling me to my feet. She, too, was noticeably ill at ease in these surreal surroundings, and her efforts to disguise her discomfort and impatience beneath a gentle tone were steadily failing.

I was entirely naked under the robe. Naked and warm as the day I was born. My wet hair was wrapped up in a white towel that wound around my head like the turban of a noble maharajah.

I loosened my grip and the white velvet robe fell in soft folds at my feet. I kept my eyes fixed on my bare toes, feeling the sharp barbs of dozens of eyes pricking me all over, like the thousands of slender arrows that pierced the tortured body of Saint Sebastian.

I was a beautiful young woman. My body, long and tall, moved with a fluid grace. My abdomen, in the first months of pregnancy, still sloped gently inward, as if collaborating in the effort to keep me from becoming a hot topic of gossip. Up until this moment, my body had kept my secret, our secret. But what would the waters do? Would they give us away? Or would they defy their nature and muffle the *ploop ploop ploop* sound that my young friends had assured me would be created, passing through a torn hymen? *Please, God,* I pleaded, as always in times of distress, directly and without any mediator, *Please make the waters keep quiet. Please. Help me. Keep my secret. And don't let me drown here either! Oh God! Help!!*

A large, heavy hand landed on my back. A hefty bosom pressed against my shoulder. When I turned around to protest this intrusion, I was enveloped by an amply built woman, a white kerchief on her head, the trace of a dark mustache on her upper lip. She took my hand and said firmly, "Don't be afraid. I'll take care of you." All at once, the voices of the Alizas faded and my trembling and anxieties subsided. The big woman cupped her hand around mine and led me, as if in a baroque minuet, to the steps leading down into the pool. I dipped my head below the greenish water once, twice, three times, and when I emerged from the pool, my mother broke over my head the ring-shaped cake she'd baked that morning and stuffed a piece of it into my mouth. Then my aunts broke into a joyful trilling—*Kulululululu!*—tossed colorful candies at me, tapped big tambourines and circled around me, swaying their hips in an Arab-style belly dance and singing the traditional song sung by Sephardi women, in our language, Ladino, to the innocent and pure virgin bride after she has immersed in the mikveh and is ready for her first experience of sexual intercourse.

Pur akeyas ventanikas m'aronjan flechas
Si son de amores vengan derechas

From those windows rolling pins are tossed on me
If they come from love they come straight*

And thus ended my first baptism of fire in the mikveh.

Twelve years later, on the eve of my second wedding, in October 1985, I returned to the same mikveh, again making my way on foot. When three stars shone in the sky, I set out from my new home on a fashionable dead-end street, within spitting distance of the modest neighborhood of my childhood. I climbed up the narrow path leading to the mikveh, toting a huge cloth bag packed with a robe, two soft towels, and all

---

*A discussion of these lyrics appears in chapter 6.

the hygienic accessories without which my cleansing would not pass muster. I was all alone this time. I'd left my mother, my aunts, and my old friends behind, because I would have felt ridiculous—now in my thirties and the mother of a son almost old enough for a bar mitzvah*—marching into the mikveh like a blushing first-time bride.

Entering the mikveh, I was greeted by three women whose body language and whispering tone put me in mind of the three witches from *Macbeth*. "Is the bride an orphan?" they asked in a soft choir as they circled me once, twice, and a third time. "No, the bride is a grown-up," I answered cynically. They completed the fourth circuit and stopped. They looked at one another with lowered glances and murmured: "Only an orphan, may Hashem† protect us from such a fate, comes here all alone on the eve of her wedding." They looked at me again and resolutely began the fifth circuit, clucking their tongues in pace with their step, muttering, "Tsk tsk tsk, it's no good, no no. It's no good for the bride to be alone."

On the sixth time around, their steady gait suddenly evolved into a kind of dance. "Well then, it is our duty to make the bride happy." They bounced around me to a *debka*§ rhythm, loudly stamping their heels on the floor, left, right, left, right. "We must cheer the bride." Their grating voices reverberated in my ears.

Suddenly I was seized with anxiety. My heart raced and I wanted to find the door and run away. As if reading my thoughts, the women abruptly came to a halt and arranged themselves before me in a straight row, forming a wall that

---

*The coming-of-age ceremony for a Jewish boy who has reached the age of thirteen; a Jewish girl becomes a bat mitzvah at age twelve.

†Hashem – literally, "The Name" in Hebrew; used by religious Jews to refer to God.

§*debka* – a traditional Arab dance.

blocked my exit. "Everything will be all right," they said, rubbing their hands together and setting to work. The eldest woman, whom I later learned was head *balanit,** stepped forward until her nose was just inches from mine and began peppering me with questions.

"Did you inspect your body?" she demanded, her blue-green eyes coming even closer as I felt my face go ashen with terror.

"You're asking if I did the purity examination to make sure that I'm clean of all bleeding whatsoever?" I replied with some boldness, though I still avoided looking her in the eye.

"Indeed."

"Well," I said, my gaze meeting her double chin, "yes, certainly." I silently repeated to myself: *You have nothing to be afraid of. You'll get through this part okay.* But logic cannot dissolve raw fear, and so there I stood, a woman of thirty-two with a good deal of life experience, quaking inside nonetheless.

I informed her of when I had my last period. I said that it lasted five days. I assured her that on the fifth day after my period began, when I felt that no more blood was coming out of the womb, or "the source" (*makor* in Hebrew) in the language of the halakha,‡ and that when I checked and the tampon I inserted indeed came out clean, I performed the examination to verify that menstruation had ceased (*hefsek tahara*), with all due meticulousness.[1]

"What exactly did you do?" she grilled me further.

I described in minute detail all the actions that I had supposedly performed, word for word as written in the instructional pamphlet *Bat Yisrael: Ma Alayikh Lada'at Bevoekh Lamikveh (Daughter of Israel: What You Must Know When*

---

*balanit – term for a woman who presides over ritual immersions in the mikveh (pl. *balaniyot*).

‡halakha – Jewish law (pl. *halakhot*).

Coming to the Mikveh), which I'd received for free at the rabbinate's marriage-registration office. I told her how after I carefully washed all the intimate areas of my body, I'd put one leg up on the toilet seat and inserted my finger, wrapped in a white square cloth, as deep as it could go inside my vagina, turning it around carefully while relaxing the cervix, then pulled it out, inspected it carefully, and found the cloth to be completely clean.

A "pure witness" (*ed tzach*) is what they call this piece of fabric. My friend Noa, who'd recently married a religious man and begun scrupulously observing the family purity laws, had shown me one. Reverently, she'd extracted a cloth from a white plastic bag with the following label:

TIDY PADS
EXAMINATION WITNESSES
SOFT AND HYGIENIC, 100% COTTON

To my amazement, the bag also contained this instruction: "In case of uncertainty and the need to ask a rabbi, keep the witness and do not stretch it out." This was followed by a partial list of recognized rabbinic authorities to whom the used cloth could be shown.*

The witness was gleaming white, soft and pleasing to the touch. Its border was sewn in a gentle zigzag to keep the threads from unraveling. A slender tail extended from one side; like the string of a tampon, it could be used to pull the cloth from the vagina—the "corridor" (*prozdor*) in the language of the Jewish sages. The white cloths are called pure witnesses because they testify to the fact that seven days after the menstrual flow has ceased, their pure bodies have

---

*According to Jewish law, a woman who finds a stain in her underwear must bring the garment to a rabbi, who will determine whether or not it precludes her from immersing.

not absorbed any discharge of any color from the woman's womb.[2]

"When did you insert the witness into your body?"

"On the fifth day, in the afternoon, before sunset. Sunset comes about eighteen minutes after Shabbat candle-lighting time for that week. After I pulled it out and checked that the witness was clean, just to be completely sure, I also inserted a *mokh dahuk* [literally, "tightly packed wadding"; another piece of cloth, perhaps a tampon] and left it inside me until nightfall, what you call *tzet hakokhavim,* when stars are visible."

"A mokh dahuk that has remained for at least a half hour and at most several hours within the vaginal canal and comes out clean confirms beyond all doubt the cleanliness of the body and the validity of the examination," Noa had explained to me. The mokh can be a pure witness or another cloth, one made of tricot, for example, as long as it is soft and absorbent. But not cotton wool, because this may contain tiny red specks that can be mistaken for spots of blood and distort the results of the inspection. The purpose of the mokh dahuk is to absorb all remnants of congealed blood, any fibers and threads contaminated with blood that may have gotten caught among the folds of the vaginal canal. When left inside the vagina for some time, the mokh reaches all those tiny crannies that the pure witness is unable to reach. "If you don't insert a mokh dahuk, there's a danger that the next morning, when you do the purity examination, the witness will come out stained, and then you won't know if the source of the staining is the leftover blood that was caught in the folds of the vagina, which does not make you ritually impure, or whether it comes from the source, from the womb, and does cause impurity," Noa said. She had taught me with admirable patience.

"After I pulled out the mokh dahuk," I continued, "I put

it aside and inspected it the next morning in the light of day. It was as white as snow."

"And seven clean days?" my interrogator pressed.

"Yes, certainly," I answered her, my mind reeling at the idea that Noa and all religious women actually do this bloody calculation month in and month out, performing all these revolting procedures that are elaborated upon in the guides to family purity and the books of sacred laws. "Yes, every day I inserted the pure witness. Twice a day I checked. At sunset and in the morning light. I assure you, there was not a single stain of an impure color. No red stain like blood or like the color of crocus or muddied earth or diluted wine, and no black stain, heaven forbid, or any other discharge that would affect the fitness of my body for immersion."[3] As I went through this recitation, my mind was flooded with awful images, and I envisioned myself sinking in the mikveh waters as stains of deep red, black, brown, and every shade of purple emerged one after the other from my "source" and floated up to cover the entire surface, exposing my learned lies about the purity examination, the *hefsek tahara,* which I had never performed. I felt the blood drain from my face as I broke out in a cold sweat, but the balanit believed what she heard and paid no heed to my expression.

Satisfied by my precise answers, she handed me over into the care of the two assistants who had been standing perfectly still nearby this whole time. Each was covered from the neck down in layer upon layer of multihued clothing. Now they came toward me in a fast-swirling kaleidoscope, like two brightly crested cocks flapping their feathers in readiness for battle over a female.

"Have you gone to the bathroom?" they asked in unison.

I was taken aback. Noa hadn't prepared me for this.

"Yes, not long ago," I ad-libbed.

"Excellent, because even if it doesn't really count as a barrier [*hatzitza*], a woman who is holding it in might not immerse properly, heaven forbid. Number one or also number two?"

"Both," I said, playing it safe.

"Did you wipe well?"

"I think so," I replied, blushing in embarrassment. The last time I'd answered such a question was when I was five years old, in kindergarten.

"Because you know that feces in the anus forms a barrier during the immersion and a woman cannot say the blessing on the immersion or any other blessing in such a state."[4]

"I know," I said, barely able to contain myself. These women have no shame. Or to be more accurate, the men who made these laws have no shame, the way they freely trespass over all boundaries of the body, and of the soul too.

"Excellent," they said, then signaled to one another with their eyes and commenced a fast, rhythmic duet, hardly pausing for breath: "In order to be clean and one hundred percent kosher for immersion, you must remove all jewelry, false teeth, and contact lenses before bathing. Remove all eye makeup and fingernail polish. Wash your hair and comb it, but don't use a brush, to avoid hairs being pulled out and sticking to your body. Clean the gunk out of the corners of your eyes. Clean your nose inside and out. Clean the ears inside and in the folds and in back. Clean the holes of your pierced ears. Clean your teeth with a toothbrush and toothpaste. Use a toothpick on the spaces in between. Clean your nipples and belly button well. Either wash well or shave the hair in your armpits and your pubic hair. Clip your fingernails and toenails. Clean between the fingers. Wash your entire body very well. Comb every hair on your body. Check again to make sure nothing is left on your body. And"—their voices rose ever higher, like a crazed sports announcer moments before the ecstatic cry of "Goal!!!"—"when you're ready, press here. Ring the bell and we'll come right away. All clear?" They took a deep breath. Thrust some Q-tips and a sponge and a bar of soap into my hands. Led me into a room. Wished me luck. Went out and shut the door behind them.

I was left alone. A shaft of moonlight shone through the tiny square window near the ceiling, merging with the glare of the bare bulb that hung from a wire in the center of the room. I smiled as the moon's silvery ambassador nuzzled against the artificial yellow light. I followed its virtuosic dance, the refracted rays scattering into thousands of slivers of light that painted the room's damp, pale green-tiled walls in a rainbow of colors. The only things in the room were a shower and a pit of water. The pit was deep, still, and menacing, and like a grave dug seven cubits into the earth, it seemed like it might suck in my naked body. Now completely nude, I warily crowded into the square space of the shower, or the "douche," as the *balaniyot* called it. The douche sprayed water with a force mightier than I'd ever experienced, as if engineered to blast off every speck of dirt, no matter how tenaciously it clung to the skin. I washed my body thoroughly, as instructed. I poured a generous amount of shampoo over my long tresses and worked it up into a growing lather, so that any lurking dirt and grease was dissolved and washed away. I plunged all ten fingers down to the roots of my hair and massaged my scalp. I rinsed well, then combed out my hair as per the balaniyot's orders, without applying any conditioner or gel, to minimize the danger that even a single hair would slip from my head to my back and disqualify the immersion. I scrubbed my skin with a braided loofah sponge until its hue went from milky white to boiled-lobster red. I inserted my fingers in every space and orifice from my toes to the top of my head. Every opening, big or small, received a thorough treatment that began with probing and cleansing and ended with rinsing.

When I'd finished cleaning myself I stood for a long while under the douche's powerful stream, eyes closed and muscles relaxed, letting the water's marvelous warmth caress and wash over me and soothe away the agitation of the cleaning inquisition I'd just been through in preparation for my wedding. When I felt mentally ready, I rang the little bell in the wall. The head balanit and her two assistants entered. The head balanit examined my body from top to bottom, while asking in a lilting but nasal voice: "Did you inspect your head? That is, you washed your hair? Your ears? Your eyes? You did? Brushed your teeth? Cleaned between the teeth?" With no hesitation whatsoever she tugged on my teeth to make sure they were permanent, since dentures would form a barrier between the body and the water and nullify the immersion. She barely refrained from thrusting her pinky in my ear to ensure that no bits of wax were stuck to the sides. She poked a finger in my belly button and said, "You know that you have to be really pure." She ran her hand down my back from the neck to the tailbone, to ascertain that I was free of any stray strand of hair, of any blemish.

When she finished, she led me down the steps to the square pit of water. I descended into the pit. The water came up to my breasts. In a soft voice, the balanit instructed me to spread my arms to the sides and splay my fingers as wide as possible. She placed her hand on my head, asked me to hold my breath, and in one swift motion pushed me firmly into the water. I sank down in a frog position and remained that way for a few seconds, which felt like a thousand years. Short of breath, I emerged from the pit and called out: "Blessed are you, O Lord our God, King of the Universe, who has sanctified us with his commandments and commanded us on immersion," reading from a laminated sheet that was affixed to the pale green wall. The balanit put a towel on my head and cried: "*Kasher! Kasher! Kasher!*" And thus I became permitted to my husband-to-be.

Two very intimate moments in a Jew's lifetime are the moment of birth and the moment of death. In both, the body is handled by strangers never seen before and never to be seen again. At birth, the baby is caught by the hands of the midwife, a total stranger the child most likely will never see again. At death, the body is handled by the people of the Hevra Kadisha burial society, the purifiers of the dead, who almost certainly did not know the person in life and surely will not have that privilege after the body has been put in the grave.

A third such moment, for me, was the moment of immersion in the mikveh. The descent into the pit of water, where my body sank with limbs splayed, and the ascent from the depths to the air of the world, wet and naked as the day I was born—seemed to me like death and rebirth.

I arose from the pit of water straight into the arms of the assistants, who wrapped me in a thick, white towel known in Hebrew as a *balnit*.*

The three women pushed a *dragée*, an almond coated with pink sugar, into my mouth, and immediately began toweling my body with surprising warmth and gentleness, as if I was their beloved baby, all the while humming Hasidic-sounding tunes. I shut off all my critical mechanisms and surrendered entirely to the pleasure of it. A supreme physical pleasure. My nude body, soft and relaxed after the blanching in the boiling hot shower, was placed in the hands of the three mothers, who, like three bacchantes in a Dionysian orgy, energetically massaged and kneaded my flesh with skilled hands, stimulating all my five senses to the edges of their nerve endings. The sweet taste of the candy; the fragrant scent of the soaps; the touch of the women's hands rubbing my body; the dense, white cloud of vapors; and the soft, monotonous, and hypnotic singing—all whirled together and suffused the room with the feel of an ancient female ritual. Out of the amalgam of the five senses a sixth was born: I was flooded with an

---

*balnit – possibly the source of the word *balanit*.

elemental emotion so stunning in its intensity, so acute, it was as if every fiber of my being was stirring wondrously to life.

This experience stood in stark contrast to the personal and cultural baggage with which I'd entered. I'd thought of the mikveh as a repellent and dirty place where numerous women immerse in the same pool of water, without the benefit of disinfectant. I'd inherited this idea from the Sephardi women of my family. Whenever I'd asked if they went to the mikveh, they wrinkled their noses in disgust and said, "Never! It's revolting! It's good for dirty Ashkenazi women who only bathe once a month." The female tradition in my family sanctified the immersion ceremony before one's wedding, and strictly upheld all the customs connected with the preparation of the bride for the wedding night, but it vigorously rejected the idea of monthly trips to the mikveh.

For me, the mikveh was also a symbol of religious coercion and the intrusion of the religious establishment into the private domain. As a secular person, I felt a deep ideological aversion; the entire marriage process, from registration to wedding canopy, seemed to be pervaded by religious coercion, beginning with the Chief Rabbinate's* dictation of the wedding date. At the marriage-registration office, I met the *rabbanit* (also known as a *rebbetzin,* the wife of a rabbi or, simply, a woman entrusted with the teaching of proper Jewish religious practice) for the first time. After locating my name on a long list, she fixed me with a cold gaze and a plastered-on yellow smile and asked: "When did you get your last period?" and "How many days does your vaginal bleeding usually last?" I was caught completely off-guard (apparently I'd totally repressed the memory of this experience from before my first marriage) and didn't know what to an-

---

*Israel's Chief Rabbinate is a government institution that oversees matters of personal status, such as marriage, divorce, and conversion, for the state's Jewish residents.

swer. As I stumbled through a mental calculation of possible dates, I was inundated by a further barrage of questions on intimate topics of the sort you only discuss with your closest girlfriends. A feeling of helplessness came over me. I feared that this stranger would schedule a different wedding date —determined solely by the timing of my bodily excretions— than the one my partner and I had already lovingly chosen. And indeed, once she'd extracted sufficient information to make her calculations, I learned that the date we'd had in mind was no longer an option.

About two weeks before the ceremony, I had to attend instruction for brides in the Jewish laws pertaining to married life. The rabbanit, a fleshy, red-faced woman with pale, watery eyes, began by describing a host of future disasters that were inevitable should we, as newlyweds, not observe the rules of family purity (*taharat hamishpaha*). Living in sin without immersion in the mikveh would bring upon us the punishment of *karet*: our children would be born with defects, would not be privileged to build a Jewish family, and would die an unnatural death, their souls permanently excommunicated from the Jewish people.

The rabbanit also foresaw all sorts of terrible afflictions that would strike us should we have sexual intercourse during our time of uncleanness. She went on to describe the relationship of the religious couple that observes the rules of family purity, likening it to one between two heavenly angels on earth. The husband is spiritual, refined, and considerate, and the wife is wholesome, delicate, and pampered. This couple lives in harmony, love, and mutual respect. In contrast, she sketched a grotesque portrait of the secular couple, depicting the husband as a crass military type who saunters home after having his way with a number of young female recruits. ("Everyone knows that the female soldiers are whores whose only job is to satisfy their commander's sexual urges," declared our instructor, oblivious to how she'd just equated all of us who'd served in the army with prostitutes.) The army man plops down on the sofa, puts his legs up on the table, turns on the television—that emblem of secular moral corruption—and hollers, "Bring me something to eat!" At night he comes to his wife for sex, whether she wants it or not, like a bull breeding with a cow. Building up to an ecstatic fervor, the rabbanit assured us secular women that unless we mended our ways, we'd end up either divorced or living in ongoing torment. At last her face relaxed into a blissful smile as she wiped a few beads of perspiration from her flushed forehead and concluded gruffly: "Go immerse in the mikveh, and, with Hashem's help, it will fill your lives with the pleasures of body and soul."

I was so angered and disgusted by her talk that I didn't want to go to the mikveh, but I had no choice if I wanted to obtain written confirmation for the presiding rabbi that I was thoroughly "kosher." Without it, there would be no wedding ceremony. The colossal dissonance between the negative emotions and prejudices with which I'd entered the mikveh and my overwhelming experience there became indelibly etched in my body's memory and embedded in my subconscious. The pleasure was indeed so powerful and intense, I felt like I was soaring ever higher until body and soul were perfectly intertwined; body and soul, I was drawn deep into the femininity and sensuality within me.

The intellect was stubbornly opposed, but the physical memory was unrelenting and continued to surface out of nowhere; it awakened in the depths of my womb and shot like a rocket into my consciousness, overtaking my dreams until I could no longer resist and returned, as if to the scene of the crime, to try to understand just what had happened to me in the mikveh.

THE PLACE

"Escorts are requested to remain at a distance from the entrance, for the sake of modesty": the large sign, appended to a high stone wall topped with barbed wire, stopped me in my tracks as I approached the rusty gate. I gazed toward the building that dwelled alone behind this wall, where rites of purity, sexuality, and fertility are performed by women and for women. Jewish women.

Three hundred and sixty-three days a year, the mikveh opens at sunset. It serves Jewish women who come to cleanse themselves of the impurity of their menstrual blood and ready themselves to have sexual relations with their husbands. Only on Yom Kippur* and the Ninth of Av,‡ days on which the halakha forbids a husband from having intercourse with his wife, is the mikveh closed. Upon emerging from the ritual bath, young women and not-so-young women hurry home to be with their husbands after two weeks of abstinence from physical contact.

A massive stone ramp, like the tongue protruding from the mouth of hell in the famous Pieter Bruegel painting *Dulle*

---

*The Day of Atonement, a day of fasting and prayer, one of the Jewish High Holy Days.

‡*Tisha B'Av* in Hebrew, a major fast day on the Jewish calendar commemorating the destruction of the First and Second Temples in Jerusalem and other tragedies that have befallen the Jews throughout history.

Griet (*Mad Meg*), accommodates the wheelchair-bound visitors to the mikveh. On either side of it, worn gray steps ascend steeply to a narrow landing.

As I stepped inside, lightly touching the mezuzah* attached to the door frame, a loud, clear voice greeted me: "Welcome!" When I turned toward the voice there she stood, as if it were just yesterday, the same head balanit. Her blue-green eyes peered intently at me from the heights of her tall, broad physique that made her seem a pillar of stability.

"Thank you," I replied with a rush of excitement. What I actually wanted to say was, *Do you remember me, the "orphan" from years ago?* Her face brightening as if she'd read my thoughts, she stepped toward me and, slowly spreading her massive hands, said with a sweet, musical intonation: "Please come in, come in, come in! Would you like a bath or a shower or just an immersion?"

"No . . . uh . . . That's not exactly . . . I mean, I . . . Yes, I am interested, but . . ." I didn't know what to say. What should I say? That the memory of an overwhelming sensory experience had impelled me to return to her? That an irresistible impulse had prompted me to investigate what had happened to me in this place, which had never happened to me anywhere else? If so, then why not immerse? Why not experience that same extraordinary pleasure once again? I wasn't completely clear on it myself at this point; how was I supposed to explain it to her? She'd probably think I was some sort of sick voyeur. "This time I didn't come here to immerse . . . I came to ask . . . to talk with you."

"With me?!" she roared, pulling on the kerchief that concealed every hair on her proud head. "Did you hear?!" She turned toward two women who'd been deep in quiet conver-

---

*A small ritual object marked with God's name on the outside and holding a parchment scroll inscribed with biblical passages (Deut. 6:4–9, 11:13–21) that is affixed to a door frame in accordance with Jewish law.

sation, sitting next to an old school desk upon which rested a receipt book and a small money box. Startled, they both quickly smoothed the folds of their faded dresses and adjusted their head coverings. "What's going on?" they asked. One of them I recognized from my first immersion. She was the one I remembered as the more pampering of the two assistants. Incredibly, despite all the years that had gone by, she looked almost exactly the same. "Why?" the head balanit asked as she thrust her head closer to me, her expression alight with curiosity and suspicion. "Are you from the newspapers or something? What's this all about? Has something happened?"

"No, no," I stuttered as I tried to find some way to answer her. Finally I blurted out the truth: "Look, I have this terrible curiosity. It's almost an obsession. I can't forget my immersion here. You supervised my immersion here about twelve years ago. You must not remember . . . So many women have been here since then. But I remember you . . . You're hard to forget. So I came especially to you . . . to ask . . . I feel drawn to this place in a peculiar way. I have to examine what happened to me. What goes on here. What the mikveh is all about. Will you be so kind as to let me come and ask questions and observe what you do here? I won't get in the way. I promise."

"Just a minute," the balanit said, shaking her head in annoyance. "I don't really understand what you want. Do you want to immerse or not?"

"No. I want to *know*."

For a fraction of a second it was as if all the planets screeched to a halt. Her blue-green eyes stared at me unblinking.

"All right." The world stirred back to life. "Sit down." She sighed expansively, pulled another chair up to the desk, and sat down beside me. "What do you want to know?"

"Tell me why you immerse in the mikveh."

She regarded me intently for a moment, and then she began to speak, her voice strong and confident. "Immersion in the mikveh is the original patent for preserving intimacy in marriage. A device invented by Hashem to keep up the love and passion between man and wife. Love—how many dreams have been woven around it? How many stories have been written about it? How many poems? But how hard it is to sustain. How hard it is to sustain love and intimacy in marriage over a long period of time. There's a saying that goes: 'Love and marriage are like a kettle that is put on the fire and taken off just when the water comes to a boil.' Meaning what? That when you get married, love blooms, it boils. Everything is afire, everything is at a peak. But unfortunately, afterwards, and it doesn't take long, the fire of love cools and gradually fades. This cooling and fading is very destructive to the relationship between husband and wife. And it also poses a great danger to the family as a whole. Hashem, who sanctifies marriage, knows that it must be preserved so that Jews will build good, stable homes, which together will build a strong and stable people. Knowing the vagaries of the human soul, Hashem concocted a magic formula which has been working for thousands of years and will never go out of date—immersion in the mikveh."

She went on to tell me about matchmaking, courtship, falling in love, and marriage. About impurity and purity and the sanctity of marital relations. She talked and talked, and it was a long time before she finally wearied. "Oy, the things I've said . . . I don't usually talk like this. I've said too much—" She broke off, glancing over my shoulder. "Hello," she said.

I turned to see a woman entering the mikveh. Her attire was breathtakingly skimpy, revealing much more than it covered. A pair of brown breasts seemed about to pop out of her tight-fitting red blouse. A bare midriff showed above swaying hips clad in a strip of red fabric no more than twenty centimeters wide. The red micro-mini gave way to a pair of long, long legs. The figure strode quickly toward the balaniyot's table. Each stiletto-heeled footstep reverberated loudly, amplified by the woman's towering height. I held my breath in anticipation, silently grateful for my good fortune in happening upon this absurd situation—a girl who appeared to have sashayed straight out of a cheap B movie mistakenly wandering into this domain of pious women. She approached the head balanit—whose name, I had learned during our conversation, was Miriam—pushed back a few strands of her bleached hair (the dark roots were showing) and said hello. I braced myself for the big explosion. To my astonishment, Miriam smiled warmly at her and, without batting an eyelid, asked in her friendly and professional tone: "Do you need a bath?"

"Yes, I need both," the woman answered softly.

"Both. Private or not?"

"Private."

"Q-tips?"

"Yes, everything, thanks."

"Come, please."

The woman was given a sponge, Q-tips for cleaning the ears, shampoo, soap, and a towel. She paid twenty-five shekels* for the immersion and another three shekels for the sponge and shampoo, gathered her things, and followed quickly after Miriam, who briskly crossed the vestibule toward the left-side corridor. The two women disappeared down the dimly lit hallway.

"She took Room 6," Miriam informed the other balaniyot when she returned. "She's new and she chose the most expensive option, a bath plus immersion in a private room. You see?" she explained to me. "The special design of this mikveh lets women choose between two options: immersion in a private room or in a common room—"

---

*At the time, the equivalent of approximately seven U.S. dollars.

"But Miriam!" I cried. "What's a girl like that doing here? I never would have expected to see a girl like her come in here . . . I'm just stunned . . . It's like a surreal scene out of an absurd play!"

She looked me up and down with the arrogant expression of a confident believer confronting a less fortunate soul, barely concealing her disdain. "Oh, we get many, many women like her here," she announced emphatically. "That's nothing! Especially now in the summer, you'll see how they look like this and that and this and that." As she spoke, she swiveled exaggeratedly, placing her hands on her thighs, her hips, her breasts, her waist, her behind. "Oh, they come, yes they do, and they keep on coming . . ." Now she lowered her voice and enunciated slowly and dramatically. "Oh, yes . . . they come . . ." And right on cue, another young woman walked in, dressed just as provocatively as the previous one, and then another and another, and they all disappeared down the corridor leading to Room 6.

"But they're completely secular! They're not brides and they still come here? For what? To immerse in the mikveh?!"

"Yes, yes, yes! Month in and month out, without fail. Every woman who understands the significance of it comes here. The mikveh is an integral part of the Jewish woman's life. It's the ABC of the Jews!" She pounded her fist on the table in her enthusiasm. "It's what sets us apart from all the other nations!"

"But if she's secular, it doesn't make sense."

"Wrong!"

"So how does it make sense?"

"A sin is a sin and a *mitzvah** is a mitzvah."

"I don't get it."

"Look, each person has two accounts in Hashem's bank, okay? In one there's a minus because of all his transgressions,

---

*A God-given commandment (pl. *mitzvot*).

and in the other there's a plus because of all the mitzvot he did. You see? It's simple. If she immerses in the mikveh and her husband doesn't touch her when she's forbidden to him, doesn't approach her and have relations with her when she's in *niddah*,* then she accumulates points in the mitzvah account. You understand?"

"But that means that her secular husband knows that he has to . . . on the day that she goes to the mikveh?"

"*Nu*, of course."

"I'm shocked."

"Why? Are you married?"

"Yes."

"For how long?"

"Twelve years."

"And you have children?"

"Yes."

"Baruch Hashem.‡ But if you're shocked"—her voice turned cold—"that means that you don't use the mikveh."

I coughed gently in my unease, feeling the trust and intimacy that we'd begun to establish slipping away. "I . . . I grew up in Mea Shearim,"§ I said finally, pulling a rabbit out of the hat. She was astounded. In one stroke, I'd placed myself firmly within her world. Saying I grew up in Mea Shearim was like saying, "We come from the same place." I saw her eyes close and her nostrils widen as the childhood scent of Mea Shearim seemed to fill the air—the sweet burnt-sugar smell of fired porcelain wafting up from the underground factory, visible through the few tiles of thick, illuminated glass fixed in the sidewalk that curved from Kikar Hashabbat toward the

---

*The period when a woman is menstruating plus the following seven days, before she has completed her ritual purification in the mikveh; also referred to as her "time of uncleanness."

‡An expression meaning "Thank God."

§An ultra-Orthodox neighborhood in central Jerusalem, founded in 1874.

Sha'arei Pinah quarter. Every day on my way home from first grade, I would step carefully upon the slippery glass tiles. Back and forth, back and forth. Then I would crouch down and press my face to the dirty glass, trying to catch a glimpse of the shadowy figures in that hidden world below. I imagined them as elves, marvelous and energetic little creatures tirelessly going about their work, spreading a dense aroma of candy throughout the neighborhood to sate the children's appetites. To grow up in Mea Shearim is something special, and I spent my early childhood there, in the same area, the same neighborhood as, I later discovered, Miriam came from. As if summoned by the wave of a magic wand, the pleasant sense of closeness between us returned.

"You grew up in Mea Shearim?" Miriam asked.

"Until I was seven," I said. "My grandfather was a very pious man. He was a cantor. We didn't live right inside Mea Shearim, but on a street next to it, where my grandfather had a nice house. I had a very enjoyable childhood there. I have a lot of wonderful memories. There weren't so many secular people in Jerusalem then," I added. "Everyone was religious, or at least traditional. My family was very, very traditional. Maybe my mother didn't go to the mikveh, but—"

"I don't believe that your mother didn't go to the mikveh. Maybe she went and you didn't know. Women usually keep it secret, and even today girls don't know that their mothers go to the mikveh. No daughter knows when her mother goes to the mikveh."

"Wait, tell me more about that. I'm very interested in the mother-daughter connection as it relates to the mikveh."

But she didn't reply. Instead, she took me by the hand and led me down the dark corridor that led to Room 6. "Come, and I'll show you the mikveh."

We entered Room 1, a private mikveh room. My heart skipped a beat. It was exactly the same room in which I'd immersed.

There were the pale green tiles, the shower off to the side, the pool in front of me. The yellow light from the dangling bare bulb suffused me with the memory of my second visit to the mikveh. I tightened my grip on the metal railing; its reflection shimmered along with mine in the murky green water.

"Two things are necessary in order for a mikveh to be kosher," Miriam explained, intruding upon my reverie, wagging her fingers in the air in a V sign. "First of all, the mikveh must contain forty *seah* of water. You know what a seah is?"

"A biblical measurement."

"Right. One seah is equal to approximately nineteen liters of water.[1] A kosher mikveh must contain about forty seah, or about seven hundred and fifty liters of water. A mikveh is not kosher for immersion unless it contains enough water to immerse the person's entire body at once. As the Torah says, 'And he shall immerse his entire flesh in the water.' During the immersion, the woman must be entirely in the water, not even a single hair on her head can remain outside, heaven forbid. The woman must stand on the floor of the mikveh and bend down with her arms and legs spread so that the water will reach every place in the body. She must slacken her mouth, her teeth, and her fists so that the water can enter every orifice and reach every cranny.

"The second condition is that the water that fills the mikveh must be 'living water' [*mayim hayim*]—rainwater that is collected in a pit dug in the earth or in a tank fixed on the roof of a building. Groundwater that is collected in special tanks and made to flow through cement pipes* into the mikveh is also kosher for immersion, on condition that it is untouched by human hands. In any case, the cistern must be a stationary, immovable receptacle. Water that is drawn by

---

*The pipes cannot be made of iron because iron is said to conduct *tum'ah* (impurity). The spigots and handles must also be made of rubber or wood. See Kehati, *Mishnayot Mevoarot*.

hand is not acceptable. As the Torah says, 'Only a spring or a cistern, a gathering of water, shall remain pure.' "[2]

"So only pure rainwater is really used?" I asked apprehensively. It seemed impossible. How, especially in this arid land of ours, could a sufficient quantity of water be collected for all the women to immerse in throughout the year? Appalled, I recalled my aunts' stories about the Ashkenazi women who bathed in mikveh water that was filthy from repeated use. If those were the rules, then maybe they were right! Steeling myself and trying to conceal my panic at the thought that I, too, had submerged my delicate, pampered body in such a collective swamp, I asked as nonchalantly as possible: "Miriam, what happens in the summer when there's no rain? What happens when there's a drought and there's no rain at all?"

"Nowadays, women don't actually submerge in a reservoir of rainwater," Miriam replied with a giggle, having read the expression of disgust on my face. "There's something that's called *hashaka* [touching, or juxtaposition]. Look," she said, pointing to a hole about six centimeters wide in the wall of the pool, just under the waterline. "This small hole gives the pool the status of a mikveh. It makes a connection between a deep storage cistern that is dug in the earth and contains at least forty seah of natural rainwater or springwater, and this pool, in which the woman immerses. In principle, a cistern of rainwater could serve as a mikveh, but since it's hard to replace the water in a cistern of that kind, and because, as you say, there also isn't enough rainwater, it generally serves as a source [*makor*] that gives the pool filled with water supplied by the municipality its kashrut* as a mikveh. All on condition that the diameter of the hole is at least five centimeters, and this, Baruch Hashem, is what we have in our mikveh.

---

*In this context, the term means "state of being kosher"; it can also refer to the Jewish dietary laws.

This way the water can be replaced every day to maintain hygiene and kashrut at the same time."

I was struck by the ingenuity of generations of Jewish sages who'd eventually arrived at this satisfying formula, whereby a hole with a minimal diameter of five centimeters could transform a pool of ordinary water from the municipal water supply into a kosher mikveh. I could see the rationale of the arrangement, though it didn't sit quite right with me on an emotional level; my sense was that this wasn't exactly God's intention. But since I didn't feel qualified to express an opinion on this scholarly subject, and admired the sages' creative virtuosity in making kosher immersion possible under suitable sanitary conditions—and also because Miriam had vanished at the sound of a deafeningly loud bell, announcing: *Hurry! A naked woman is ready and waiting to immerse!*— I turned and went out into the long, dark corridor.

As I continued to reflect on the process by which the divine imperative had been adapted to twenty-first-century reality, a rhythmic clicking of heels echoed down the hallway, growing louder and closer. Out of the shadows a woman appeared. She was a head and a half taller than me, and her hips swayed in time with her stride. When she noticed me standing there, she bathed me from above in the warmest of looks. Her broad, beautiful face was beaming. Above her sharply sculpted cheekbones, her dark, almond-shaped eyes were protected by fluttering black lashes. Her wet hair was pulled back and rested on her regal neck. Something about her reminded me of the provocatively dressed woman who'd been escorted to Room 6, but this woman looked completely different. Her face bore no trace of the heavy makeup the other had worn, and her body was modestly encased in a pink cotton tracksuit. Only the noisy high heels told me that the brazenly attired woman who'd been assigned to Room 6 and this princess coming toward me were one and the same.

I blocked her path. "Um . . . I saw you earlier . . . when you

came in . . . I was just asking the balanit some questions . . .
Can I ask you too?" I stammered into her belly button.

"Pardon me?" She reared back slightly, her heels squeaking to a halt as she stopped and leaned down toward me.
"What did you say?"

"I want to know what immersing in the mikveh does for
you. I'm curious . . . Can you tell me a little about it?"

She lifted her right foot, bent forward, and with the gracefulness of a long-limbed stork, elegantly adjusted the red vinyl strap of her high-heeled designer sandal.

"What is there to tell? Go immerse and you'll feel it yourself." But then she relented and said, "Okay, but make it
quick because my husband is waiting. You understand?" Her
eyes twinkled mischievously.

"Sure," I said, still trying to reconcile the flamboyant-looking woman who'd entered the mikveh earlier with the
quietly radiant figure now looming over me.

She laughed gaily. "Listen, I'm telling you, today it was
really dangerous. I was late getting out of the house because
I cooked all the foods my husband is crazy about. And when I
was about to leave he stopped me right by the door. We came
this close to sinning, God help us. Luckily, I kept a grip on
myself and slipped out of his arms. Talk about a close call!
And now he's waiting for me. Starving—if you know what
I mean," she whispered conspiratorially. "So I'm really in a
rush to get home. You know how it is."

"I don't know. Tell me."

"All right, but come, let's sit over here," she said, leading
me out of the corridor. We sat down on white plastic chairs
that were grouped in the vestibule.

"Look," she said, clasping her knees and staring down
at the polish-free toenails that poked from the front of her
shoes. "Today is a special day. Today I went from being impure to pure. When I came in here I was impure, you know?
For twelve days—five days of bleeding and seven more clean

days—I was impure and could also spread the impurity to others. My husband wasn't allowed to touch me or have any kind of sex with me, of course, because I could, God forbid, make him impure—you get it? After I immersed in the pure waters of the mikveh I became pure myself. The immersion makes it okay for me to have sex with my husband again. He's even obligated by the Torah to make love to me tonight when I return from the mikveh; otherwise he's committing a really big sin. You know what kind of a feeling this is? You know what a burden is lifted from your soul when you leave here after bathing in the mikveh? It's just incredible! Unbelievable!"

"No, I don't know. I don't use the mikveh."

"It's impossible to put into words. No words can describe this amazing feeling. It's the most incredible kind of foreplay—you really ought to try it. I'm telling you—you're really missing out if you don't use the mikveh."

"Why? What happens?"

"Lots of things, but to keep it short, because I'm in a hurry, going to the mikveh is what keeps sex with my husband so exciting. Between you and me, he's not exactly one of the world's red-hot lovers . . . It's not like he melts every time I touch him, no, even though we've been married just two years and are still very young. He's twenty-six, and I'm only twenty-four. But it's not just the sex; it's everything. All the wooing, the loving, the tension before and after and during. It just adds so much to our marriage and our sex life. Believe me, it works a whole lot better than all sorts of advice from the 'sexologists' or whatever you call them."

"What does it do?"

"I don't know how to explain it exactly, but for those two weeks that you're keeping apart, you're just, like, so eager for this day. There are days when you're just dying for it, you know? Hey, we're human, and we have our lusts and our desires and suddenly you want it—and you can't have it!

It's absolutely forbidden! A sin you can't atone for. And let me tell you, this prohibition really stirs up your desire. It's such a turn-on. You really appreciate this thing when it's not like you can just come home any time and do it because you happen to feel like it just then. You have these two weeks, and you can only do it during these two weeks. So each day becomes really important and each night is like a wild celebration. You tell yourself: *Oh shit, that's another day gone; pretty soon this time will be over.* And when you feel your period coming on, you think: *Shit, now for two weeks I'll want it when I can't have it.* You see? It makes it so much more special."

"So, what will happen tonight?"

"Tonight will be, like, totally mind-blowing. I told you how we almost sinned when I was on my way out the door. But when I come home from the mikveh, he doesn't pounce on me, we don't go to bed straightaway. Uh-uh, no way. There's a whole long ritual, you know? Everything moves in slow motion. And the greater the desire, the longer we stretch it out. When I come in he'll pull me close and start kissing me, but then, when sparks are practically flying from all our making out, we'll stop ourselves and sit down at the table I set before I left, with the gorgeous tablecloth I got in Istanbul and the special dishes we got as a wedding present—you should see them, they're all decorated with symbols of love and marriage. Like, my aunt gave us a napkin holder embroidered with two hearts in blue and red. And my husband's aunt gave us a teakettle—the lid is shaped like a nest with two kissing lovebirds inside. At lunchtime I also bought special roses, very expensive ones, red and white, and I put them in this vase that's shaped like a woman's body—it's so sexy!—and then I sprayed them with this fabulous perfume.

"Anyway, so we eat, and the meal is always something special, always something that my husband is really crazy about . . . I don't usually cook that much, I have a very demanding job in television and it saps all my energy. But on this night, after we've finished off the meal with this delicious, thick cherry liqueur that my mother makes, I light scented candles and have tons of energy and desire for sex. Also, it just feels so great to have sex when you're so incredibly clean and purified, you know? That's how it is for me, anyway. I have much more patience for all the caressing and licking when every inch of my body is clean and washed, inside and out."

"Licking?"

"I'll tell you something that's very personal, and I mean really personal, but it has to stay between us, okay? My husband has this thing about licking. He loves to lick every part of my body, as if I was a never-ending dish of whipped cream. First he whispers in my ear the kinds of things you only hear in the movies and I just melt, and then he inserts his tongue in my ear, then he moves on to my neck. He takes his time, and I can't tell you how much it turns me on . . . His warm, sweet tongue glides into my armpit, wets my breasts, my stomach, my belly button . . . He even sucks my toes, one at a time, just like in that Indian sex guide—*nu*, what's it called?"

"The *Kama Sutra*?"

"Yes, that's it. And you know, what he likes the most is to kiss my lower lips, to lick and insert his tongue . . . you know where . . . and the only time I let him do it all—lick, bite, do whatever, wherever he wants, and as much as he wants, and that I really enjoy it, is on the night I come back from the mikveh. Not only is my body clean—I could do that by taking a bath at home—but my soul is too. After you've been in the mikveh, stuff that might otherwise seem crude and pornographic becomes a real exaltation of body and soul. The physical pleasure is so profound and intense, it's like your very soul has been cleansed. Like heaven and earth are completely as one. That's what happens to us when I come back from the mikveh."

Her body trembled with emotion, her voice cracked, and her eyes filled with tears. "I don't know what just came over me," she sobbed. "It's like I lost my brakes. When all your inhibitions are released you feel out of control. It's scary. You know, you're not really supposed to talk about this kind of stuff. Aside from your husband, no one is supposed to know these things or talk about them. It's forbidden. And you shouldn't think that it's just all about sex. It's a lot more than that. It's an intimacy with God and with your soul, and it's so weird that suddenly I'm telling you all this. I don't even know who you are. Okay then," she said as she tried to pull herself together, to stopper her unleashed emotions, "now I have to run home to my husband."

She gathered her things, turned, and hurried to the exit, leaving me awash in her sensuality. I couldn't believe what I'd just heard. I never imagined that such openness was possible between two strangers. Even the closest friends might never expose themselves to that degree. If I hadn't felt the sanctity of the moment as it occurred, I'd have deemed her words a cheap pornographic invention. But that wasn't the case. It had been a rapturous, genuine confession. Now she'd vanished into the outside gloom, the tapping of her shiny heels on the wide floor of the entranceway momentarily sustaining her physical presence.

I sat glued to my chair, dumbfounded. In under an hour, I had seen a woman undergo an astonishing physical and emotional transformation. A brash-looking, skimpily dressed stranger had entered the mikveh and emerged from it transcendent and aglow. And having covered herself modestly, she'd removed her mask and proceeded to bare her naked soul to me, opened a window and invited me into the labyrinth of her hidden garden, taken me into her bed, shown me every inch of her body, inside and out, let me peek into her "house of secrets" (*beit hastarim*), where her husband makes love to her body and God makes love to her soul; she'd given me a glimpse into the most fragile, sensitive, and sensuous part of her and enticed me to know more. She'd entered the mikveh dirty and come out clean, entered impure and come out pure, entered it forbidden and come out permitted, entered it a stranger and come out familiar and ready to expose herself to me completely and utterly, as if a blood pact had been sealed between us, a pact of trust between two women otherwise unknown to each other but brought close by virtue of their common gender.

Such is the mikveh. It is a place where one is stripped down on both the physical and spiritual levels, where women undergo a transformation from girl to woman, from virgin to bride, from impurity to purity.

Judaism is very precise in defining categories and drawing boundaries in all areas of life. Between sacred and profane, meat and milk, *hametz* and *matzah*,* male and female, impure and pure, forbidden and permitted. The world of nature must go through a process of classification and separation. Each natural thing must undergo a transformation in order to enter into the realm of culture; that is, to enter society and become part of it. Through the conversion ritual, for example, the non-Jew who is off-limits and outside the society becomes a kosher Jew who is a part of the society. The immersion ritual transforms the impure woman, who is ruled by the forces of nature and consequently banished from society, into a kosher woman, who is under cultural control and so included in the community of Israel.[3]

---

*Hametz is the term for food that cannot be eaten during the Passover holiday; *matzah* refers to the unleavened bread eaten on Passover and, more generally, signifies the opposite of *hametz*; i.e., all that is permissible to eat on Passover.

The clanging bell, announcing that another woman was ready for her ritual bath, jolted me out of my reverie. I looked around and saw that the broad vestibule, though poorly lit and lined with bare gray walls, was bustling with life. Women were coming and going down the hallways. Balaniyot hurried back and forth among the rooms, perspiring in excitement as they murmured the final words of blessing over one immersion and prepared to greet the next woman in line. Some women left the mikveh soon after they were finished, mumbling a quick good-bye to the balanit. Others, their heads wrapped in towels, lingered in the vestibule, in front of the prayer sheet displayed on the wall near the entrance to the right-side corridor, reciting the words in hushed tones:

Dear Lord! With a fervent heart I observe the mitzvah of immersion for the sake of purification. I have striven to be faithful to your commandments and hope for the sanctity of your name, and as the waters of the mikveh purify me spiritually, so I pray to you that you wash away from me all sin and transgression, all sadness and sorrow.

Dear Lord! Who holds every living thing in your hands, grant me, my family, my relatives, and all of the Jewish people your blessings, for long life, health, happiness, good fortune, and gratification from my children, bestow upon me your pure spirit and divine presence.

May it be thy will, O Lord, that our home be one of peace and brotherhood, and may your kindness never desert our people, and that I always be worthy of the purification appropriate for the daughters of your people, the House of Israel. Amen!

The women pray with eyes closed, with full concentration, sometimes gently swaying to and fro. I watched as three women dried their hair with the hair dryers attached to the wall next to a large horizontal mirror in the corridor to the left of the prayer sheet. They gazed at the reflection of their purified selves as they primped in preparation for their return home.

If the private thoughts of all the women here were magically voiced, what would we hear? What goes through the minds of these women, all gathered in one place at one time for one purpose—sanctifying themselves for the act of love? Each has her own life story, her own desires and dreams. But all of these Jewish women here in the mikveh at this moment are united by two common denominators: All have a husband waiting at home who has been sexually starved for two weeks and is now eager to remedy that (or perhaps apprehensively anticipating the fulfillment of his obligation). All of these women are now halakhically purified and tonight all will observe the most important of the Torah's imperatives— the commandment to be fruitful and multiply. Tonight, when the egg in their ovaries is, theoretically at least, optimally ready to meet their mate's sperm.

2

THE BALANIYOT

A terrible wailing rose from the corridor as a young woman, a girl of about nineteen, rushed out of the immersion room. With her wet hair plastered to her face, towels slung over her shoulder, she ran straight to Miriam, crying: "I've come to say good-bye to you! I won't be coming here again! I'll never, ever, ever come here again!" The girl collapsed into Miriam's massive arms, and Miriam held her in a firm embrace before guiding her into the room used for counseling brides.

"I couldn't stop her," panted the balanit who came running after her. "As soon as she came out of the water she collapsed into this awful weeping and started shouting: 'I won't come here anymore! I loved coming here so much! But now I'll never have the chance to have another child!' So I said to her, 'Come, get dressed first of all. Let's get dressed. It's not right to talk like this, all naked.' And she was drying herself and crying, drying and crying. And I helped her dress, trying to calm her down. I know her well. I myself was the one who immersed this sweetheart when she first got married, and afterwards, when she conceived right away on the wedding night, just like it should be, she came and told us. And we congratulated her and wished her good health and that all would go well and that she would have an easy birth and a healthy baby. Then she came to us after the birth and showed us a picture of her with the baby, a boy—may he live long—and with her husband—so wonderful, such a pleasure—and said she wanted to have a baby every year. Every year she wanted to get pregnant and bring a kosher child into the world. And all of a sudden, not two months later, the problems started. Her period wasn't regular and she was bleeding all the time. So she went to the doctor and now she has come here with the terrible news—may we be spared such a fate—that they found a tumor and her uterus has to be taken out. *Tse tse tse*"—she clicked her tongue against her teeth—"such a tragedy. So tough, so tough. And I dressed her, trying to comfort her, but what can I say? I can't find the words. And as soon as she was all dressed, she rushed out of the room yelling at the top of her lungs. I hope Miriam can calm her down."

A few minutes later, the two women emerged from the brides' room. The young woman was a bit calmer, though she still leaned on Miriam, who escorted her outside to her husband's car.

"I feel so bad for the poor girl," Miriam sighed when she returned.

"How did you get her to quiet down?" the other balanit and I asked.

"Very simple. I said to her: 'Listen, honey. You have a son, may he live long. There are many women who come here for forty years and have no children. Not even this one child that you have. So you should thank Hashem, who brought this evil decree upon you after your son was born and not, heaven forbid, before. Then you wouldn't even have this boy. You should give thanks for what you have and not cry over what you have not.' And then she started to quiet down, and I hugged her and blessed her and tried to convey to her as much of my inner strength as I could, until she calmed down some more. And now she's calmer and going to be with her husband. But she's transferred her trouble to me. I'm taking it home with me. It doesn't stay behind here. It comes home with me. It sits with me at dinner and comes into bed with me with my husband and, *oy vey,* I won't sleep the whole night because of it. I tell myself that I won't ever see her again and it's hard for me . . . It's very hard for me to know that for this little girl, this was her last immersion as a woman, and she's only nineteen."*

Normally, when a woman leaves the mikveh after her immersion, there are no tears. She says good-bye to the balaniyot and the women sitting with them, sometimes lowering her eyes in embarrassment as the women bid her goodnight with a sly, meaningful smile. They all know what awaits the woman who has just immersed, and sincerely wish for her to have a wonderful and fertile night. Whenever a woman walks out of the mikveh, the gentle general feeling of warmth and sisterhood is momentarily heightened.

"Is balanit a profession?" I asked Doris, who immigrated to Israel with her family from Morocco forty-two years ago, at the age of eighteen, and has lived near the mikveh ever since. For seven years now, since becoming religious and leaving her job at a national institution, Doris has been working at the mikveh alongside Miriam, whom she holds in boundless esteem, mostly for her mastery of Jewish law. Finding a halakhic solution for each and every problem posed by the women who visit the mikveh is what gives Doris's life meaning and provides her with the greatest emotional satisfaction.

"It most certainly is, but it's not just a profession. It's a calling, and not everyone is chosen for it."

"How is one chosen to become a balanit?"

"Hashem decides who is worthy of being a balanit. It doesn't just happen." Doris held her head high, exuding pride.

---

*A woman without a womb does not menstruate, and without menstruation there is no need for monthly ritual immersion.

"What does that mean, 'Hashem decides'?"

"Look, where a person wants and deserves to be, that's where he's led . . . I'll tell you my story. You can believe it or not," she said, her nose still pointing self-importantly upward.

"I'll believe you."

Now she lowered her gaze and the deep lines etched across her weathered face were softened by the joy that lit her eyes.

"What brought me to the mikveh? The truth? This is something that you really ought to write down. One day, about seven years ago, I was sitting around with some friends. One of them was a balanit. And I didn't even know that she was a balanit, and I opened my mouth and said: 'You know what I really ought to do? I should become a balanit. I want to immerse women in the mikveh.' As a matter of fact, I didn't even know this word 'balanit.' I just said: 'I need to immerse women in the mikveh. That's really the thing for me, I think.' And everyone laughed. This one giggled and another one said: 'What's she going on about the mikveh for? What the hell does she have to do with the mikveh?' Because I worked as an administrator at one of the Jewish institutions; I was a manager there for about eighteen years. That's what I did all the time. A whole lot of nothing is what went on there, a lot of nothing. We were just spinning our wheels there. Three days later I get this phone call out of the blue from Rabbanit Cohen herself, of blessed memory—she passed away a few years ago. She was responsible for all the mikvehs in the city. She called me and said: 'Are you Doris Cohen?' I said, 'Yes.' She said: 'A course for balaniyot is about to start. Are you interested?' I thought: *What in the world? How does she know who I am? Or anything about me?* But I told her: 'Yes, as a matter of fact, I am interested.' Then she said: 'The course is starting today. So come at four, come and sign up.' And that's how it went. Suddenly I find myself surrounded by all these very *frum** ladies, wondering: *What am I doing here? What do I have in common with them?* Because I was like an alien there, you see? No matter what, I looked like an alien among them, like something that didn't fit in. But, Baruch Hashem, the course was very interesting, and I did very well in it and was certified as a balanit."

"What did you study?"

"There's a whole book by Rabbi Yonah Yinon. He's a great authority on the laws of family purity and niddah and you have to learn his whole book." Doris's neck stretched proudly toward the ceiling again. "And then there's a test, about twenty questions, all oral. What do you learn? Everything. All the halakhot."

"I thought that only men were allowed to study the halakha, that it was absolutely forbidden for women," I said, touching on what I saw to be the balaniyot's Achilles' heel, the prohibition against learning Torah.

"Sure she studies—she studies what pertains to her. A woman is permitted to study the areas that pertain to her," Miriam interjected, coming to the aid of her protégé, deflecting my subversive attack and catching me out in my patronizing ignorance. "And there's a lot to learn. A woman can reach the level of prophecy. A woman is permitted to study only the written Torah. It is forbidden for her to study the Oral Law. She is forbidden to study Talmud. That's the man's area. Talmud is very deep study and she wouldn't understand."

"So she's chosen by God to immerse women in the mikveh but limited in her capacity for understanding?" I asked defiantly.

"It's true," added Michaela, the philosopher of the group, pouring a little water on the fiery argument that was about to ignite. Michaela had grown up in a Hassidic home. In 1967 she'd boldly bucked the norms of Hassidic society and en-

---

*Yiddish term meaning "devout."

listed in the Israel Defense Forces. Today she is married and has eleven children, "like the eleven kinds of incense that the high priest lit every morning and at twilight in front of the tent of meeting and in the holy of holies, may they all be healthy. The balm, the cloves and galbanum, the frankincense, myrrh, and cassia. Spikenard, saffron, and costos, aromatic bark, and cinnamon. These eleven spices make up the incense, and I love them more than anything. They say their scent was so strong, you could smell it all the way to Jericho."

"What's true?" I asked her.

"*Hakadosh Baruch Hu** chose me, too, to serve in the mikveh," she whispered, eyes aglitter. "I, too, am 'chosen.' "
She humbly bowed her head as her lips spread into a shy smile that brightened her drab, buttoned-up front. Michaela works full-time during the day as a caretaker for the elderly, and in the evenings she immerses women in the mikveh. From the first day I entered the mikveh, she formed a deep attachment to me. Whenever I sat down behind the desk with the balaniyot to discuss mikveh matters, Michaela would drink in the stories and listen intently to the debates that frequently arose. When the bells tolled for her to go immerse someone, she would reluctantly pry herself from her seat, hurry off to fulfill her mission, and then rush back to take her place beside me, eager to catch up on anything she'd missed. Her unusually large eyes, taking up a third of her translucent, thin face, would hone in on the heart of the polemic, her ears attuned to its rhythm. Every so often, her tongue would shake off its bonds and she would come out with stories illustrating the profound essence of the Jewish religion, tales about the symbiotic connection between God and his Jewish people, and about the unique traits of the chosen people, the jewel in the crown of nations. She held all the women there rapt. Michaela often wondered aloud about a woman's place

*"The Holy One, Blessed Be He," a substitute name for God.

in Jewish society in general and about her place in her family in particular.

"How did you know that you were chosen?" I questioned her.

"I had two small children and I had to help my husband earn a livelihood, and I absolutely didn't want to give the children to a babysitter. I prayed hard and said: 'Hashem, What shall I do? I'll have to work in the evenings.' But what work could I do? I had no profession because, Baruch Hashem, I married young. And then the idea came to me, right from Hashem. A new mikveh had just opened in the neighborhood and they were looking for a cleaning woman. I went to talk to the balaniyot and they said: 'Take an apron and start cleaning.' And that's what I did. For years, I just cleaned. Then suddenly, one evening, apparently because Hashem, the All-Seeing One, saw that I had reached such a level where I could serve as a balanit, the rabbanit in charge said to me: 'Michaela, go learn to be a balanit.' I took the course and now I'm a balanit, and I have no words to describe the miracle that happened to me, Baruch Hashem. It's a very great privilege."

Her Cinderella story thrilled the women: God, the mighty ruler, saw and loved little Michaela, the humble cleaning woman; he wanted her to become his holy servant, and by virtue of God's will, Michaela achieved her destiny and went from scrubbing tiles to serving God with holy work. God redeemed Michaela, just like the prince redeemed Cinderella.

The story of Doris, another chosen one, who, thanks to God's mysterious intervention, was transformed from an administrative manager to a balanit, is also brimming with motifs from Jewish tales of holiness originating in the Islamic lands.[1] Doris, the heroine, worked in a negative secular environment, which contributed nothing to society ("We were just spinning our wheels"). Once she expressed a desire to become a balanit, God, "the granter of wishes," sent her a "messenger" in the form of the Rabbanit Cohen. She called upon the heroine and commanded her to enlist in God's work: "Come and sign up for the balaniyot's course." Doris was surprised but answered the call. The language, the behavioral codes, her conceptual and cultural world—all were utterly different from those of the ultra-Orthodox world she would enter, but Doris met the challenge and overcame all the obstacles that God placed in her way in order to test her. She adapted herself to the other women in the course, passed it with flying colors, and was certified as a balanit. In the course of her studies, Doris became very religious. She always strove to go beyond the minimum of what was expected in fulfilling each of God's commandments, and he, "the granter," repaid her accordingly. Now she is engaged every day in saving the souls of Jewish women, who submit themselves to her ministrations as if on a conveyor belt: they arrive impure, immerse, and emerge purified. And this is her reward. The reward of a *tzaddika* (righteous woman), which will be hers in the world to come.

The balaniyot tell me that, in them, God has strengthened and enhanced the feminine qualities that, according to tradition, are imprinted in every Torah-observant woman from birth: compassion, generosity, and dedication. God has given them remarkable healing powers that enable them to bring succor to anguished women who enter the mikveh. "I think that a doctor is nothing compared to us," asserts Lily, the "pampering assistant" from my second immersion, in a heavy Moroccan accent. About sixty years old, she, too, became religious late in life, and is concerned above all with helping women in distress. "The whole trick is to be warm and welcoming. When they see a trustworthy face, trustworthy hands, and after a few times in the mikveh they see that there's someone to talk to, that there's someone who will listen and not a brick wall that doesn't answer, then they open up and talk. We convey Hashem's strength to them and soak up their pain when they break down in our arms from all their troubles. This is part of the purification process for the women who enter the mikveh all burdened and troubled and leave calm and relieved."

The balaniyot's outlook on life, their maturity and their rich life experience, both personal and professional, all combine to create a team of skilled women who fulfill an important communal role. They are able to identify women who are physically and emotionally abused, and refer them to social services that provide first aid and professional care.

"Ninety-nine percent of it is psychology," says Lily. "You have to get to know each woman. To be a good listener and know where it's possible to help them. It's not like they say, that every woman who immerses in the mikveh is a queen in her daily life. That she has all she needs and is perfectly happy. Absolutely not. It's not like that at all. You need to know how to approach a woman. For example, we don't go right up to them. We can tell who is in distress and before she even opens her mouth we make her want to come to us and talk. Immerse a woman? Any twelve-year-old girl could do that. But the real expertise of it is to get a feel for the woman, to listen well and know what to latch on to and where to help. When you see a battered woman, when you see actual signs of a physical beating, you can't just walk up to her and say, 'What is this here? What's happening to you?' You sometimes have to wait months until she opens up and tells you about it. And once she opens up, I help her with all my heart. I have the patience of a woman who has been through a lot in life. I know about this sort of thing. I know how to listen and to talk to them and I can help them and refer them for help, each in accordance with her needs. Women have no shortage of pain and troubles, and this help that I give I think is very important."

The balaniyot have ties with religious organizations that assist women. "We have a lot of girls who have this calling, to work with these women," Lily tells me. "They're not social workers from the state; no, they're volunteers who work with private organizations that ask us, 'Have you seen a battered woman? Send her to us; we can take care of her.' And that's what we do. Every day we refer women in distress to rabbis and different institutions. There are a lot of places we can refer them to, Baruch Hashem."

The balaniyot are also the halakhic authority in the mikveh. They are the ones who permit or prohibit a woman from immersing in the mikveh, according to their judgment. They rely on the dictates of the halakha, Jewish law, which outlines clear boundaries in the life of the observant Jew. The permitted and the prohibited, the impure and the pure, positive and negative commandments—all is laid out in minute detail. For the simplest actions in life there is a halakha regarding how to behave. The ideal is to fulfill all the commandments and laws properly, to come closest to what is required by the Torah and the halakhic texts, in the faith that this world is just a corridor to the world to come. On their way through this corridor, individuals accumulate as many "good points" as possible, so as to ensure themselves the place due a *tzaddik*, a righteous person, in the next world.

The halakha was and is created in an exclusively male world that operates separately from the world of women. It addresses every aspect of a Jew's lifestyle, including the most sensitive and personal matters of married life and sexual relations. Through the laws concerning family purity and immersion in the mikveh, the male-formulated halakha permeates every nook and cranny of the "hidden places" (*beit hastarim*)* and takes control over every intimate detail. But there's a

---

*Also called the "house of secrets," the term refers to those parts of the body whose form may prevent the mikveh water from entering, e.g., the armpits, under the breasts, the inside of the ear and mouth, etc.; also a slang term for "genitals," i.e., the "hidden organs."

catch. The authors and arbiters of Jewish law are precluded from personally enforcing these rules, since they are strictly forbidden from entering the women's mikveh. So, having no other choice, the men delegate authority to the balaniyot, who conduct the male halakha concerning the purification rites into the exclusively female world of the mikveh.[2] This is the one and only instance within Jewish communal life where such momentous authority—the prerogative to sanction or deny approval of someone else's adherence to halakhic dictates—is placed in women's hands.

My mikveh is staffed by eight balaniyot: Miriam is in charge; Michaela, Lily, and Doris are *matbilot,* women who oversee immersions; Leah and Dina are a mother-and-daughter team specializing in the immersing of disabled women; Paula is Dina's apprentice; and then there is Sarah, who counsels brides.

A clear hierarchy exists among the balaniyot in terms of their authority and importance. At the bottom of the pyramid are the apprentices and the regular matbilot—Paula, Michaela, and Doris. They possess a basic knowledge of the pertinent halakhot and are relatively new to the profession. They are led by Lily, who has seniority after many years in the mikveh. On the next level are Leah and Dina, who are thought to possess supreme strength, both physical and emotional, that enables them to cope with the difficulties of tending to the disabled women, some of whom have suffered grievous disfigurement. Leah is thought of as something of a saint. "Dina's mother, Leah, is a national asset," proclaims Doris, causing Leah to stare at her feet in embarrassment and her dark complexion to redden until beads of sweat trickle off her face. Ignoring her mother's discomfort, Dina tries to top Doris: "Only a national asset? She's an international asset."

Sarah surpasses Leah and Dina in importance because of her extensive knowledge as an instructor of brides and her

unflinching devotion to this cause, despite the perilous encounters it requires with many stubbornly secular women,
which she undertakes for *kiddush Hashem*—purely to sanctify the name of God—and not for any material reward.
Finally, at the top of the pyramid stands the head balanit,
Miriam, the supreme arbiter in the mikveh. Only very rarely
does her expertise prove insufficient, compelling her to turn
to a rabbi for a halakhic ruling. For thirty-eight years Miriam
has been a balanit in the mikveh, fulfilling all the roles there.
She is an instructor of brides and oversees immersions, including those for disabled women. Miriam is a walking ency-
clopedia of Jewish law and life wisdom for whom conveying
the message of family purity is a hallowed cause. Her sacred
mission is to see that every Jewish woman meticulously car-
ries out all her divinely imposed obligations, "because the
actions of the individual are what build the collective Jewish
future and hasten the coming of the Messiah." The balaniyot
call Miriam "the rabbanit," even though the ultra-Orthodox
woman was never certified as such by any religious body, nor
is she married to a rabbi. She earned this title by virtue of
her vast knowledge of the halakhot pertaining to women and
the great respect accorded her by her subordinates. To them,
she is the true exemplar, the ultimate woman, from head
to toe, so much so that, when Michaela is trying to explain to
me about the morning prayer service and comes to the *asher
yatzar* blessing,* "Blessed art thou . . . who formed me with
many openings and hollows . . . " she cites the body of her
rabbanit as an example. "The word 'hollow' emphasizes that
the opening must be a hollow hole and not blocked, heaven
forbid, because if the hole is blocked, if an ear is blocked with
wax, say, or the urethra is blocked with a stone, or a lump
hardens in the intestines and blocks the opening of the anus—
may we be spared such a fate—then it is terrible and awful.

---

*A prayer recited by Orthodox Jews upon exiting the bathroom.

Take Miriam, for example; she's such a real *tzaddika*—every year, after the fasts of the Ninth of Av and Yom Kippur, the hollows of her intestines get blocked and the poor thing goes through pure agony and horrible pain, but it doesn't stop her from fulfilling the mitzvah of the fast."

Miriam's rulings in the mikveh are like the words of the Living God. When Miriam gave her seal of approval to my regular presence in the mikveh, the balaniyot warmly took me in, saying, "We will do and we will listen," like the Israelites at Sinai. They opened the doors of their hearts to me with complete trust, and I respected their ways. Little by little, their smiles and gestures became less formal, and more genuine and affectionate. Little by little, I got to know them, and they got to know me.

3

A DOSE OF IMPURITY

It was obvious to the balaniyot who welcomed me into their mikveh that I was a secular person, and I had to tread very gingerly in this encounter between our different worlds. I always dressed modestly and showed them respect, emphasizing what a privilege it was for me to sit in their company and the importance I ascribed to the mikveh, and to their views in particular. At times, I felt that I offered some of them a glimpse into another world, one they would never personally experience. And they were eager to explain to me every little detail of their work, so that I would understand their holy calling and accept their worldview, which glorified observance of the mitzvah to immerse in the mikveh.

The balaniyot also turned out to be tireless missionaries. Every time I came they asked: "*Nu,* what about you? Don't you want to go in the mikveh?" They longed to immerse me and thus chalk up one more mitzvah in their tally with God. They laid out all sorts of arguments in favor of using the mikveh, from warning me that my descendants were in danger of extinction to assuring me that I would enjoy a better love life. This ongoing challenge served to sustain a positive tension that helped me win their cooperation every time I entered the place.

One night, when I was giving Miriam a lift home after the last of the women had finished her ritual bath, she asked me:

"Tell me, why don't you immerse in the mikveh? You, who grew up in Mea Shearim?"

"I'm like Tevye the milkman," I replied. "I converse directly with God."

"Tell me about Tevye the milkman," she said.

I was flabbergasted. "You don't know the story?"

"I know that Shalom Aleichem wrote it, but this literature is forbidden in ultra-Orthodox society. For us, every book and every written page is censored. 'Tevye the Milkman' is forbidden literature."

I cringed inside at this injustice, and I felt terrible for this sharp-minded woman—it pained me to think how the rules of Miriam's society had suppressed her tremendous natural abilities. With her keen intelligence, social awareness, and knack for leadership, there was no telling what Miriam could have accomplished if other avenues had been open to her.

I told her about the seven circles of hell that Tevye endured with his seven daughters; I told her how he stuck to his faith in God despite the endless troubles that befell him and how he laid out his trials and tribulations before God as he drove his milk wagon.

As I talked, Miriam sat silent and alert, gazing out into the deep gloom of the night, thirstily drinking in each word.

"You see?" I said, moved by the wonderful intimacy that enveloped us. "I believe in the existence of God, but my connection with him is direct, and I make my requests directly to God, like Tevye, without mediators. I don't need to stick a note in the Western Wall,* to pray in a synagogue, or to immerse in a mikveh in order to put my requests to God. I believe that he hears me from everywhere, and there have been times when I really felt that the hand of God intervened

---

*It is customary for visitors to the Western Wall in Jerusalem, Judaism's holiest site, to place notes inscribed with prayers or messages to God in the cracks between its stones.

on my behalf and helped me solve the problem at hand. There were times when I felt that he bestowed upon me some of his infinite wisdom and showed me the way, that he illuminated a vague feeling, granted my wishes, and did not leave my pleas, big or small, unanswered. Sometimes, when I'm at a crossroads and torn and don't know which direction to take, I feel like an unseen hand gently and wisely guides me to make the right choice, to discern between good and bad, between what really matters and what's not so important, between darkness and light . . . You understand what I'm saying?" I choked up a little, overcome by the intensity and holiness of the moment.

The shadowy figure to my right abruptly turned to face me. Miriam's eyes flashed like a cat's gleaming in the night, and her tone was pure ice: "That you talk with Hashem might be good for you, but I don't think that he accepts the way you turn to him or the way you run your life, especially your sex life with your husband."

In a flash, my euphoria evaporated and my spirits sank. A hard lump caught in my throat. "I feel close to him and that means he's close to me, right?" I spluttered. "After all, didn't the sages say: 'Each in his own faith shall live'? Isn't that so?" The pleading in my voice was undisguised. I yearned for her to take back her words so the magic moment between us could be restored.

"I think that's horrible frivolity," she said unwaveringly. "There is a whole system of rules that determines how we live and how we communicate between our world and Hashem's world. 'I am your Lord, I set down my Law and my decree, and it is not for you to question.' Observance of the laws is the stronghold of faith in Hashem's Torah. Every doubt and question and deviation is from the devil, from the evil impulse [*yetzer hara*]. The laws of the Torah and the halakhot elaborate on the positive and negative mitzvot down to the smallest detail. On the simplest thing in life, there is a halakha that shows a person how Hashem wants him to behave, that shows him the right way. And all a person has to do is follow the instructions in the spirit of *na'aseh venishma* ['We shall do and we shall listen'] without asking unnecessary questions."

"But it doesn't work that way anymore in today's reality."

"Whose reality are you talking about? Yours or mine? Yes, the Messiah will come only when all human beings, all of us, fulfill the commandments and the laws and the halakhot as Hashem requires. But until then, and in order to hasten the coming of the Messiah, there has to be effort, striving. It is written that if a person strives and does his best, at least one can't fault him. But what if he doesn't do the maximum? Well, then, what do they say? Then he is to blame. The goal is to perform the mitzvot exactly as commanded out of faith that this world is just a corridor to the next world, to the world to come. And on your way through this corridor you accumulate as many points in your favor as possible in order to obtain for yourself the place of a righteous person in the world of truth. Hashem didn't give us these rules for nothing."

"I won't argue with you about the halakhot because I don't know as much about that, but I do understand what I do with my body and what is good for my soul," I insisted.

"But don't you understand that it's all connected? Hashem is the one who created us and he is the one who knows what's good and what's bad for us. Look, when you buy an appliance, you get an instruction manual from the manufacturer, right? And you're careful to follow exactly what the manufacturer tells you, because an appliance that is properly maintained functions best, right?"

"Yes, of course, but what does that have to do with anything?"

"That's exactly the point," Miriam replied. "The human body is an appliance manufactured by Hashem, and we have operating instructions from the manufacturer. All that is written in the Torah that was given to Moses at Sinai are Hashem's operating instructions. Now you come and say: 'I don't care what the manufacturer's instructions are. I'll operate my body and soul as I see fit.' But every time there's a problem or a breakdown, you get distressed and then you pester Hashem and ask him to fix it. But it doesn't work that way. In order to maintain the appliance you have to follow the operating instructions and do proper upkeep. This is the duty of every Jew."

"Manufacturer's operating instructions! I wonder what appears in red, where it says 'Warning!'" I scoffed.

"It says 'Do not touch the impurity of niddah'—this is the most important warning of all," Miriam lectured, sternly rebuffing the scorn in my words. "Touching this impurity is the greatest danger of all. Listen, the most important imperative, without which the continuity of the Jewish people would not be possible, is the imperative to maintain family purity. With her body, the Jewish woman fulfills this vital duty. Therefore, when you do not maintain purity, you are niddah, and your body is defiled from the blood of niddah and your children are defiled and your entire household is defiled, and this is worse than the defilement of the dead." Miriam's voice filled with fury. "And it's not only you who are impure—your impurity affects your offspring and their descendants for generations to come, and worst of all, with the blood of your niddah you defile all the people of Israel and bring the danger of karet upon the entire Jewish people. You understand how far this goes?!" She was shrieking now. "You understand what a calamity women like you are bringing upon the entire Jewish people?!"

Shut up! I wanted to scream. With my right hand I gripped the steering wheel tightly to keep from slapping the face of this woman who was glaring at me like a fire-breathing dragon in the close confines of my tiny car, her massive girth drooping over the sides of the passenger seat as her head seemed about to poke through the roof. With my left hand, I pinched my thigh to try to cool my anger.

"But I don't have relations in sin," I said through gritted teeth. "I am married in accordance with Jewish law. That's not pure enough for you?"

"It's a good thing that you're properly married, because in Judaism, marriage is considered a divine imperative. But that's just the beginning. Why do you think people marry and have intercourse? Why does Judaism sanctify sexual relations on condition that they only take place within the framework of marriage? Why do you think the bride and groom, weeks before the wedding, receive precise sexual instruction on how to act and what exactly they are supposed to do on their wedding night? For the sole purpose of enabling them to perform the mitzvah of 'Be fruitful and multiply,' to bring children into the world and continue the chain of Jewish generations—"

I cut her off mid-stream. "Pardon me, but my children are Jewish in every way!"

"Your central role as a Jewish woman, as it was for your mother and her mother and the mother of the mother of the mother of the mother of your mother, going back through all the generations up to Sinai, is to bring generations of Jews into the world and to raise them in the spirit of Judaism," she continued, smothering me with her torrent of words.

"I am raising my children in the spirit of my cultural values. The fact that I pray to God in my own way doesn't make me less Jewish than you!" I said furiously.

"You are not less Jewish than me, but the difference between us is that I'm a kosher Jewish woman as far as possible, Baruch Hashem, who brings kosher children into the world, and you are a sinning and impure Jewish woman, who delivers children in impurity. Do you understand?" she said coldly. "The main point of the laws of the Torah is to maintain boundaries, to say what's permitted and what's forbidden. The laws of purity and impurity, first and foremost, preserve Jewish society and distinguish it from all other societies in the world. Look, just look around you. In a Jewish neighborhood, for instance, before anything else, a mikveh is built. A Jew can survive without a synagogue—he can pray at home. He could pray in a hut, or like your Tevye, on a milk wagon, wherever he is. But without a mikveh? There is simply no continuity for the Jewish people. No continuity. It's what differentiates us from the rest of the nations in the world. How are we different essentially? What is the unique strength of the Jewish people?"

"The Jewish genius that comes up with nifty inventions," I said, mockingly reciting a popular old Israeli saying.

"And where does this special genius come from?" she continued with fervor. "How is this 'Jewish genius' created? What is its origin? There has to be a reason for it."

"Okay, how?" I said, humoring her.

"From immersion in the mikveh, plain and simple," she replied triumphantly.

"Nonsense. The Torah says you have to use the mikveh because, once upon a time, there weren't sanitary conditions. That's all."

"That's completely made up. It's a total lie. It's lack of knowledge," she thundered. "That's just total ignorance. Just take a little bit of our history—in the time when the Temple was in existence, was the high priest dirty? He didn't have sanitary conditions? You know what construction was like two thousand years ago? Our engineers today stand in awe of how they ever did what they did. So your argument is sheer bunk."

"*Nu,* really, Miriam. So there were public baths, but people couldn't bathe at home. It wasn't like today."

"What are you talking about? Now you're really being an ignoramus. Immersion in the mikveh is the ABC of the Jewish people. A Jewish child, even before his conception and birth, is different from those of all the other nations, because his mother purifies herself before the wedding. The man doesn't approach her as long as she is not pure. Today in Israel there is a law that requires this. But throughout the history of the Jewish people? Whoever knew any other way? To come to one's wedding without having been in the mikveh? You'd never hear of such a thing! That would be a wedding ceremony conducted in niddah! And that would mean he could not come close to her, on penalty of death! He shall not approach her in her niddah! And if he cannot approach her then there are no children, no children—the whole Jewish people would become extinct!"

"You're saying that the Jewish child is different from the non-Jewish child because it is born pure?" I said, my skin crawling.

"Definitely, definitely, that's the unique strength, the special quality of the Jewish people. From time immemorial, the Jewish brain has been brilliant. Why? Because it really is different, because its conception and birth are different. The mother purifies herself and the child is created and born pure. And then his soul is a pure soul. What does it say in the morning blessing?"

" 'A pure soul that you have given me.' "

"And what else does it say?—'For you are a holy people to Hashem, for Hashem chose you to be a treasured people from all the peoples on the face of the earth.' Pure children for a pure nation. The best quality children for a chosen people. Plain and simple."

"Tell me, do you hear what you're saying? Are you out of your mind?" I said, by now so livid that my eyes felt as though they were bugging out of their sockets. "Do you know how awful that sounds? Do you know what it sounds like? Like Hitler, may his name be erased, who touted the supremacy of the Aryan race and murdered millions of people who, according to his criteria, were inferior and polluted the air of this world with their inferiority!"

"I mean every word and I don't understand what you find so terrible. What does Hitler have to do with a chosen people? That has nothing to do with it. In any case, I didn't make this up. These are Hashem's words, not mine, so I am not out of my mind, and you, who don't cleanse yourself in the mikveh, are impure. And I'm not the one who says so, either. It was determined thousands of years ago at Sinai."

Stunned, I remained silent.

"You have a good night," Miriam said brusquely as she got out of the car and shut the door. I watched as she strode down the street, like a battle-hardened warrior off to relax after racking up another vee in her daily victory tally.

The shocking dogma that had just been hurled at me out of the blue kept me nailed to my seat, unsure where to turn. My head spun. The Jewish "chosen people" produces a special breed of children who are pure from birth, so Miriam had told me. The reproductive mechanism of the Jewish people, which resides in the womb of the Jewish woman, undergoes a continual process of purification from the punishments of original sin. "Be fruitful and multiply and fill the land and subdue it" (Gen. 1:28), God commanded Adam and Eve, the first creatures made in his image and the mythological parents of all mankind. But they received the punishment of mortality for having eaten the forbidden fruit of the tree of knowledge.

Menstrual bleeding, which occurs cyclically once a month, is a sign imprinted in the biological mechanism of the female body that on the one hand symbolizes the potential it holds for the creation of life, and on the other signifies the destruction of life—the mortality that Eve's sin brought upon all future generations. However, at Sinai, when God presented his contract with the descendants of Abraham, he defined them as his chosen people and he became their God. God wanted to cleanse his chosen people of the impurity of original sin, and thereby distinguish them and elevate them above the other nations. How? By commanding them to cleanse their bodies after any contact with the blood of death. He set down rules of kashrut* to ensure that the blood of a dead animal never enters the body of a Jew. "For the life of any creature—its blood represents its life, so I say to the Children of Israel, You shall not consume the blood of any creature, for the life of any creature is its blood, whoever consumes it will be cut off" (Lev. 17:14). And he commanded that when a woman's body is discharging menstrual blood—blood that embodies death—she shall not have physical contact with her husband until the bleeding has ceased and her body has been purified before God. Fertility and reproduction, God commanded, shall be accomplished in purity.

> And if a woman has her discharge, and her discharge in her body is blood, she shall remain seven days in her separation, and anything she touches becomes unclean until evening . . . And when she has become pure from her discharge, she shall count for herself seven days and after that she becomes pure. On the eighth day she shall take for herself two turtledoves or two young pigeons and bring them to the priest, to the entrance of the Tent of Appointed Meeting. The priest shall offer the one as an offering that clears [she who brings it] of sin and the other as an ascent offering, and the priest will effect atonement for her before God for the discharge of her uncleanness. (Lev. 15:19–30)

This is how God purified from the blood of death, which was discharged for the first time from the body of Eve, all the succeeding generations of Jews, and they are born, according

---

*In this context, term refers to the Jewish dietary laws.

to this thinking, into a code of divine purity that distinguishes them from all the other nations. You are a chosen people, the Lord told the flesh-and-blood beings who accepted his covenant. You are a select people, my Children of Israel. Elevated over all the other nations. A superior nation of pure beings, and your primary obligation is to maintain and preserve the purity of your nation, lest it be defiled in any way, heaven forfend. And how shall you do this? "So now, do not give your daughters to their sons, and do not wed their daughters to your sons, and do not seek after their peace and their well-being forever, so that you may possess and eat of the goodness of the land, and bequeath it to your sons forever" (Ezra 9:12). God in his beneficence gave the Jews a long list of rules designed to keep them distinct from and unassimilated in the other nations. The various strands of observant Judaism accept God's laws in the spirit of *na'aseh venishma*, "We shall do and we shall listen." They are exacting in adherence to God's dictates of purity. They proclaim themselves to be God's true chosen ones and the perpetuators of dynasties of "pure" Jews. But I and my children, who, like many others, define ourselves as secular, nonobservant Jews and nevertheless see ourselves as an inseparable part of the chosen people, are, as Miriam informed me, considered impure and defiling, doomed to extinction, not to mention responsible for delaying the coming of the Messiah.

This is outright discrimination between one Jew and another within the Jewish people! I thought. *Singling out the children of us women who don't use the mikveh and marking them as outcasts doomed to suffer various forms of extinction . . . Whoever heard of such a thing? What is this horror?!*

My instinctive reaction was that it was racism of the first order. But even in the midst of my emotional turmoil and anger, I was wary of using that term, which is so routinely invoked by many of Israel's enemies both at home and abroad.

In the halakhic Jewish outlook, the concept of a chosen people has nothing whatsoever to do with the racial doctrines developed in the nineteenth century by a group of Jew-hating intellectuals. Aryeh Kaplan, the noted scholar and exponent of Judaism, explains that, from the start, when man was created, all of humankind was destined to be "the chosen people."[1] When Adam sinned, the evil impulse became a part of human nature, and thus all of his descendants lost the opportunity to be chosen. Three times after that the human race missed out on the opportunity to be a chosen people. The first was in Noah's generation: the people were sinners and unworthy of redemption; therefore, instead of being purified by the waters, they and their impurity were washed off the face of the earth in the Flood. The second time was in the generation of Abraham, when his contemporaries joined forces to build the Tower of Babel. Instead of following the path of Abraham, who had begun life as an idol worshiper only to discover the divine truth and impart this to his offspring, they sought to build a great tower to challenge God. In response, God confounded their common language and dispersed them to the four corners of the world. The third missed opportunity occurred when, prior to giving the Torah to the Jewish people, God offered it to all the other nations, who declined it. God saw that no other nation was capable of preserving his Torah for thousands of years without abandoning it, and that only the Jewish people could answer his call and say, "We shall do and we shall listen," and thus it alone was worthy of receiving the Torah and becoming the chosen people.[2]

The only way for the chosen people to maintain its special character is through observance of the laws of purity. "[The purity laws] preserved Israel more than Israel preserved them," wrote Rabbi Isaac Halevy Herzog, the chief rabbi in Palestine from 1936 to 1959, in the preface to a booklet on marriage distributed at the offices of the Israeli rabbinate, explaining that it is these laws which have enabled the Jewish people to maintain their intellectual and spiritual powers and inner vitality in a way unmatched by other nations.[3]

The *Guidebook for the Jewish Family in Material and Spiritual Matters* provides the formula for "giving birth to nobler and happier children." It upholds the view that the purity laws are at the core of the Jewish people's spiritual character, and that these laws not only constitute the source of the so-called Jewish genius, but also account for the Jews' extraordinary capacity to endure hardships both in the Diaspora and in Israel. The guide also posits a direct link between the rise in the rate of violent crime, and moral decline in general, and a lack of adherence to the purity laws.[4]

A chosen people that does not permit any non-Jew to penetrate its ranks . . . I was reminded of a surreal scene I witnessed at the mikveh:

"The water cannot be cleaved or broken"—I recalled the loud, clear voice of a young blond American woman as she cited the wisdom of her favorite writer, Paulo Coelho, from his *Warrior of the Light: A Manual.*[5] The contours of her face were incredibly lovely, as if carved by an artist: sensuous heart-shaped lips, the chin delicate, yet firm and decisive. A white cotton tank top stretched tautly over her magnificent cleavage was emblazoned in black with אלד—the Hebrew letters alef-lamed-daled. The red silk shawl wrapped around her strong shoulders matched the simple thread tied around her left wrist. A gold cross rested in the recess at the bottom of her neck. She strode forward, leaned her pelvis against the edge of the balaniyot's table, pulled out a twenty-shekel bill, offered it to Miriam, and said in slightly ungrammatical Hebrew: "One immersion, please."

"If the Warrior of the Light was a Jew, he surely would have mentioned water's most important characteristic—'the power to restore a thing to itself,'" Dina said to the young woman, gaping in astonishment at the crucifix that lay gracefully against her fair throat.

"And if he was a Torah scholar who knows *gematria** he would also be able to prove it mathematically," Michaela said, inspired by the possibility of converting the Warrior of the Light. "For every child knows that water's power of restoration is imprinted in the gematria of the word *mayim* [מים, water]. Mem-yod-mem is ninety in gematria. Mem equals forty, yod equals ten, plus another mem equals forty—all together it equals ninety. Nine plus zero is nine and the number nine always restores a thing to itself. You can check it with all the numbers in the world. Take any number and add nine to it and it returns to itself. Dina, pick a number."

"Seventeen," ventured Dina.

"Seventeen is one plus seven equals eight. Add the number nine to the number seventeen and you get twenty-six. Two plus six also equals eight. The sum of the numbers in seventeen is eight, and when you add nine, the sum of the numbers in twenty-six is also eight. The same thing happens with every combination of numbers in the world."

"And if you, young lady, had even a drop of respect, you wouldn't dare set foot in this building." Miriam scolded the young American woman in a harsh voice, pushing away her hand as she attempted to pay for an immersion. "I ask you to leave this place at once," Miriam demanded, pointing with her right index finger at the door. "Out!" she shouted.

"Why? What's the matter? What's wrong?" the young woman stammered in a mixture of Hebrew and English, as she gathered her shawl around her and placed her hands over the letters printed across her breasts, as if they might protect her from the woman who sought to banish her. Her painted tiger eyes became veiled with tears.

---

*Hebrew numerology in which each letter of the alphabet is assigned a numerical value and is used to derive hidden meaning.

"May Hashem protect us," Miriam intoned, clutching her face, pinching her cheeks, and pulling at her puckered lips until they puckered even more from the pain. "Madam comes in here adorned with this vile symbol of abomination"—she pointed a furious finger at the shiny crucifix—"and then she has the nerve to ask why?! Christians are forbidden to enter this place, Madam. You are defiling it with your presence."

"Huh? What?" The blonde struggled to keep up with Miriam's rapid cascade of Hebrew.

"But she's not even impure," Paula ventured gamely, peeking out from behind Dina's broad back. "The Talmud says that someone who comes near a non-Jew's corpse does not become defiled, because the non-Jew isn't considered a human being."

"Even better!" Miriam clapped her hands. "You're not even human. So is Madam ready to leave here at once?!" Again she pointed sharply at the door.

"Please, I must immerse today! I have to!" said the young woman. "I don't understand what your problem is."

"That." Four raised arms pointed simultaneously at the gold cross. "That's our problem," Dina, Miriam, Paula, and Michaela chimed in unison.

"Listen, this chain was given to me by Grandma, by my great-grandmother, when I turned twelve."

"For the bat mitzvah?" The four balaniyot were stunned.

"No. For Communion. It's like a bat mitzvah. And I've worn it ever since. It's always with me. I got bigger and the chain stayed small, as you see." She picked up the crucifix and held it closer to them.

"*Shema Yisrael!*"* The cluster of balaniyot reared back. "So you're a real Christian?"

"I'm an atheist. I'm not with any religion. No church, no

---

*"Hear O Israel," an exclamation of horror uttered in the face of imminent disaster.

synagogue. For me this is just a souvenir from Grandma. A childhood keepsake. It's not religion."

"So what in the world are you doing here? You're not religious, you wear a cross, and you've come to immerse in the mikveh?" Dina asked.

"I must immerse. I have finished seven clean days and I must do an immersion," she said, clasping her hands in desperation. "Please. If there was a sea or a river around here, that would be like a mikveh and I would immerse in nature. But there isn't."

"From where does a Christian like you know all this?" one of them asked as the balaniyot's defensive barricade eased ever so slightly.

"From the Kabbalah Center. Here"—she pulled a slim booklet from her purse, printed with the title: *Dialing God: Daily Connection Book; Technology for the Soul*[6]—and showed it to the balaniyot, explaining: "The mikveh is a pool of living water. The water in the Kabbalah Center mikveh comes from underground wells. They say that all the wells on earth are connected. So, when we immerse ourselves in the Kabbalah Center mikveh, we are immersing body and soul in the same water that fills the mikveh of Rabbi Yitzhak Luria, the sixteenth-century Kabbalist of Safed. It's like we're touching the waters of Jerusalem's Shiloach spring, which were used by the high priest in Solomon's Temple up until about two thousand years ago."

"What a nice thought," murmured Michaela.

"The Kabbalah says that water has powers of mercy, sharing, and healing."

"I don't understand the English," Miriam said to Dina, and Michaela promptly translated for her. "Please, could you speak only Hebrew? Miriam doesn't speak English and it's a little hard for us to understand too."

"Okay. I go to the Kabbalah Center regularly," she continued in Hebrew for Miriam's benefit. "There I learn about a proper way of life, about the connection between spirit and body. Kabbalah for me is a way of life. It's not religion. Immersing in the water and observing family purity is one of the most important conditions for maintaining a balanced and healthy way of life. I'm on vacation in Israel and I must purify myself. I never imagined that I'd have a problem here—in the Holy Land, of all places."

"Is that where you learned your excellent Hebrew, too?" Miriam inquired.

"Thank you." The woman smiled with pleasure, and it was apparent this wasn't the first time she'd received this compliment. "No. The Hebrew is from college. I studied a little Judaism."

"And what do you do for a living?" Miriam inquired.

"My profession is singing," she said, batting fair eyelashes coated with pale green mascara.

"I knew it!" Michaela's eyes opened wide, followed by her mouth, and she forgot to close both, like a teenager suddenly finding herself within touching distance of the pop star who graced the silvery poster taped to her bedroom door.

"Knew what?" A gleam of hope flashed in the young woman's eyes.

"Hold on a minute—are you married?" Miriam inquired.

"No," the young woman answered. "I'm not married, but I have a man, and I'm a mother. I have two children."

"You know that we don't immerse single women, divorcees, or widows."

"But it's like a common-law marriage, and I'm kind of well-known . . ."

"Are you a Jew?"

"No."

"Then who knows you? I'm sorry, but here we only let Jewish women immerse in the holy waters of the mikveh. It's strictly off-limits for Christian women."

"But look," the young woman protested, extracting a

carefully folded paper from her colorful, crystal-studded Swarovski purse and waving the paper in Miriam's face.

"What have you got there?" Miriam narrowed her eyes. "A black Star of David with 'kosher' written on it? Give that to me." She reached out and snatched the paper as if trying to rescue the sacred Jewish symbol from the non-Jew's hands.

"This paper was attached to my meal on the airplane. I only fly El Al because of the kosher. I eat only kosher food. That's not enough for you to let me immerse?"

"What does one thing have to do with the other? There's no connection," ruled Miriam as she examined the piece of paper. "I'm sorry, young lady." She handed the paper back to her. "Try somewhere else. Not here in my mikveh."

Tears welled in the young woman's khaki-colored eyes, and one trickled down, gathering on its path a bead of perspiration from a nose reddened by shame, and the two blended together into a single large droplet that clung to the tip of that delicate nose, as the woman's head bowed further.

"Tell me . . ." Michaela maneuvered herself so that her head was just below the young woman's face, and the droplet plopped from the sorrowful nose right onto the lens of Michaela's eyeglasses. "*Oysh*," she said as she wiped her glasses with her skirt before putting them back on. "You're not by any chance . . . the singer . . . who was supposed to come to Israel right at this time but canceled because of the threats against her?"

"Yes . . . Madonna . . ."

"I knew it! Oh, Miriam! I don't believe it! This is Madonna herself! Madonna, in the flesh!" Michaela squealed with joy, jumped out of her seat, stretched out her arms, and began twirling around in circles like a Sufi dervish, her white dress floating like a bright halo around her body.

"What's got into her? It looks likes she's possessed by a dybbuk, heaven forbid. I've never seen her like this." Miriam looked at Michaela as if she'd lost her mind.

"I don't believe it! It's Madonna!" Michaela lifted her head skyward and covered both ears with her hands and called out to the gray ceiling: "Oh my gosh, I'm going to tell my children that Madonna came to Mommy's work. They'll go nuts!"

"Where's Madonna?" asked Dina, who'd just returned from immersing another woman. "Who? You?" She scrutinized the young woman, who'd now paled, and her expression changed abruptly. "Oh my gosh! You're right! It is Madonna!"

"What's a Madonna?" Miriam raised an eyebrow at all the fuss.

"The mother of Jesus," answered Dina. "The one who they say gave birth to him as a virgin."

"Jesus?!" Miriam's eyes bulged from their sockets. "That terrible name! Michaela, stop bouncing around already! What is this demonic dance?!"

"Don't worry," Dina hastened to reassure Miriam. "Now Madonna has changed her name to Esther."

"Esther? Why in the world did this shiksa* choose the name of the queen who saved the Jewish people from the wrath of the evil Haman?‡ Thank goodness she didn't choose my name." Miriam was horrified.

The blonde hurried to Michaela, who was still caught up in her wild dance. "It's not me," she said, trying to stop Michaela's celebration. "I mean, I'm me, but I'm not Madonna. My name was originally Maria, but I changed it to Miriam."

"Paula, bring me a glass of water," Miriam moaned.

Michaela abruptly ceased her whirling. "Huh? What do you mean you're not her? I have eyes, don't I? The nose is the

---

*From Yiddish, an often disparaging term used to refer to a non-Jewish woman.

‡In the Book of Esther, chief minister of King Ahasuerus who sought the Jews' annihilation.

same nose, the eyes are the same eyes, the hair is the same hair. You're probably just being modest. You don't want publicity. Don't worry. You're safe here. This place is airtight. Here there is absolute discretion. Nothing leaks out of the mikveh. Ever."

"I'm sorry, but I'm not Madonna," the non-Jewish woman quietly repeated.

"They say that everyone has a double somewhere in the world," Michaela sighed, the light in her eyes dying out and her body sagging with disappointment. "So you're just Madonna's double . . ." She looked at her thoughtfully. "How lucky you are; she's so beautiful." Michaela smiled and a glimmer of love restored the light to her eyes. "Like you, Madonna is not Jewish, and she's also very deep into Kabbalah, right?" she asked, attempting to sprinkle the double with stardust.

"You won't believe it, but the two of us are also mystically connected to water. Madonna is a Leo, and I'm a Scorpio. In the Zohar* it says that the energies and strengths of these two signs are so great they could uproot the works of creation. In the Talmud, in Tractate Berakhot, it says: 'At the time when the Holy One, blessed be he, wanted to bring a flood upon the world, he took two stars from Kimah and brought a flood upon the world. And when he wanted to stop it, he took two stars from 'Ayish and stopped it.' 'Ayish is likened to a lion and Kimah to a scorpion." The blond woman basked in the glow of her temporary stardom.

"For us, worshiping the stars and the zodiac is idolatry," Miriam snapped.

"Both of us also make sure to drink pure water that's sold at the Kabbalah Center. Most of our body is made up of wa-

---

*The most important Kabbalistic work, attributed to Simeon Bar-Yochai, who lived near the end of the first century AD; considered by critics to be a thirteenth-century compilation.

ter. When I drink this special water I'm purifying my body from inside. I believe that my body is like a miniature cosmos and I flood my cosmos with holy water. This water goes in through the mouth, cleanses my entire system, and finally goes out—"

"Through the urine," Michaela said triumphantly, completing the sentence for her.

"No," the blonde responded. "Through the vagina. We women are like a flowing spring. Our vagina is always moist, but especially before intercourse a lot of fluids are secreted into the vagina, which wet it and prepare it for penetration, and afterwards, when I experience an orgasm, my vagina is flooded with fluids that come from within the womb, that wash the vagina and flow and spill out. It's like a self-purification system that cleanses the vagina and prepares it for the next intercourse. The mikveh waters purify me once a month from the outside and my body's waters purify me regularly from the inside and ensure that every experience of intercourse happens in purity."

"Sheer nonsense," Paula remarked, unable to contain herself.

"So why do you think the vagina dries up for postmenopausal* women? Because they're done menstruating. They can't get pregnant anymore so there's no need for the body to cleanse itself. Since God didn't create anything superfluous in the body, the self-cleansing mechanism ceases to operate and they dry up."

"To each his own," said Michaela, mesmerized.

"Why don't we get back to Madonna?" said Dina, bored with the direction the conversation had taken. "Does she even know that you exist?"

"Yes. I saw her once at one of the lectures at the center.

---

*This status is referred to in Hebrew, in the context of the family purity laws, as *mesuleket damim*, literally "free of blood."

Very modest. Very neat. And when she came out her eyes gleamed with a passion to learn more and her aura was very tender, like she was overflowing with love. Her eyes shone with a radiance that suffused all of us there."

"What is this place? A center for non-Jews who want to come back to the Jewish religion . . . um, I mean . . . to convert?" asked Miriam.

"No. Kabbalah is not religion. It's a way of life. We needn't be Jews to join the circle of believers. The Kabbalah teaches us how to live in a better, more correct, healthier way; it shows us how to take responsibility and attain full control of our lives. All with the help of heavenly guidance. This combination of letters"—she pointed to the אלד on her chest—"is one of God's seventy-two names. Each one has a special meaning and purpose. This combination guards against the evil eye. And this red string also protects me"—she held out her slender wrist. "It's not just any string. It's a sacred string that we buy at the center, and it's not cheap either, but it's worth every dollar, because it protects us from the evil eye. At the center there's a mikveh and we come to immerse. There are two types of immersion. Spiritual immersion and physical immersion. Spiritual immersion can be done as many times a month as you like. Physical immersion is done for the purpose of family purity. The immersion that purifies us from the niddah of the blood allows us to have relations with the man. I keep two weeks a month; no one comes near me. We believe very strongly in the water's power to change worlds, to cleanse, to purify, to preserve sanity, to repair. Water is the most important part of our rituals."

"It sounds like the end of the world to me," muttered Miriam. "Complete chaos."

"Actually, that's just a small part of the whole mess," said another woman, who had stopped on her way out of the mikveh and had come to bid the balaniyot good-bye. "I moved to Israel from Long Island, and some of the single women in our community there immerse in the mikveh before going on a date. They purify themselves before going to have sex with their boyfriends, even if their lovers are not Jewish. They have a need to purify and sanctify the sexual act that's performed without the benefit of marriage and they feel that the holy waters in the mikveh do just that."

"And the balaniyot in the mikveh let them do this?" Miriam was aghast.

"First of all, who knows better than you that there is no way to really control these things?" the woman said. "After all, you don't question each woman about whether or not she's married. And second, it's really become the fashion, and the religious institutions can't withstand the tide. The public is expressing its demands and bending the halakha to its needs. And a third reason is that the Jewish communities in the Diaspora are very eager to preserve any affinity for Judaism and its symbols. So if lots of young Jewish women feel a need to immerse in the mikveh, they mustn't be turned away, because it's better than them not coming at all and assimilating with non-Jews and forgetting their Jewish roots."

"*Oy Gevalt!** I don't feel well," Miriam cried, clamping her hands over her heart.

"Why, Miriam?" asked Dina. "This is news to you? Here, too, we have a serious problem with lots of girls who come and want to immerse. They're secular, they're not married, and they want to immerse in order to receive a blessing from the waters. The rabbis themselves send us these single women. Not a day goes by without a woman showing up who was sent by some rabbi and then we have to turn her away. We are absolutely unwilling to cooperate with these rabbis who totally cheapen the sanctity of immersion. But we can't

---

*"Help!" or "Oh dear!" in Yiddish.

always resist the pressure, and it's becoming more and more of a problem. These beliefs are spreading among the young people, among the secular especially, who are searching for roots and searching for answers and come here because they think immersion is the way to find spiritual and emotional satisfaction."

"You know what? Better they immerse in the mikveh than go and worship some guru in an ashram in India," said Michaela.

"There's a reason why they want to immerse here," Paula said. "Water really does have amazing healing properties. My grandmother told me that the inhabitants of Jerusalem believed so strongly in the seawater's ability to heal the sick, enhance masculinity, and help the childless that they impatiently awaited the summer months when they could go down to the Jaffa shore and immerse."

"An excellent idea!" Miriam suddenly brightened. "And you, young lady," she said, turning to the Madonna look-alike. "You go right down to the sea in Tel Aviv or Jaffa and immerse. There it's just between you and the Creator. Here I must obey the rules of the halakha, the rabbis, and my conscience. I cannot put a non-Jewish woman in the waters and afterward, heaven forbid, immerse a bride, or any woman, lest the impurity adhere to her."

"Are you sure that it's forbidden? Maybe you could ask the rabbi first?" the blonde pleaded.

"Sorry, but I have no intention of asking any rabbi, because I know what the answer will be," said Miriam. "And you know what? In this case it doesn't matter to me what the rabbi would say. What matters is what my conscience says, and I'm not about to take even the tiniest chance that my mikveh will be polluted by the flesh of a non-Jew and defile a Jewish bride on the eve of her wedding, heaven forbid. Farewell, young lady," Miriam concluded in a cold, clear tone. "This discussion is over."

The blonde exited shamefacedly without saying good-bye. Total silence descended upon the mikveh. No bell rang. No one spoke. All movement ceased.

"There's no end to the tests that Hashem puts us to," said Miriam, breaking the silence. The bells announcing the next immersions clanged loudly once more, the balaniyot responded, and life in the mikveh returned to normal.

[4]

BLOOD AND BANISHMENT

Ten curses God brought upon Eve after the serpent tempted her: "I shall greatly multiply thy pain and thy travail; in pain thou shall bring forth children; and thy desire shall be to thy husband, and he shall rule over thee" (Gen. 3:16).

The Jewish sages counted seven: "I shall greatly multiply" (*harbeh arbeh* in Hebrew) contains the first and second curses, which relate to the two types of blood secreted through the vagina—the blood of niddah (menstruation) and virginal blood (when the hymen is rent for the first time). The others are as follows:

"thy pain"—the hardship of raising children;

"thy travail"—the hardship and sickness of pregnancy;

"in pain thou shall bring forth children"—the hardship of labor;

"thy desire shall be to thy husband"—the longing a woman feels when her husband is not with her;

"he shall rule over thee"—the prohibition against a woman's openly expressing her desire for sexual relations; the man dictates when, how, and where this takes place.

To these seven curses, the Talmudic sage Rabbi Dimi and his commentator Rashi* added three more:

"covered like a mourner"—it is a disgrace for a woman to go out with her head uncovered;[1]

"forbidden to every man"—she is forbidden to all men except for her husband, while the man may have multiple wives;[2]

"jailed in a prison"—in the spirit of the phrase from Psalms, "All the honor of the king's daughter is within," meaning it is a woman's duty to be modest and introverted, in order to prevent a repeat of the original temptation and sin.

All of these curses are connected to a woman's physicality and sexuality. All are insulting, hurtful, and humiliating to her being, as they underscore the inequality between her and the man, an inequality that comes as punishment for the terrible sin she committed in the Garden. Terrible, because it shattered the vision of human perfection and immortality and led to mankind's expulsion from the heavenly paradise to the earthly, impulse-driven, flawed world that required individuals to be constantly on guard against the inherent potential for sin. Thus man and woman became mortal, and she inferior—lacking control and enslaved to the man and to her menstrual cycle, month in and month out.

Two curses, that of the blood of niddah and of the virginal blood, are related to the blood of the woman's body: they are her punishment for having caused Adam to sin and spilling his blood, "the blood of the world," by making him mortal. The niddah blood that is spilled from the woman's

---

*Rashi is an acronym for the famous eleventh-century biblical and Talmudic commentator Rabbi Shlomo Yitzhaki.

body is "blood that amends or atones" (*dam tikkun*) for her having spilled the blood of the world (of Adam). Therefore, the woman must be careful in her time of niddah, and thus she may bring remedy (*takana*) to the world.[3]

God marked the bodies of Adam and Eve with signs of the punishment for their sin. Adam and Eve did not accept the divine rules that prevailed in the Garden of Eden; with their bodies they broke the rules and trespassed when they ate the forbidden fruit of the tree of knowledge. They received their knowledge via the mouth and for this their bodies were punished by becoming mortal: "For dust thou art and unto dust thou shall return" (Gen. 3:19).

The origin of the word "niddah" is the Aramaic word *nadu*, meaning to throw, to distance from, to remove; to reject, to ban, to ostracize, to expel from the community; to deny a person the right to derive pleasure from something.

The root of the Hebrew word "niddah" is nun-daled-daled, or *nadad*, which reflects the woman's continuous wandering from one state of being to another over the course of her life cycle: from fertility to barrenness, from permitted to forbidden, from excluded to accepted in the community, from nature to culture.

In the Bible, the word "niddah" is used metaphorically in the sense of filth, abomination, and revulsion,[4] and menstruation is perceived as an illness. *Isha dava* (Lev. 20:18) is a woman who is ailing in her impurity and her illness is contagious. The deeply negative meaning of "niddah" became an inseparable part of the woman's negative image in patriarchal Jewish society throughout the ages.

Sociologists, anthropologists, folklorists, and other researchers of human civilization distinguish between nature and culture. Culture comprises an array of symbols, concepts, perceptions, and rituals that give meaning to the actions of human beings. Culture explains reality, instills order, and helps people interact with the world. Culture transforms nature; it conveys what is in nature to the realm of culture. It transforms something from a "raw," uncontrolled, wild, and natural state to a "cooked" state that is controllable and deemed acceptable. Everything from nature that undergoes an acculturation process matures and changes in accordance with the understandings and beliefs that guide human behavior.[5]

Ever since the destruction of the Second Temple, the Jewish people, a nation that dwells alone, lived as a social and cultural minority among the Gentiles. The constant threat to the Jews as a distinct minority is reflected in their tenacious efforts to preserve a certain isolation, to maintain a physical purity that is untainted by their surroundings. Naturally, the body's orifices signified areas of vulnerability and peril for the Jews, who compulsively set boundaries that separated them from their surroundings. Bodily discharges were perceived by them as contaminating and hazardous. They differentiated between discharges that are subject to control, such as tears, saliva, mucus, urine, and feces, and those that are not subject to control, such as semen and menstrual blood. Of all the bodily secretions, menstrual blood is considered the most perilous. Semen is perilous when it is discharged to no purposeful end, when it is not completely ejaculated into the woman's womb, where it could potentially fertilize the egg.

These two bodily secretions are connected with death. Their loss symbolizes the potential loss of the creation of life. The blood of niddah is a metaphor for death because it is created as a consequence of the death of an egg in the woman's womb. If the man's sperm is spilled in vain inside a menstruating woman's womb, a potential human life is lost. Therefore, said the Jewish sages, having intercourse while the woman is menstruating falls in the category of transgressions that carry the penalty of death, such as adultery, incest, and homosexuality. All of these transgressions constitute a threat

to the continued survival of the Jewish people. The prohibitions against sexual relations with a woman in niddah derive
from the act's lack of usefulness. A woman in niddah cannot
become pregnant. Therefore, she is not to be approached. In
Judaism, all that is not purposeful is considered wasteful and
is consequently forbidden.[6]

At Sinai, the chosen people received the Torah, God's
"cookbook." The Torah gives exact recipes that enumerate
in minute detail how the Jewish nation can preserve itself
as separate and pure, elevated above all the other nations. A
common thread running through the Torah is the concept of
categorization and separation. Sociologist Nissan Rubin explains that Jewish culture is scrupulous in defining categories
and setting clear boundaries and does not allow for even the
slightest exception or deviation from them.[7] The most basic
classification differentiates between Jews (culture) and non-
Jews (nature). Whoever takes upon himself the burden of the
Torah leaves the realm of the raw, undefined state of nature
and enters the defined and cultured realm of Judaism.

Within itself, Judaism posits further differentiations—
between male and female, between one kind of blood and
another, between male blood and female blood.

Male blood is "pure" blood, that is, blood that is subject
to control. The blood from a wound (*petzia*), such as from
circumcision, ritual sacrifice, or the ritual slaughter of animals, falls into this category. Not only is it not defiling, but
it is also considered holy. In the patriarchal Jewish world
there is complete control over an array of customs associated
with the spilling of blood. Male blood is willful (*retzoni*); it is
spilled from the body in a conscious manner, at a preset time,
in the course of a rite that is conducted solely by man and in
which each and every step is planned and timed and known.
There are no surprises and no exceptions. All is under control. Male control.

Female blood is the menstrual blood that is discharged

from the woman's womb into the "corridor" (*prozdor*); that is, the vaginal canal. This is blood that is not subject to control, and hence is defiling, contaminating, and desecrating, and deemed hazardous to the set social order. This female blood erupts in a wild, uncontrolled manner and crosses the body's set boundaries. It flows into the realm of uncontrollable nature and threatens the man, who exists at all times within the realm of culture. It provokes him to try to exert control over the woman's rebellious body from which it comes forth, as well as over her soul, which, like the blood, transcends borders and becomes a wild, uninhibited, sexual, lustful entity that constitutes a physical and spiritual danger to male society.

As long as the woman's blood is discharged from her womb, the man sees it as his duty to set behavioral boundaries (*siyagim*) for her, along with all sorts of rules to control the conduct of the bleeding female within the society and the family, in the belief that he is thereby minimizing the destructive influences of uncontrolled nature over disciplined culture. In the time that a married woman has her period, she is subject to the "blood ban" (*herem hadam*), meaning that she is required to withdraw from society and to abstain from all contact with those around her. Thus are the negative energies of menstrual blood restricted to her realm and prevented from spreading and endangering her soul and the souls of her family members. When the woman's body ceases bleeding, it's as though it has become tamed. It passes from the realm of nature to the realm of culture, and the woman is permitted—after having cleansed herself from the impurity of the blood—to return to being a part of her environment and of her family.

The blood of childbirth is not defiling like menstrual blood. Its impurity is not seen to be as serious as the impurity of the dead, because birth does not symbolize an abrogation of life.[8] When the Holy Temple was in existence, women whose postpartum bleeding had ceased would bring a sacrifice of two turtledoves. Bringing this sacrifice would purify them from their blood. The purification of the blood of childbirth with the blood of the sacrifice amounted to a purification of un- controlled bloodshed by means of controlled bloodshed. The controllable blood of the sacrifice compensated for the blood of childbirth, which is not subject to control.[9]

Since the destruction of the Holy Temple, blood is no lon- ger purified with blood, but with water. Immersion in the ritual bath stands in for the offering of a sacrifice. The im- mersion ceremony, like the sacrifice, is a ritual that is subject to male supervision.

God commanded that immersion and purification be done in "living water" (*mayim hayyim*)—water that is in a "natu- ral" state, untouched by human hands. On the most funda- mental level, women who immerse in the mikveh have a faith in the water's power that is derived from an ancient Hebrew concept of the divine presence in water. Water, which accord- ing to Jewish belief contains and reflects God's strength, is considered a pure substance. Only a substance that is itself pure can serve to cleanse one of impurity. The great folk- lorist and ethnographer Raphael Patai distinguishes between two types of impurity: "physical impurity" and "ritual im- purity."[10]

Physical impurity is defined as "impurity that can pass from one person to another, such as illness, dirt, and so on." Human beings' belief in the power of water to remove physical impurity from them received corroboration in daily life. Water rinsed and cleaned their food, their utensils, their clothing, and their bodies.

Ritual impurity is defined as "a special condition of a per- son or an object that does not allow it to come in contact with God." Water has the power to purify only certain types of temporary ritual impurity. If the impurity is of a permanent nature, then water has no effect on it. Water cannot make impure animals* pure or purify a corpse, which from the moment of death enters a state of permanent impurity.

Someone who is affected by a (temporary) ritual impurity needs to undergo immersion—*tevila* or, as the Torah says, *rehitza* ("washing" or "cleansing"). In the mikveh, women remove both types of impurity: they remove the physical impurity when they clean their bodies so very thoroughly in preparation for immersion, and the ritual impurity is lifted from them during the immersion itself.

The myriad instructions regarding classification and distinction between one sort of blood and another, between one stain and another, between one type of vaginal discharge and another are all drummed into the head of the Jewish bride before her wedding. And the fact that these extremely intimate matters have been dictated by male rabbis from Talmudic times up until the present may easily cause any thinking woman to shudder. The Torah's injunction is simple: a woman in niddah requires *tahara,* purification. But then the Jewish sages came and added extra stringencies and essentially poked and prodded and stuck their noses into a woman's most private, intimate parts, into her house of secrets (*beit hastarim*), her hidden places, deep into her sexual organs, and came up with a multitude of classifications and intricate rules whose entire purpose is to ensure that the woman does indeed know her body and recognizes and understands the results of her *tahara* inspection. These male-dictated rules clearly imply that a woman's intellectual abilities cannot be relied upon.

God, on the other hand, trusting in the wisdom of the being he created from Adam's rib, gave a clear instruction:

---

*Impure (unkosher) hoofed mammals are those, such as pigs and horses, that do not meet the two criteria of having a cloven hoof and chewing the cud (see Lev. 11:26).

> And a woman who has a discharge of blood for a number of days during a time that is not part of her [period of] separation—or if, after having passed her [period of] separation, she has a discharge again, then all the days of the discharge of her uncleanness shall be as in the days of her [period of] separation; she is unclean. Any bed on which she lies on any day of her discharge shall be for her like the bed of her [period of] separation, and any article on which she sits shall be unclean like the uncleanness of her [period of] separation. And whoever comes near to [i.e., touches] them becomes unclean; he must wash his garments, bathe in water and remains unclean until evening. (Lev. 15:25–27)

God had confidence in the woman's ability to properly implement his instruction. The Jewish sages, however, feared that in her innate foolishness, ignorance, and simplemindedness, a woman wouldn't know, God forbid, how to accurately interpret the discharges she saw with her own eyes, that she wouldn't be able to distinguish between the blood of niddah and another sort of blood or another kind of discharge from her vagina, that she wouldn't be able to decipher the workings of her own body—and that as a result she herself would sin and also cause her entire community to sin.

So what did they do? They set about composing an elaborate system of rules and conditions relating to every possible form that a woman's flow of blood could take. They wrote vivid descriptions of how each potential stain that may be absorbed by a woman's undergarments would look and smell, and of how each and every one should be treated. They also characterized two types of fundamental feelings, differentiating between the feeling that a woman has upon the onset of her period, before her blood comes out: "fatigue, nausea, stomach ache and so on," and the feeling she has just when the blood comes out from inside her, when "her source is opened" (a feeling that the cervix is opening) "and her body is shaken by a kind of chill and something moist flows between her legs."[11] Every married woman is obliged to learn by heart, to fully grasp and absorb with all her soul all the signs and sensations that indicate niddah, maintained the Jewish sages; she must internalize them so well that they become an integral part of her being. Only thus can she predict her time of impurity and withdraw from society on time, as required by the blood ban.

The scent of menstrual blood, said to possess a unique smell, apparently intoxicated the Jewish sages and blinded them from recalling that it was actually the daughters of Israel who originally imposed upon themselves draconian strictures regarding the stains of menstruation. The women, who customarily brought sacrifices to the Temple as a group, were so careful to remain pure that they counted seven full menstrual days followed by seven clean days to avoid the slightest danger of entering the Temple in a state of impurity. The rabbis also did not realize that the women adopted this strict approach in order to have a uniform method of counting and thereby avoid confusion regarding the calculation of an individual woman's unclean days. It appears that the Jewish sages appropriated from the realm of female custom and tradition these extra strictures regarding the stains, and enshrined them as unassailable halakha.

Or perhaps it was the fear of blood that led the Jewish sages to impose the rules of the blood ban upon women. For they were males and, like many males the world over, they evidently were affected by castration anxiety. The cultural researcher William Stephens argued that this type of anxiety affects a man who sees—or even just thinks about—a woman who is bleeding from her genitals.[12] Fear and feelings of inferiority are, according to Stephens, what propel males to impose a blood ban and thus keep women removed from all prestigious forms of activity and mark them as inferior.

The psychoanalyst and cultural researcher Bruno Bettel-
heim believed that "vagina envy"—male envy of the woman's
fantastic capacity for giving birth—inflicts a greater fear than
does castration anxiety and is what lies at the root of men's
feeling threatened by women's menstrual blood.[13] A feminist
approach might find an answer in the male need to preserve
the "proper" social order within his community, a need that
may have driven rabbis to wallow in the halakhot of the
blood of niddah, devising ever more stringent and intricate
prohibitions and bans with which to burden women.

The blood of niddah is a dominant factor in the personal
and formal relations between a Jewish husband and wife.
Niddah blood may be likened to a red flag hoisted over the
battleground in the war between the sexes. It is that which
calls for the marking of boundaries within the Jewish family.
It is that which proclaims that the time has come for isolation
and separation between husband and wife and demands the
creation of a demilitarized zone. It is that which threatens
that the punishment for the infiltrator beyond the permitted
boundary is death and which assures those heroes who con-
quer their impulses and observe secure boundaries domestic tranquility (*shalom bayit*), as well as eternal security and
stability for them and their descendants for generations to
come. The laws of niddah are cold and rigid and scrupulously
demanding of women and constitute a central aspect of the
definition of the Jewish woman and the shaping of her identity. "A hedge of roses" (*suga bashoshanim*)* is how the sages
referred to these halakhot, cloaking in misleadingly pretty
language the debasing rules of separation, which include the
following:[14]

It is forbidden for husband and wife to sit side by side
on one seat. It is forbidden for them to touch one an-

---

*The phrase comes from Song of Songs 7:3.

other, even indirectly, via an object that is passed from hand to hand, with the exception of a baby that expresses a desire to move from one parent to the other.

It is forbidden for husband and wife to touch the other's clothes while they are being worn—to brush off lint, for example.

It is forbidden for husband and wife to toss an object from one to the other.

It is forbidden for husband and wife to sit together on a seat that moves when sat upon, such as a rocking chair or a sofa with a single cushion, unless another person sits between them or a visible object is placed between them.

It is forbidden for the wife to make her husband's bed in his presence.

It is forbidden for the wife to lie on her husband's bed; it is forbidden for the husband to lie on his wife's bed or to use her pillow.

It is forbidden for husband and wife to eat from the same dish or drink from the same cup; when dining at the same table, husband and wife must make some change from the ordinary, such as placing between their plates something that isn't needed for the purpose of the meal; or having the wife sit somewhere other than her regular spot or having another person (or more) sit between them.

It is forbidden for husband and wife to drink from the same bottle, even if using two straws.

It is forbidden for husband and wife to eat directly from the serving dish, with the exception of foods that are taken from them occasionally such as bread, fruit, and so on. Other foods should be placed on separate dishes before each spouse.

It is forbidden for husband and wife to pour a drink for or serve food to one another unless some change is introduced, such as pouring with the left hand instead of the right or placing the dish some distance away.

It is forbidden for the husband to pour wine for his wife. The wife is permitted to drink the Kiddush wine,* even directly from the Kiddush cup, on condition that the husband puts it down on the table and does not pass it directly to his wife; a wife may pour wine for her husband, but only in a way that is out of the ordinary.

It is forbidden for husband and wife to sleep in the same bed, no matter how wide; their two beds must be separated so that neither the beds nor the blankets are touching. Optimally, there should be at least arm's length distance between them; during the day, when not in use, the beds may be pushed together.

It is forbidden for husband and wife to prepare bathing water for the other, including adding water to the bathtub, in the other's presence. They may prepare water for one another for the ritual morning hand-washing.

It is forbidden for husband and wife to behave in a way that might arouse passion; during niddah, the woman should still take care to look pretty for her husband, but not too attractive or tempting.

It is forbidden for the husband to see parts of his wife's body that are usually covered; therefore, it is forbidden for a wife to get dressed in front of her husband.

It is forbidden for the husband to intentionally sniff his wife's perfume, either on her or her clothes.

It is forbidden for the husband to hear his wife singing.

It is forbidden for husband and wife to discuss inti-

---

*The wine over which the blessing is recited at the Friday night Sabbath meal and holiday meals.

mate subjects that might arouse sexual impulses. It is permitted to study and discuss the laws of niddah. Husband and wife are to maintain the rules of separation even when one of them is ill and needs the other's care. However, if no one else is able to care for the ailing spouse, the healthy spouse may do so, while avoiding words of affection.[15]

It would appear that the woman is a passive victim of a male conceptual system that torments her with a wide range of prohibitions and social exclusion.

So it would appear, yet this is not the case.

5

PURITY AND SEXUALITY

The rabbis needn't enforce the blood ban on devoutly religious women. Most ultra-Orthodox women willingly accept the excommunication associated with their niddah blood. With the onset of her menstrual bleeding comes the blossoming of a girl's sexuality, as she goes from being an "unripe fruit" (*pri boser*) to a fertile woman.

The balaniyot at the mikveh speak of menstruation in positive terms. "As yeast is good for the dough, menstruation is good for women," says Doris the balanit. "A woman without a period is as impotent as a man without an erection," pronounces Miriam. In the religious world, fertility, femininity, and sexuality are integrally connected. Since fertility is not possible without blood, women's niddah impurity proclaims their fertility potential loud and clear and validates their sexuality.

Ask an ultra-Orthodox woman to describe a woman at the height of her femininity and sexuality and she'll describe a woman who is teetering under the weight of her advanced pregnancy. Ask her to provide a caption for this image and she'll say, "A wondrous device manufactured by the Holy One, blessed be he, for giving birth to children."

"When my womb is loaded with eggs and all ready to absorb and fertilize my husband's sperm, when I'm not having my period and am fertile and ready to glide into a state of pregnancy and nursing, I'm in my primal state as a woman," explains Shlomit, a modern Orthodox woman who has recently immigrated from Long Island and who instructs young mothers in the art of breast-feeding. "In the past, women were hardly ever in a state of niddah. They got their period once or twice over a period of a couple of months, something like that, but afterwards, when they got pregnant, they nursed until the child was four or five, because this was the most important food, and they would become pregnant again while still nursing and continue to nurse, so that a woman might only go to immerse in the mikveh four or five times her whole life, that's all. I'm that way, too. I have eight children, may they all be healthy, and altogether, I've immersed in the mikveh maybe ten times since the day I got married eleven years ago. Every time I immersed I returned to my natural primal state as a woman, a state of readiness for pregnancy. A state of fertility."

The religious woman's sexuality is identified with pregnancy. Conception is the result of a sexual act. A woman who has conceived is a blessed woman whose husband desires her and has intercourse with her. Only when new life begins to sprout in her womb is her femininity maximally fulfilled. A woman who does not bring children into the world is not considered a real woman, in the eyes of her community and in her own eyes, in the ultra-Orthodox view. A barren woman, no matter how beautiful, will turn green with envy at the sight of a graceless, homely woman who is hugely pregnant and has a gaggle of small children trooping behind her as she pushes a baby carriage.

As powerful as menstrual blood's negative association is, its positive connotation is just as strong. Menstrual blood is a metaphor for life. It is a uniquely creative force and a reminder of the fact that the Creator, when he created us in his image, chose to imprint his most exalted trait—the ability to create life—exclusively in the body of the woman and not in the body of the man. This divine characteristic is reflected in the amazing changes and transitions from one state to another that occur within the woman's body and are intrinsically tied to the blood that flows in her. There are three such phenomena: the onset of menses, pregnancy, and lactation. The onset of menses transforms the girl into a woman. The anthropologist Carol Ochs describes this change as qualitative rather than quantitative.[1] Menstruation brings a fundamental change in a girl's social standing. The moment her body is capable of receiving the man's sperm and being fertilized by it, she enters the circle of women who are designated for marriage, those who will give birth to the next generation, which will continue to build their husbands' family trees.

For a fertile woman, the cessation of menstruation signifies the start of a pregnancy. In many traditional societies, the fetus is considered a product of the blood. The Jewish sages also believed that since the menstrual blood does not come out of the woman's body during pregnancy, it is "building" the fetus during this time: "A woman's womb is always full of blood and still, drops of sperm fall into it and immediately the offspring is formed."[2] After the birth, the blood turns into the milk that flows in the woman's breasts and nourishes the baby. Developmental psychologist Erich Neumann maintains that the woman's amazing capacity to transform her body's blood into milk that nourishes her babies is what made her responsible for transforming raw nutrients from nature into actual foods through the processes of cooking, baking, and fermentation.[3]

The Jewish sages believed that as long as she is nursing her baby, a woman is not fertile and will not become pregnant. Rabbi Meir explained the cessation of menstruation during pregnancy as follows: "The blood is decomposed and turns into milk," hence, in his view, a woman does not conceive while lactating, for "because of the milk, the blood disappears."[4]

In a thirteenth-century disputation with the Christians, as part of his argument against the idea of Mary's Immaculate Conception, Rabbi David Kimhi (called Radak) contended that "even fools" know that every female from about the age of thirteen has a time of blood each month, and when a woman conceives, she does not see any blood, since during pregnancy the blood is helping to nourish the offspring in the womb. He added that a few days after the woman gives birth, that same menstrual blood goes to the woman's breasts, where it turns to milk.[5]

Without blood there is no fertility. A woman without a menstrual period is like arid ground that thirsts for the fluid of life, for blood, to fertilize it. Blood and not water. Carol Ochs explains that the biblical story of Cain and Abel, in which God accepts Abel's offering of lambs from his flock but rejects Cain's offering of fruit from the ground he tilled, illustrates the intrinsic connection between the spilling of blood and the fertilization of the earth. Cain, the tiller of the earth, thinks his offering is not acceptable to God because the produce of his land is not good enough. He must perform a rite of atonement in order to avert divine rejection. He must spill blood in order to infuse his soil with new life.[6] Only earth that is saturated with blood undergoes a mysterious process of renewal in which it is transformed from barren and arid to fertile and fruitful.

The Talmud teaches that there are three partners in the creation of the human being—the Holy One, blessed be he, the father, and the mother: "The father supplies the semen, from which are formed the white elements of the body, that is, the bones, sinews, nails, brain and the whites of the eyes; the mother—'Mother Earth'—supplies the red elements, out of which are formed the skin, flesh, hair, blood and the dark of the eye; and the Holy One, blessed be He, supplies the spirit and the soul."[7]

The ultra-Orthodox woman's femininity is subject to the strict rules of the halakha. The couple's initial sex life is shaped by expert male and female counselors on the subject. Their job is to teach the bride and groom, in thorough and intimate detail, how to perform the act of love in accordance with the Jewish religion's dictates. Nearly all ultra-Orthodox girls meet their husbands through an arranged match (*shidduch*). Usually, the husband is the first man in their lives, and they marry as virgins.

"In principle, a girl is not supposed to know anything about sex," Miriam explained to me. Her tone of voice and behavior toward me held no trace of our heated exchange in the car.

"She's not aware of what happens in her parents' bedroom?"

"Heaven forbid! The mother does her best to see that her daughter shouldn't know anything about the parents' sex life. I want to tell you that my husband and I lived in a one-room apartment, and my eldest daughter was sixteen and she never knew when I was pure and when I wasn't. I never passed anything to my husband by hand,* and as a rule our beds were separated all the time, and there was always a cabinet separating the beds, like the halakha says. So even when he was asleep, if he stretched out his hand, he couldn't reach me. Not even by mistake, while sleeping.

"My daughter never saw me going to or coming back from the mikveh, so she had no awareness of the pattern of the sex life between my husband and me. It's forbidden. Ultra-Orthodox girls might know that there is such a reality as sexual relations, but they don't know what to call this reality or what it looks like."

---

*See chapter 4 for an elaboration of these prohibitions.

About two months before the wedding, the girl receives, through a tutor, the first lesson in her sexual education: the laws of niddah.

"The first thing she's taught is when she needs to go to the mikveh," explained Miriam. "Without this, there is no sex. She learns what it means to count the clean days, when she needs to consult a rabbi, when she's permitted to hand something to her husband, when it's forbidden for her to hand something to her husband. She memorizes a whole book on the laws of niddah. The boy also learns. With us, the first week of the honeymoon, as you secular call it, is set aside for learning the halakhot—by both members of the couple. The two of them together study the subject."

"That's what the poor things do on their honeymoon? Study the halakha? We make love," I remarked snidely.

"You secular folks make love?! How brilliant!" Miriam responded, incensed. "What happens to each and every one of you the first time she has intercourse? After all, every girl, secular or religious, is born a virgin, and every girl has her first man, and no one, secular or religious, is born with the knowledge of how to do what. But with you secular, there is no answering to a higher authority. Your society does not intervene and take responsibility for what happens in the individual's intimate personal life. With you secular, there's total lawlessness, which you like to call 'permissiveness,' but you don't have the same openness which, in the end, we have in our conservative ultra-Orthodox society, which has something to say about each and every subject, public and private, big and small.

"This is the openness that derives from the Torah, and the concern of the individual is the concern of the society as a whole. The community intervenes, directs and teaches what is to be done and what is not to be done, especially when it comes to relations between husband and wife. Because the marital relations between the couple affect not only their personal life, but the life of the whole community, and here, too, must be implemented the commands of Hakadosh Baruch Hu, whose whole desire and intention is to preserve and protect the individual in the community and direct him to conduct himself in accordance with the dictates of the society, some from the Torah and some from the sages, and, with Hashem's help, to create a proper society and to hasten the coming of the Messiah."

"What you say isn't totally accurate . . ."

"It's very accurate. You, who live in sin and have sexual relations in impurity and before marriage—show me who teaches your young generation how to behave sexually with one another, both emotionally and practically!"

"Every eleventh-grader, without exception, receives a series of lessons in sex education—"

"I beg you," she said, vehemently cutting me off, "don't tell me about the lesson that you get in school, where they explain to the children—heaven help us—about the different kinds of sexual diseases and AIDS and safety measures and, even worse, about contraception. I've heard about how they bring in male dolls and teach the children, may Hashem have mercy, to put condoms on them. This is an absolute horror! Not only do they teach you how to live in sin, but they compound the sin by teaching the boy to spill his seed in vain. Did you know that a man spills *seventeen million* sperm in vain every time?" Her voice rose to a shrill crescendo. "This is the source of all the Jewish people's troubles! Because what is this? It's wasted seed [*zera lebatala*]—a terrible sin!! And this is the reason why young men in Israel die by the hundreds. Wasted seed is the cause of all of the Jews' troubles. And how long will it go on? How long? Tell me!" She clasped her hands together and wailed like a mother grieving for her child.

"They explain the structure of the sexual organs and about getting your period and maintaining physical hygiene," I said.

"Collective sex education for a class of forty children? You call that serious? I'm talking about education for the sexual act itself. Who in secular society takes responsibility in an orderly fashion for a sixteen-year-old girl who finds herself naked with a man, who, if she's lucky, is her friend and beloved and if she's not, and there are many such cases, is just some man she happened to meet who seduces her and then goes on his way? Who explains to her what she must do? What recommendations does your society give to a seventeen-year-old boy about, as they say, foreplay? About hugging and kissing and caressing and preparation for this important act? I haven't seen you secular ever talking about the first time, which is a sacred time, not to mention that you do it in sin, but let's leave this point aside for the moment. Who among you explains, with true openness, with genuinely giving respect to the act, without being embarrassed, and prepares the young couple for this important event in their life?"

"Our children are exposed to everything through literature, and movies . . ."

"Is that why eighty percent of the brides who come to me are pregnant? You know what? Over eighty percent come to me pregnant, because life is not a nice story or a movie."

"That may be," I argued, "but those who come to you are not sixteen years old. They're usually in their late twenties and getting married only after having become pregnant intentionally."

"Just like I said. Total lawlessness! Living with their men without the benefit of holy matrimony. They get pregnant, get married, and then they suddenly find that the shine is off, and it's no great bargain. 'Why doesn't Gadi act the same way anymore?' one bride who I immersed when she was in her seventh month asked me, when she came back again two months after the birth." Miriam mimicked the perplexed girl's voice. "'He was so sweet before, and now everything's changed. He's not the same Gadi anymore.' With all their impurity and their sin, they are delaying the coming of the Messiah. This is exactly what's happening! With you secular there's no theory, there's only practice, which ends in failure. No honey and no moon."

"So tell me, what do these religious couples learn on their honeymoon?" I asked, wanting only to bring the pointless argument to an end.

"Look, there's theory and there's practice. How does the virgin girl who has never touched a man know what to do? It's explained to her that this is the way of the world and this is how it's supposed to be. That she shouldn't think of the groom as a criminal, because she could really think that he's some sort of maniac if she knows nothing about sex. She might have some idea that there is such a reality—otherwise, how is it that a married woman gives birth and an unmarried girl doesn't? Basic logic says there has to be something going on. But the two of them don't know exactly how to make this 'something' happen. The honeymoon is the time for the couple to learn how to do it. We call the acts of love on the honeymoon 'learning.' "

"And just how does the virgin groom know what to do with his bride?" I asked.

"Our boys receive guidance a day or two before the wedding."

"What does this guidance consist of?"

"They receive written material with detailed instructions on how the new couple should perform the first act of intercourse. The young man must memorize these instructions and know them perfectly when he comes to his wife on the wedding night to fulfill the commandment to be fruitful and multiply."

"Which instructions does he receive? What does he need to know that isn't already dictated by nature?"

"Nature exists, but it must be directed and fulfilled under the right conditions. Intercourse should be preceded by deliberate intention, and should be an entirely conscious act. There is a list of rules for the young couple regarding how to have sexual relations for the first time." Miriam pulled out a sheet of paper and began reading the rules to me one by one:

"*During the fulfillment of the mitzvah, the room should be in total darkness.*[8]

"*For the sake of holiness and preparation, both should wash their hands three times before and three times after fulfilling the mitzvah.*

"*Before performing the mitzvah, they should recite the bedtime* kriyat shema *prayer, and after fulfilling the mitzvah, they should say the* zer hatehilah *prayer.*

"*The groom must recite: 'I wish to fulfill the mitzvah to be fruitful and multiply as Hashem, blessed be his name, commanded me.'*"

"With us Sephardim," I interrupted, "the men say a prayer for success in sexual intercourse: 'May you infuse me with your heroic spirit and give me the courage and strength in my limbs and in my body to fulfill the mitzvah of my conjugal duty [*onah*], and may my limbs and my body and my desire not contain any weakness or any limpness or any coercion or any faltering or any confusion of thought or any exhaustion that may negate me, so I may fulfill my desire with my wife, and may my desire be available to me at any time I wish without any hesitation or any limpness of the member, forever and ever, Amen.' And some people go to a rabbi and get a charm against impotence and hang it on the wall above the groom's head."[9]

"For us Ashkenazim it's forbidden to have any holy writing in the room at the time of intercourse. And I was just coming to that," said Miriam, continuing with the list of rules:

"*No holy book is permitted to be in the room while the mitzvah is fulfilled.*[10]

"*After coming out of the bathroom prior to the mitzvah,*

*the groom is to lightly tap the bride on her knees seven times,
so she shall not be distracted from the sanctity of fulfilling
the mitzvah, and then wait two minutes before fulfilling the
mitzvah.*

"*Also, two white cloths need to be prepared ahead of
time*—I'll explain why later," she said, glancing at me before continuing with her list. "*Once all of these preparations
have been completed, the couple prepare themselves for the
mitzvah itself. The groom turns off the light so that it is completely dark in the room and the bride gets into the bed and
removes all of her clothes, keeping on only a tunic. Then the
groom does the same. He removes all of his clothes except
for the tunic . . .*" Miriam fell silent.

"*Nu?*" I prodded her.

"Here"—she handed me the page, which was faded from
use and bore the following heading in red pen: "Instructions
for the Young *Hared* [ultra-Orthodox Jew]"—"Go ahead,
read it yourself."

I proceeded to slowly read her meticulous handwriting, in
which she had recorded the rules in an orderly list: "*There
shall be no intercourse that is not preceded by embracing and
kissing. Prior to intercourse the groom shall do this forcefully to subdue the bride and he shall also do it afterwards,
during intercourse two times, and to a recalcitrant bride four
times.*

"*The bride must lie on her back, move her legs apart, and
raise her pelvis. This helps to ease the fulfillment of the mitzvah. Then the groom shall enter as far as possible between
her two legs while kneeling. It is natural for the member to
turn hard on its own. If the member is limp, the groom shall
instruct the bride to do as Rahab did, as is written in the Torah, as the bride was taught by the righteous rabbanit . . .*"

I paused. "What did Rahab the prostitute do?"

"It's not referring to Rahab as a prostitute exactly,"
Miriam said, squirming uncomfortably. "It's because of her

name.* Look, it is written that a pleasant wife, a pleasant home, and pleasant furnishings broaden a man's contentment. If the member is limp, and it happens, it can happen to any man . . . Some of our people just get a complete shock the first night. And hardly any of them succeed the first time to—as they say—open up the hymen. So the girl is taught not to panic if the member is limp, that she just needs to arouse him so it will turn hard."

"So just what did Rahab the prostitute do with the limp member?"

"When they say 'Rahab,' it's not referring to the biblical prostitute, but it's a hint to the bride that she must be erotic. Stimulating, as they say. To use all kinds of ways that are from nature to bring him to a state of arousal. That's all. Because the impulse is there in the person. It just needs to be aroused, that's all. Let's keep on, I see that you find this very interesting . . ."

"But what exactly do you tell her to do?"

A mischievous twinkle flashed in Miriam's eyes, but she immediately controlled herself and the spark faded out. "Continue," she said tersely.

"Then the groom must ask the bride in a clear voice to grasp his member with her hands and guide it to the place that she herself examined for the entire week before. This is the way to the fulfillment of this difficult mitzvah. Because that place is very far down and below it lays the 'mouth of sin' . . .

I stopped again. "What does that mean—'the mouth of sin'?"

"That's what the rabbis call the opening of the woman's sexual organ. It's also called 'the mouth of the grave.' And

---

*From the Hebrew root *rahav* ("broad"); Miriam alludes to the Hebrew expression *leharhiv et da'ato,* literally, "to broaden his mind," meaning "to please him."

why? Because this is the place from whence she can cause someone to sin. Hashem cursed this place when Eve sinned and caused Adam to sin. The niddah blood is spilled from this place and the pain of childbirth is in this place. This is why the woman is obligated to zealously guard the opening where 'sin lies at the door' [*hatat rovetz*—Gen. 4:7] so that only great souls shall come out of it into the world. You may continue," she ordered.

"   . . . *and it is also narrow and cramped and it is impossible to insert the organ without assistance. The bride knows that it is incumbent upon her to perform the deed and to ensure that the groom is successful in fulfilling the mitzvah.*

"*Extra care must be taken to remain covered all the time so that no part of their bodies is exposed outside of the covering . . .*" Once again I stopped. "Pardon me for asking, Miriam. Is it true that they must make a hole in the sheet in order for her to remain covered while he is penetrating her?"

"That's total rubbish," Miriam replied. "That's an ancient, malicious rumor that refuses to die. The opposite is true. During penetration, the couple is not permitted to be dressed. Only at the beginning, he and she keep just a tunic on their body, but before he penetrates her they must remove the shirt and be as naked as the day they were born. For what is the meaning of 'And you shall be as one flesh'? How can they be as one flesh when they're wearing a shirt? Or she is covered with a sheet? They must cleave together while completely naked. And the sheet? It's to cover their nakedness. On top of them, not between them. That's all. You get it? Okay, you may continue," she concluded, leaning back in her chair, gazing up at the ceiling and clasping her hands together.

"*The aperture is very narrow and cramped and also causes the groom much trouble and the member does not enter it very easily either. Therefore, once the tip of the member is at the opening, the member should then be pushed gradually and somewhat forcefully until it enters the 'gate.' If pushed too abruptly, the member will very likely slip out of that place and still not go in. Then the bride must be asked again, more insistently, to guide the member to that place.*

"*For the member to enter easily, it is good for the bride to lubricate that place on the inside with some kind of oil, and the groom should carefully lubricate the member using one of the two cloths he prepared.*

"*In that place there is a very thin membrane called the hymen** *and the groom must tear this membrane with his member and this is how the blood is produced. Sometimes it hurts her a little and she has to be soothed and reassured three times, and told that it only hurts the first time, for her mind rebels during the act until she understands that this is the way of the world and that this mitzvah is as important as the mitzvah of* tefillin.\‡

"*If the member has entered and the sperm has not yet come out, then the member should be slid carefully in and out, in the place where the seed will come out, taking care that it does not slip out and go limp. Before the member enters the place, the groom must forcefully admonish the bride to act in accordance with nature's way so that the groom may succeed in fulfilling the mitzvah. And after the sperm comes out, they must wait until the member goes limp and he feels that no more drops of sperm are coming out. At that point, the member nearly comes out on its own and need not be taken out. After the member has emerged, it should be wiped with the other cloth, and then the groom should immediately get out of her bed and then she is in a total state of niddah.*

"*The member should be washed with a wet cloth or water and the tunic should be changed and the hands should be*

---

*In Hebrew, *or habetulin*; literally, the "skin of virginity."

‡The donning of prayer phylacteries.

washed three times and clean water is to be poured before
the bride and she shall be commanded to bring a cooked dish
that will please the groom and praise him to his face."

"Openness" is what Miriam called these chauvinistic rules,
dumped upon the young woman with the first budding of her
sexuality, which suppress and seize control of her blossoming
impulses and channel them to the man's needs, directing her
to be his maidservant in the coital act. She must surrender to
his kisses, emulate a prostitute—all to fortify his limp instru-
ment of desire. She must push his member inside her, keep
silent when the pain of her torn hymen shoots through her
body, and continue letting him move inside her aching body
as he murmurs words of conquest—all so he may duly spill
his seed into her womb. And after all that, when his desire
is satisfied, she must lovingly accept his abrupt parting from
her because her torn hymen has put her in a state of niddah.*
And then, while still reeling, bruised, and sore, she is to pull
herself together to serve his majesty a good meal and massage
his male ego and tell him what a great, fantastic, wonderful,
and successful man he is.

"The biggest challenge for the ultra-Orthodox young man
is to breach the hymen on the first night," says Miriam fer-
vently. "Many fail. The majority fail."

"So what do they do?"

"*Nu,* what do they do?" Miriam opened her bright eyes
wide and curled her lips downward. "They ask their coun-

---

*Immediately after the sexual act, the bride and groom are obliged
to follow the rules of niddah, even if there was no blood. But the bride
does the examination (*hefsek tahara*) on the fourth day (instead of
on the fifth as after the end of a menstrual period) and then counts
seven clean days. The difference is that there is no issue of "impurity
of the dead" (*tum'at hamet*). Impurity of the dead applies to the blood
of menstruation, which is related to the loss of potential life. If the
woman continues to experience bleeding in the days following the first
intercourse, or in subsequent intercourse, she must consult a rabbi.

selor again, and they receive detailed and relevant instructions again, and again and again and again, until they succeed."

"It sounds a little too erotic, this learning . . ."

"It's not in a group. Ever. Usually, every groom receives guidance from a personal instructor until . . . Baruch Hashem, you see that everyone, Baruch Hashem, in the end, they know what to do."

"And how do you know that they're really doing it right?"

"Fact. There are results."

"Pregnancy is the result?"

"It's not just the pregnancy. It's also the relations, if they're normal and okay. Only pregnancy is the result? Do all women get pregnant right away? How many women don't get pregnant right away? That's no proof at all," Miriam admonished. With her finger she wiped the beads of sweat that had begun accumulating on her forehead as a result of all my questioning.

"Is the fact that she's not a virgin the proof?" I said, gently coming to her aid.

"Of course, of course," she answered wearily. "The proof is that she's not a virgin."

"Is the man obligated to cause the woman pleasure?"

"What's that supposed to mean?" Miriam furrowed her brow and clenched her jaw. "There's the act itself, and there's the act of preparing her . . . what's called . . . foreplay, and there's also the matter of causing her pleasure during the act of coitus itself. Look, that's the business, as they say, of the two people in the couple themselves."

"Are there laws that command the man to cause her pleasure?" I persisted.

"Yes, certainly there are . . ." She bit her lips hesitantly. "There are laws, what's permitted for him and what's forbidden," she mumbled. Then her eyes widened once again. "There are laws that it's forbidden to him, for example, to get hard when he's not with her," she said in a moment's inspiration.

"What's forbidden to him?"

"It's forbidden for him to reach a state when the member is, as they say, in a state in which he could couple with the woman, when he's not with her. He is forbidden to even think about the woman in that way when he is not with her. All of his thoughts should be only when he is with her, and not about anyone else in the world. That would be an abomination verging on adultery. You understand? It's no trivial matter. These are the issues of the highest importance for the Jewish world. Apart from that, on this subject there are also detailed halakhot that the man has to learn. When she has to return to immerse in the mikveh if there is penetration and when she doesn't. All of these things are very intricate halakhot. A third of the halakhot of the Talmud revolve around women. A third of the Talmud! Do you know what this means? In my house there are six or seven books like this." She spread her thumb and forefinger to illustrate the thickness of the texts and began counting them out on her fingers one by one: "There is Sota and Niddah and Gerushin and Gittin* and there is . . . so much! There is so much learning on this subject, it's endless.

"I, as you know, am also a counselor of brides. Therefore, while it's unusual, I instructed my own daughters when the time came. The truth is that a mother cannot convey this whole subject in a good way. Because of all the prohibitions and the duty of modesty and concealment. In general, the whole subject of niddah is problematic. Mothers don't always tell their daughters what to do when they first get their period. First, because the daughters often haven't told their mothers about it. Besides, mother and daughter are ashamed to talk about the rules of family purity, because it means that

---

*Tractates of the Talmud.

they have to talk about sexual relations, and this embarrasses them both. My daughters were very lucky, because this is my profession and they'd heard me giving lessons at home to newly religious women, so they were much more aware of the subject, which was discussed theoretically at home. And so they grew up with it, and so at the time, I sat down with my daughters and taught them the whole subject very freely.

"Now I have two granddaughters who've married, Baruch Hashem, and both went to a counselor. I couldn't take them on, because I don't have the same patience anymore, or the time, and I'm not in shape, as they say, like I used to be. My younger daughter, for instance, it took her two and a half months until she finished with the hymen. Two and half months! But I didn't worry at all. I knew that it would come. He was just a Slonim hasid, as they say—he was as cold as ice in this matter. And the ice had to melt . . ." She tossed her head back with a free, hearty laugh. "You understand? So it took time, but, Baruch Hashem, they have five wonderful children."

Miriam explained to me that once the bride is thoroughly versed in the rules of niddah and of intercourse, the rabbanit teaches her a lesson in feminine manners. Miriam tells the bride the story of the two sisters Rachel and Leah, and the love they had for their shared husband, Jacob:

"Seven years Jacob worked for Laban in order to marry Rachel, Laban's younger, beautiful daughter. The Torah says that to Jacob these seven years were like just a few days because he loved her so very much. On the day of the wedding, Jacob was deceived and married Leah, the tender-eyed elder daughter, instead of Rachel. Seven more years Jacob worked in order to win Rachel. 'And Jacob loved Rachel over Leah . . . When Hashem saw that Leah was the hated one, He opened her womb but Rachel was barren' [Gen. 29:31].

"Let's put ourselves in Leah's shoes for a moment," Miriam might say to her student. "What would you do in her place?"

"I'd weep over my misfortune," the virgin bride responds, trembling at the thought. "My husband loves my young and beautiful sister, for her sake he worked seven years, and in the end he got me, the older and ugly one. *Gevald!*"*

"But that wasn't Leah's way," Miriam will tell her, proceeding to quote from the Bible in a tone of voice befitting a bedtime story. "Reuben went out in the days of the wheat harvest; he found mandrakes in the field and brought them to Leah his mother; Rachel said to Leah, 'Please give me some of your son's mandrakes.' But Leah said to her, 'Was your taking my husband insignificant? And now to take even my son's mandrakes!' Rachel said, 'Therefore, he shall lie with you tonight in return for your son's mandrakes.' When Jacob came from the field in the evening, Leah went out to meet him and said, 'It is to me that you must come for I have clearly hired you with my son's mandrakes.' So he lay with her that night" [Gen. 30:14–16].

"Wow, that's so cheap . . . Leah behaves like a prostitute," the young bride will remark, not knowing that she is reacting exactly in the way that's expected of her.

"Hashem didn't think that she was a prostitute at all," Miriam will explain, savoring her student's healthy response. "'Hashem hearkened to Leah, and she conceived and bore Jacob a fifth son. So she called his name Issachar.' The commentators say: Issachar means *yesh sachar* ['there is a reward']. What did Leah do to earn this reward? Because she went out like that to meet Jacob, Leah earns the privilege of becoming the mother of the tribe of Issachar. Who was Issachar? A man imbued with special wisdom and understanding. Every great Torah scholar that you see to this day is from the tribe of Issachar."

———

*A common exclamation of alarm in Yiddish.

Two key messages about the religious woman's perception of sexuality are contained in this story: First, a woman's sexuality is not necessarily dependent on the man's sexual desires. Leah, the rejected one, demonstrates and realizes her sexuality, regardless of Jacob's wishes.

Second, sexuality is "kosher" when it's connected to fertility. The woman's sexual and emotional urges receive divine approbation solely because they are a means to the fulfillment of the most sacred mitzvah of all—the commandment to be fruitful and multiply.

Leah is presented as a model of the ideal woman, who fights for recognition of her femininity. She does not disdain any means to satisfy her sexual needs and desires, and purchases from Rachel the privilege of having sexual relations with Jacob. After the deal is struck, she takes great care to groom and adorn herself as a woman should in anticipation of being with her husband. She goes out to meet Jacob and informs him, "Today you are mine." Jacob's point of view is not related in the story because it is not relevant. God's attitude is the only thing that matters.

"Rachel, desired and beloved, belittles her husband's bed and blithely sells the privilege to couple with him in exchange for the mandrakes. For this, she is punished. She is not buried alongside Jacob in the Tomb of the Patriarchs, but interred all alone on the road to Bethlehem," Miriam explains to the bride.

"And Leah? On the face of it, the purchase of the privilege to couple with her husband seems an act of abasement. But this act reveals the feminine side of Leah. It reveals her to be a strong, emotional, hopeless romantic who pursues an action that goes against nature and social conventions. She rises above the frustration of rejection, takes action to change her situation, and makes possible the holy union of her and Jacob. 'And they were as one flesh.' "

"Through this story, I convey to brides the importance of

building the relationship with their husbands, the importance of having sexual relations for the sake of building intimacy in marriage," Miriam tells me.

"You mean that the importance of fulfilling the commandment to be fruitful and multiply justifies the means," I insist.

"Certainly not," counters Miriam. "I teach the new bride not to be timid and not to be afraid to be assertive and to insist on her conjugal rights. It's not a sin. Just the opposite, it's a mitzvah that is rewarded with a successful pregnancy."

Women are permitted to be open about their desires as long as they fulfill their femininity by having children, is the lesson Miriam seeks to impart.*

Similar action was taken by Ruth the Moabite, who seduced Boaz and exposed his nakedness. Ruth's sexual assertiveness saved the dynasty of Elimelech from extinction. Although this was done in sin, Ruth was rewarded by giving birth to the grandfather of King David.

Now, after she has learned the way of a man with a woman and is thoroughly familiar with the halakhot between husband and wife, the young woman is ready to build her family. Immersion in the mikveh is a necessary condition for building a home with strong foundations. The central ceremony in the fulfillment of her femininity—that is, having sexual relations and readying herself to realize her fertility potential—takes place primarily in the mikveh. Thus, most religious women go there happily, with love and a sense of purpose.

"Simply put, a woman goes to the mikveh to purify herself for her husband, and with Hashem's help, she will have a child. This brings joy to the home. It builds the home and strengthens the family. And all the little cells of good fami-

---

*Contrary to the prohibition against a woman's openly expressing her desire for sex, one of the ten curses enumerated in chapter 4 (following from "he shall rule over thee"), the balaniyot actually encourage new brides to be assertive in this regard.

lies build and strengthen the community," says one religious woman who's come for her monthly immersion. "Believe me, I'm speaking on behalf of all women. This is an integral part of the proper functioning of every religious Jewish home."

The religious women I can understand, I think to myself, *but why, for God's sake, do secular women relate to this whole bloody story?* What compels them to stick their healthy heads into a sickbed and to choose to define themselves as niddah? Why do they accept the label of impurity and thereby collaborate with the chauvinistic, patriarchal attitude that brands an entire category of women as "impure," denigrates them, and criminally discriminates against them?

"The man's life is saved before the woman's,"[11] mandate the sages in the Mishna, setting the social norms that to this day serve as the beacon for the Jewish people. "The beauty of the king's daughter is within" (Psalms 45:14), they wrote, using poetic words to justify the draconian order essentially imposing house arrest on all women. For "a woman's wisdom is only in her spindle,"[12] and "anyone who teaches his daughter Torah, teaches her frivolity,"[13] cried the men, adding "may the words of Torah be burned, than that they should be handed over to women,"[14] thus shutting out the excellent minds of an entire population of women who thirsted for understanding and knowledge. At the same time, they shut their mouths, too, declaring, "a woman's voice is temptation,"[15] forbidding them to interject and make their voices heard in public, to speak their minds, lest their ideas be heard, heaven forfend, and so influence the ways of the greater society. Thus was a terrible personal and social injustice done to Jewish women over thousands of years of history.

Of the balaniyot I had come to know in the mikveh, Miriam was raised this way, but Doris was another story. Less than a decade ago Doris was a modern, independent, opinionated woman who was a senior full-time public servant. Why would she choose to cross over to the side of stringent religious Orthodoxy at a time when feminism is flourishing in the enlightened West? Why, at a time when women are freeing themselves from the patriarchal social structure and making their voices heard in the fields of science, philosophy, and literature, when they are fighting to open the gates of Jewish learning that have always been shut to them and gaining recognition of their rightful place in the synagogue and in public rituals through certification in public religious roles? Why, at a time of major upheaval in the status of women, who are freeing themselves from the binds of biological fatalism and the traditional order that links their sexuality to religion and society, who are disregarding the religious interpretation of concepts like impurity and purity, temptation, niddah, asceticism and exclusion, marital relations, sin and punishment, modesty and ignorance—concepts that were prevalent and unchallenged in the patriarchal world?[16] Why in this day and age would Doris, and many other women like her, choose to travel back in time and willingly place herself in a world whose societal rules are so medieval and unenlightened? Why in this day and age are these women enthusiastically choosing a lifestyle centered on the concepts of purity and impurity? Why do they readily accept being "untouchable" for about two weeks of the month—for half of their fertile lives, in other words? Why, in this day and age, are these women ready to shackle themselves to the conventions of a religion whose essence is discrimination between the sexes, all to the man's benefit?

Doris, what in the world motivates you to do this?

"I'm a Jewish woman and the mikveh is an integral part of the life of the Jewish woman," Doris explains, answering my question by serenely chanting the "mikveh mantra" regularly recited by the balaniyot. "I'm about to get married— I know there's the mikveh. There are some girls, you're just shocked when you see them. Arriving for their immersion practically naked. Sinning and sinful in their immodesty.

You can't understand what they have to do with the mikveh. Sluts that come to immerse. Forgive me—I do wrong by calling them sluts. To tell the truth, these secular women, for whom immersion is an unbreakable rule, are more righteous than the women who were raised religious, and the ones who became religious, like me, because they choose to immerse even though they weren't born into it. In the center of their wanton secular life, they create this island of holiness and purity. This means that they are in a process of *tikkun*, of repairing the soul. I only hope that Hashem will repair their ways. Because as long as the candle is still burning, repair is possible."

"What are they looking for here, Doris? Why do they come?" I ask.

"Why? There's no one simple answer. A lot of factors come together to bring secular women to the mikveh. At the root of the phenomenon, of course, burns the flame of faith. Without faith there is no immersion. What motivates the secular women is not religion, but rather a faith in a higher power. Faith in Hashem's power to intervene in our lives and to affect them for good and for bad; faith in our ability to communicate with Hashem and pray for our lives. To this basic faith are added thousands of reasons that fall into two categories: reasons from the halakha and personal reasons. As numerous as the secular women who immerse in the mikveh—and they are quite numerous—are the reasons why. Each has her own reason, her own interest, her own personal story. It's amazing to see how so many women going through the same immersion can react to it in a totally different way.

"As for 'impurity'? Excuse me, but I think you're overreacting to this term 'impurity.' To me, the impurity of niddah is a part of the cyclicality of nature. Like the way a tree sheds its leaves before it blossoms, that's how I view blood. I don't see in my monthly change of seasons all this negativity you're talking about. No humiliation and no discrimination and none of all that rubbish you say. And I'm not alone." She turned to a group of young women who were waiting in the vestibule for an immersion room to become available.

"Come, girls, tell us, how do you feel about the impurity of niddah?"

The girls were eager to share their experiences, and a symposium on purity and impurity erupted on the spot. Each and every woman there had something to say.

A lean young woman of Yemenite extraction humbly lowered her dark eyelashes at me as she spoke. "Menstruating women cause plants to wither, wine to sour, pickled vegetables to spoil, dough to ferment, and all kinds of other damage, because menstrual blood contains chemicals that poison the environment. My husband and I have a hothouse in which we grow delicate spice plants. That's why I purify myself in the mikveh. So as not to hurt the plants."

I glanced, aghast, at Doris, who stifled a giggle as the woman smiled mischievously.

"Oh, I was just pulling your leg!" The Yemenite girl, Sima, laughed, and the other women laughed along with her. "You're so in thrall to all these stupid theories of purity and impurity that you can't tell the difference between reality and imagination. I study Jewish philosophy at the university, and I know about all the concepts of purity and impurity that are mentioned in the Torah. About how the body's symbols illuminate a society's cultural texture and influence the perception of personal boundaries and the individual's place in society. All these interpretations derive from the philosophical constructs of the cultural researchers who've informed your views. I think you've also been poisoned by the halakhic male attitude toward blood and impurity. We see these things through female eyes—at least I and some of my secular girl-friends do. For me, immersion is something very intimate that I choose to do with my body. It's not about being subject to the authority of some man who wrote the halakha. I have to acknowledge the impurity because this is the only way to reach purity. How can I be purified if I am not first impure? Otherwise, there's no difference."

"This 'impurity' business doesn't bother me at all. It just comes from the halakha and I have no argument with that," declared a lanky redhead with an American accent. "With time and experience, you come to understand the logic of the halakha."

"Well, the whole idea of the impurity of the blood really repelled me at first; I was totally grossed out," a young, dark-complexioned woman stated. "All this snooping around inside the vagina, examining the cloth, if there is or isn't a stain—it seemed like some kind of weirdo ceremony conducted by witches looking for blood to use in a pact with the devil. So instead of calling myself impure, I like to say I'm just 'slightly stale,' and instead of pure—'fresh.c

"Do you know how they used to check whether or not a woman was impure?" asked Sima. "They would take a metal tray, lay her bloodstained underpants on it, scatter red lentils over the stain until it was completely covered, and then count them. If it took less than seven lentils to cover the stain, it meant the woman was pure. Eight or more lentils meant the woman was impure."

"You know how women used to get revenge on unfaithful men?" added a bespectacled short-haired woman with a French accent. "In primitive societies, menstrual blood is believed to be toxic. The witches of the tribe would mix menstrual blood in the unfaithful man's food, and it would kill him right away."

"On the other hand, blood also has life-giving powers," said a fortyish woman. "It's a unique substance that contains the opposite qualities of blessing and curse. This ambivalence really intrigued me. At first, I immersed just out of curiosity—I wanted to see whether I would really feel a transition from impurity to purity. And let me tell you—I was bowled over by the intensity of the transition that I felt in the mikveh. That's why I decided to keep on following this mesmerizing fluctuation between impurity and purity."

"I heard that there are tribes that use menstrual blood as a deadly love potion," said a long-legged American, whose smile revealed a row of teeth covered with orthodontic braces. "My mother used to tell me this horror story that I always got a big kick out of, about Uncle Skinny and Aunt Fattie:

"Uncle Skinny screwed a lot of women behind Aunt Fattie's big fat back. Aunt Fattie was afraid that Uncle Skinny would fall in love with another woman and leave her. She went to an Indian sorcerer and he advised her to put a full tablespoon of her monthly menstrual blood in Uncle Skinny's coffee. 'If you do this for all five days of your period, only death will part you,' the sorcerer told her—and collected a hundred dollars. For five days, Uncle Skinny drank coffee mixed with menstrual blood, and on the sixth day, right in the middle of an orgasm, he died in Aunt Fattie's arms."

"Disgusting!" The other women grimaced.

"For me, the whole purity thing really comes down to a matter of hygiene and aesthetics, nothing more," said a scantily clad girl. "All this stuff about impurity and filth that the halakha ascribes to women in niddah is irrelevant to me. It's primitive stuff from the time of the Jewish sages that has nothing to do with the twenty-first century. To me, it's just as irrelevant as the prohibition against lighting a fire on Shabbat.* Once, making fire was hard work but today it's nothing. Maybe, long ago, when women sat at home and cooked and men went out to hunt—then, maybe, the scent of menstrual blood would adhere to men who came in contact with a menstruating woman and scare off the animals and hurt the family's livelihood. Maybe that's why they imposed a whole bunch of rules on the women. But nowadays the woman is

---

*The Jewish Sabbath.

liberated and the man goes to work in an air-conditioned office."[17]

"I identify menstruation with emotional pollution. When I'm impure, I'm cleansed of all the emotional garbage that's excreted along with the blood. For me, it's like sweating in the sauna," said another woman, blissfully stretching her arms upward.

"When I was eighteen, an old crone took my hand in hers, studied it, and told me: 'You will never have children,'" said a plump young woman who reminded me of Guy de Maupassant's Ball-of-Fat. "She said my womb would be affected by a serious illness and I would never get pregnant. I went into such a panic! I didn't tell anyone, and for years I lived in fear that I would never be able to have children. Before my wedding, when I was forced to go to the rabbanit, she explained to me about the healthiness of impurity: 'You know that terrible plagues that felled tens of thousands of victims hardly touched the Jews, who kept themselves separate? That Jewish communities, which avoided contact with the *goyim** and strictly followed the Torah's rules of kashrut and hygiene, were hardly affected by these diseases? Even nowadays, not a day goes by without some doctor calling to tell me that the mikveh saved his female patient. It's all anchored in scientific reality. It's not superstition,' she told me. 'The human body has certain mechanisms to repel all kinds of harmful organisms so they won't enter the body. The internal organs are protected by the skin. The eye is protected by moisture. If a grain of sand gets in the eye, the eye tears right away and washes it out. The ears are protected by wax, et cetera. What happens with a woman's sexual organs? They, too, have a connection with the outside world. Germs can also penetrate inside there and cause infections and diseases. That's why inside there's a protective layer that's acidic. The moment a

_____

*Non-Jews.

woman's period appears, the whole protective layer, this mucous substance that covers the cervix and the vagina, is secreted. When is this protective layer formed? Studies show that it's formed *exactly a week* after the menstrual bleeding stops. When you keep these seven days, you're guarding your health. Look,' she said to me, 'the human body is like an appliance. When you go to buy any appliance, you get a manual from the manufacturer, right? It's the same with a human being,'" she said, echoing the lecture Miriam had given me in my car. "'You get a manual from Hashem who created you. I promise that if you follow the instructions Hashem gave you, he will watch over you and, with Hashem's help, you will have not only one child, but every year you will have pure and good Jewish children.' That's what this rabbanit said and she had no idea what a mitzvah she'd done! On that day I was reborn. All my fears and anxieties disappeared. On the wedding night I conceived, and nine months later I gave birth, and now I'm a mother of three. This is what I call the blessing of impurity."

"I could care less about the so-called physical impurity. What I love is the feeling of joy that comes with the purification," enthused a pretty, petite young woman named Shuli. "I don't understand it when I hear women moan about all the sacrifice involved, about how they'll observe the purity laws no matter the price. What price is there? Immersing is just one great big pleasure."

"Look, it happens sometimes with secular couples that the husband gives his wife hell over it," explained Doris. "He doesn't want to accept the 'fast' that's being imposed on him, and it creates lots of trouble, and a woman who insists on sticking to her beliefs is sacrificing herself on the altar of immersion. She's endangering her marriage in order to maintain family purity. I know someone whose husband isn't willing to abstain at all, and whenever she gets her period, off he goes to another woman. Right in her face. And it kills her. It makes her ill. But you should see how he waits for her when she comes back from the mikveh. And the craziest thing is the way she says she gives herself to him with love, as if he hadn't cheated on her. That's not dedication?"

"But that sort of thing is quite rare. For the most part, a woman who maintains family purity brings lots of positive things to the home: a good livelihood, a successful marriage, domestic tranquility—*shalom bayit*—and all that goes along with that," said Sima.

"Because, *mon dieu,* there's so much blessing in the whole process of getting your period, keeping separate and then the cleansing afterward," exclaimed the Frenchwoman, whose name was Claudine. "I just feel so blessed when I come to immerse after two weeks of impurity so severe it's compared to the impurity of the dead. Not that I feel impure, oh no. I don't go around with such thoughts. But when I bathe and immerse I feel pure. And blessed. My menstrual blood is a sign from my body that it's ready to create new life. It's part of my body language. It's the power of life."

"My mother is a nurse and she explained to me once that impurity is a part of the body's cyclicality. It's like this," said the American, Tamar, sketching a horizontal line in the air. "During the five days of menstruation the body is neutralized, and then"—she drew an ascending line—"for seven days it's on the rise, and then"—she jabbed the air with her index finger—"it reaches the top between the twelfth and the fifteenth day. At this top point, the body is at its most fertile and able to absorb the sperm. On immersion day the body is in its optimum state.

"My mother says it's also good for the husband to abstain two weeks a month, because then he has more potential. His sperm is better preserved. Stronger. The time of impurity acts as a warning to us about the body's weakness; it's like nature's sign language," she added.

"You know, that's exactly what Meir Shalev says in his

book *Fontanella*,"[18] the plump girl interjected. "The main character complains that every time he reaches orgasm, the ejaculate takes a part of his memory with it. Whenever he sleeps with a woman he temporarily loses his memory. His wife, knowing her darling husband all too well, asks him to recite their children's phone numbers whenever she suspects that he's been cheating on her. If he can't recall them, she asks him: 'So, who sucked out your memory this time?'"

All the women laughed.

"They say that menstrual blood also takes with it a part of the brain when it's spilled. And that's why menstruating women are all muddled," said Sima.

"Men's nonsense," one of the women scoffed, smiling, and the others expressed their agreement.

"Do you have any idea what sort of worldview you're associating yourselves with?" I finally asked, growing impatient with their lighthearted banter. "Do you know why, for example, you keep seven clean days after the menstrual bleeding stops and not eight or ten? Because seven is a number that symbolizes the seven days of creation. When God created the world, he superimposed the order of civilization on the chaos of nature. That's why the period of seven clean days is the transition period that symbolizes the enforcement of order over chaos, the enforcement of purity over impurity, the enforcement of life over death, the enforcement of the man's rule over the woman.

"By the mere fact of your upholding with your body the counting of the days and your being so scrupulous about performing the purification rites, you are essentially accepting the decree of your inferiority in men's eyes. You are subject to the laws of the blood ban, which remove you from the community; you are not counted in a prayer quorum in the synagogue and your testimony is invalid, you are enslaved to their draconian laws that keep you far away from any possibility of active participation, no matter how small, in a religious ceremony at home or in public. At home you are prevented from any contact with sacred objects, like laying on phylacteries, or reciting the Kiddush blessing over the wine or the blessing over the challah;* and you are only commanded to perform three mitzvot that you received from God because of your primary duty on earth, to atone with your body for the unrestrained actions and desires of our legendary mother in the Garden of Eden, and they are: niddah, challah, and lighting the Shabbat candles. Niddah—she spilled the blood of the world and therefore she must be circumspect in her niddah and thereby bring repair to the world. Challah—she caused the downfall of Adam who was the 'challah of the world,' and so she must separate the challah from the rest of the dough. Lighting Shabbat candles—because she extinguished the soul of Adam, she is given the mitzvah of the Shabbat candles, in which she restores the light to the world, the light of the soul."[19]

"None of that has anything to do with me, because I'm not religious, and my whole worldview is different," said Sima.

"It certainly does have something to do with you!" I insisted. "Do you have sons?"

"Yes. One boy, he's six years old, may he live long," she said carefully.

"Well, are you aware that you are absolutely forbidden from taking part in any active way in his bar mitzvah?" I exclaimed. "You are banished to the women's section, and there, behind a cage of bars or a curtain, you can participate by listening alone, lips sealed, because your voice is sexually tempting and it is forbidden to be heard lest it contaminate this important ceremony for your son, who is completely in the domain of the men. The boy you raised so lovingly un-

---

*The special bread eaten at Shabbat meals.

til finally he reached the age of mitzvoth is led by his father alone, within the community of men who impose the culture, to one of the most important rites of passage in his life, and at the same time he is completely removed from your domain, you, his mother and his parent, who are ruled by the forces of nature, and he is taken into the domain of culture, abandoning you in your wooden cage or behind the cloth curtain."

"That's not how I imagined it," Sima said softly, and then she fell silent, as did the rest of the women, each retreating into her thoughts.

"We're not obliged to do a bar mitzvah in an Orthodox synagogue," the redhead said, breaking the silence. "We had my son's bar mitzvah in a Reform synagogue. What respect we women were given there! The whole family was on the *bima,** without any discrimination. My daughter and I put skullcaps on and prayed and it was wonderful. Whoever chooses an Orthodox synagogue should accept the rules there, but she has the option to choose, free of coercion, because today there are alternatives. It's the same with immersion. We immerse for the sake of purity, but we don't all follow every little one of the Orthodox rabbis' rules. Right, girls?"

"Right," they all agreed.

"We find the rules of separation excessive. There's no reason to be that extreme. Even Lisa, the strictest among us, who is practically ready to become observant, sins against the halakha and sleeps next to her husband during niddah," the redhead continued.

"We don't have a 'Jewish bed,' I admit," said Lisa, blushing. "I mean, we don't have a double bed that can be separated into two single beds. Our bed is a big king-size and we like to sleep together all the time. When I have my period, each of

---

*The raised platform in the synagogue from which the Torah is read.

us turns toward his own side and we do our best . . . Look, I'm not going to pretend that I don't suddenly feel like kissing him. I do. Badly. When that happens, I will kiss and hug him. Sometimes I get the urge for more than that . . . So what? Lust won't kill you. We restrain ourselves. There's no other choice. We've been married just three months, and I expect that as the years go by, when we get older, we'll be more relaxed, and when we're more relaxed we'll grow even stronger."

"We also sleep in the same bed, but there's no contact—none. Maybe sometimes just a slight touch of the hand or a little good-bye kiss on the cheek, but no more than that," added shy Nurit, a mother of two.

"No—no separations. Sleeping apart is out of the question. As it is, my husband barely puts up with this whole family purity thing. Separate beds would be the last straw," admitted Claudine, the Frenchwoman.

"To me, separating the beds seems idiotic, repulsive, and artificial," declared Tamar.

"I think the whole point of separation is self-restraint and overcoming one's impulses. So when we sleep in the same bed it's harder to hold back and that enhances the mitzvah," explained Sima.

"I kiss and cuddle with my husband and sleep in just my underwear . . . a thong usually. This family purity business isn't going to make me change my habits," Shuli said dismissively.

"My mother and grandmother didn't bother with any of this. They didn't follow all of these separation rules from the rabbis," interjected Yehudit, the young dark-complexioned woman.

"So what did they do?" I asked.

"They did what is written in the Torah—literally. They completely removed themselves from the community. They left their houses and went to another house. A 'blood house' is what they called it."

"I've never heard of a blood house," said Lisa. "Where is there such a thing? In Bnei Brak?"*

"No," laughed the young woman, who looked like she'd stepped out of a picture of the Queen of Sheba on her visit to King Solomon. Her dark, taut skin glistened in the pale yellow lamplight. "Not in Bnei Brak, in Ethiopia," she explained, a row of snow-white teeth illuminating her smile. "In Ethiopia, a woman who has blood is impure and must actually physically remove herself from the community until the blood disappears. Only the Jews act this way with blood. Not the Christians. Absolutely not. They make fun of us Jews for making it obvious to one and all when the women are menstruating so that everyone knows when the husbands are having sex with their wives. But for the Jews, this is an inviolable law. In each village, people got together and built themselves a blood house for use by a few families. A blood house is a cone-shaped hut built out of long wooden poles covered with straw and leaves. Around the house, at a radius of about a meter and a half, stones are placed in a circle to mark the boundaries of the impurity zone. When a woman got her period she would move into the blood house for seven days, until she was clean. Mothers with babies took their infants with them to the blood house.

"During this time it is absolutely forbidden for anyone to come near her, let alone touch her. My grandmother and mother's women friends would cook meals for them. They wouldn't come close either. They'd pour the food into special vessels for the niddah period—just like there are separate Passover dishes,‡ there were separate niddah dishes—and leave them beside the circular stone barrier. The impure women stayed in the blood house until sunset on the seventh

---

*A city in Israel with a largely ultra-Orthodox population.

‡Only separate kosher-for-Passover dishes and utensils can be used during the Passover holiday.

day, even if their bleeding stopped before that. At sunset they went down to wash their bodies and their clothes in the river. After dark, they were permitted to return to their homes and be reunited with their husbands."[20]

"Your grandmother must be in menopause already and not need it, but what does your mother do now that she doesn't have a blood house to go to?" I asked.

"She goes crazy. It's still very hard for her. Ethiopian women in Israel can't get used to the new rules. For them, no bathing in a bathtub or immersion in the mikveh is going to cleanse the impurity. As long as they haven't left home for the duration of their period, they consider themselves impure. They're impure and their house is impure and anyone who comes in contact with them is impure. Some women can't tolerate this feeling, it makes them ill. They say that some have even committed suicide. They would rather die than live in impurity. The men took it very hard, too. They couldn't sleep with their wives. The Jewish men—called Falasha—believed that having intercourse with a woman in niddah would cause the child to be born mentally retarded and physically crippled. 'You slept with your wife when she had blood? No wonder you got a retarded child,' a Falasha would taunt a Christian man, who is called Amhara."

"And what does the Falasha say when his child is born retarded and with a birth defect?" I asked.

"The Falasha don't have any children like that. All of our children are healthy and whole. Only the children of the Amhara are leprous and defective," Yehudit asserted. "The blood house also served as a maternity house," she continued. "After the birth of a son, a woman stayed there forty days, and after the birth of a daughter, eighty days. For all that time, the other women take care of her from a distance. Usually, a woman wasn't all alone in the blood house. There were other women in niddah to keep her company. They would sit together and relax and laugh and enjoy a break from the men's

company and from the burdens of caring for the family. For
them, the time of niddah was a break from life's chores. It
was a vacation. The break gave them space and freedom. And
they miss that very much, too."[21]

"For us, too, these two weeks of separation also provide a
little breathing space," remarked Lisa.

"There's no question that these two weeks give you a little
time to be with yourself," offered Shuli. "I'm not saying that
otherwise you're preoccupied with sex all day long, but when
you abstain from being with your husband you have this feeling that you're on your own. You don't have any obligation
to get up at night or anything like that. You feel peaceful.
Two weeks of peace. To me, the sense of space is very important. The menstruation time delineates boundaries for me
and frees me from having to comply with my husband's desire
for sex, though he's not the sort of red-hot lover who wants
it all the time."

"For me, these days are actually very busy and tense,"
confessed Claudine. "My husband doesn't accept this whole
niddah thing. For years now we've been living in purity and
it still feels strange to him and upsets him, and during the
separation time he freaks out and keeps me occupied with
a thousand and one things. During the day, he has me running around on all sorts of errands and at night he turns into
a needy hypochondriac. Once, he had shortness of breath,
another time it was chest pain and another time, *mon dieu,*
he was certain he'd found a cancerous lump in one of his
testicles. A few times, I've ended up calling an ambulance
and spending the night with him in the emergency room. But
on the night when I immerse, as if by the wave of a magic
wand, he miraculously recovers. The mikveh is like a magic
potion for my husband, it cures all his terminal illnesses. This
doesn't mean that he makes love to me that night. Oh no, he's
stubborn and he punishes me for my stubbornness, and often

I come home and he's sleeping like a log and I go to sleep beside him, purified and frustrated."

"Are you aware that all the rules of separation between man and woman are a product of the blood ban that is meant to differentiate between holiness, which is ascribed to the man and identified with the spirit and intellect, and nakedness [*erva*], which is identified with the woman, with the body and lust? That all of this has been imposed by men for the sake of fertility and reproduction?" I asked.

"I don't feel that way at all," objected Sima vehemently. "I consider myself an early product of the feminist movement that began in the sixties and fought the notion that having children is the central defining factor in a woman's identity. My definition of femininity is modern and derived primarily from sexual attraction and beauty. Fertility is just one aspect of my self-definition as a woman and how I view my relationship with my husband. For me, a woman who forgoes her fertility potential and doesn't bring children into the world is still a feminine and sexual woman in every inch of her body."

For the secular women in this group, attention to physical grooming plays an integral role in their perception of femininity. Beautification of the body is often felt to be inextricably linked with beautification of the soul. "We are beautiful," the women say, scrubbing their bodies; "we are clean," they say, washing every hidden spot, rubbing off every stubborn stain or bit of dirt; "we are feminine," they say, removing every strand of body hair, also associated with masculinity; "we are blessed," they say, immersing in the mikveh waters and purifying body and soul. "We are new." They emerge refortified.

Meticulous grooming of every part of herself gives the woman an intimate familiarity with her body and bolsters her self-image. The preparation performed by the woman who has immersed for the encounter with her husband elevates their physical intimacy to a spiritual level. Even seriously disabled women, some disfigured by terrible injury, are able to connect with their femininity in the mikveh, in part because of the compliments and encouragement they receive from their friends, the other women there.

"How can you go [to your husband] with a mustache? Aren't you ashamed of yourselves?" one Tunisian aunt scolded a bunch of young women who hadn't removed their body hair before going to the mikveh.

"The night before the immersion I take some time for myself. I remove all the hairs—you know, legs, armpits—I'm very scrupulous," boasts newlywed Gili, a successful cosmetician. "I know a lot of girls who neglect their bodies in the winter. They don't take the hair off around the crotch, because who's going to see? They don't give a damn, because they already feel comfortable enough with their husband, you know, they don't have to impress him anymore, so they get neglectful. But someone who always goes to the mikveh doesn't neglect herself." Trimming and cleaning the fingernails, shampooing the hair and conducting a thorough and painstaking cleaning of every inch of their bodies once a month, before the immersion, is part of a regular ritual aimed primarily at enhancing the sense of femininity that infuses sexuality. This special bathing and cleansing make the woman feel more delicate and sensual and, she believes, makes her husband see her that way, too.

Most of the secular women who immerse in the mikveh are young, in their twenties and thirties. Many are college students or professionals who define themselves as independent women, free to choose their way of life and to adopt components of the religious lifestyle to suit their needs.

"I'm completely independent. I do what I want. I don't come from one of those religious families that raise women to be submissive. I observe only a few fundamental things that the religion dictates. I light candles on the Sabbath. My husband puts on *tefillin*. I come to the mikveh and we recite Kiddush,"* says the young mother Nurit.

"I'm a free woman—I work, I study, I'm independent, and I can do what I want. Still, I like the other side, the side of religion, even though I find the Bible to be very chauvinistic. But that's the source. And my ideal is to be able to live according to this source. Right now it doesn't seem feasible because of my husband, and without him I'll never do it. So in the meantime I imbibe from the religion what I can. I call it 'selective faith,'" remarks Gili.

"I'm a marathon runner. I train on the Sabbath and eat *treif.*‡ But I feel a connection to religion and I've chosen to observe the mitzvah of immersion because it's the only one that seems truly important and relevant to me. All the others seem outdated," says a woman named Orly.

"There are certain things in religion that I agree with, like the mikveh, for example. Keeping Shabbat I don't agree with, so I don't do it, or keeping milk and meat separate§—I don't do that, either," admits Shuli.

"Renewal. That's what they're looking for," says Doris, the balanit. "To be renewed each time. To feel the excitement each time anew. To come to your husband each month as fresh as a virgin. A young couple that has no physical contact for twelve days a month goes through torture. But these twelve days give more meaning to what she's going to do on this night . . . all

---

*A prayer recited over wine, which proclaims the holiness of the Sabbath or a holiday.

‡Nonkosher food.

§Jewish dietary laws (kashrut) require that meat and milk be kept separate. Separate utensils and dishes are to be used for each, and one must wait several hours after eating meat before having any milk products. The prohibition is derived from the biblical injunction "Do not cook the flesh of an animal in its mother's milk" (Exod. 23:19).

the anticipation . . . her husband desires her so much . . . she can see this desire . . . he's eager . . . he wants her . . . he's longing for her . . . it's hard for him to hold back . . . especially when he's a young man. This whole feeling that the man has been waiting and waiting—it's conveyed to the woman and really raises her self-regard. I'm not just a vessel that anyone who wants can have intercourse with. I'm master of my body. I decide when my husband will be inside me."

"But Doris," I protested, "not everyone who doesn't use the mikveh has intercourse during menstruation. A lot of secular women abstain from sex while they're menstruating, for all kinds of reasons. Most of them have plenty of self-respect and feel that they're masters of their bodies. So what difference does it make if they immerse or not? What does the immersion really do?"

"The truth?" She smiled mischievously.

"Only the truth," I said, tensing in anticipation.

"Give me your ear." I bent my head closer and she pulled my ear to her mouth: "The truth is that immersion is done only for the sake of 'Be fruitful and multiply,' " she said confidentially, her breath tickling my ear. "This was Hashem's sole intention when he commanded us about immersion. Today's young people think the main purpose of immersion is to preserve passion. They believe that good sex is what preserves their marriage so they run to immerse. But that's rubbish. Sex doesn't bind a couple together at all."

"What do you mean, it doesn't bind them at all?"

"Shh," Doris hushed me and pulled my ear back to her mouth. "Hashem, may he be blessed, created carnal lust only so that human beings would be fruitful and multiply and fill the earth. That's all. The whole purpose of intercourse is just to be fruitful and multiply. That's the essence of the matter. But what happens? The heads of young men and women who get married are filled with thoughts of lust and sex. So, fine. Hashem has no problem with them thinking about sex. As long as they immerse and mate in purity and bring kosher Jewish children into the world."

"Wait a minute." I turned my face, cupped my mouth with my hand, and whispered in her ear: "You're saying that sexual attraction is just a divine trick? That it's simply a biological mechanism whose whole purpose is to make people 'be fruitful and multiply'?"

"Precisely. But only in purity. The essentialness of purity mustn't be forgotten."

"So all the earthly sexual desires that mix with heavenly feelings to create a sensuality unique to him and her, all the magic, all the yearning and sweet longing in the Song of Songs—'Let him kiss me with the kisses of his mouth—for thy love is better than wine'; all the pining for one another's beauty, all the raging desire and erotica that fills billions of lines written by poets with the blood of their hearts and the sweat of their passions, that ignite the minds of millions of people throughout the whole world—all that is nothing but the product of a fertility trick?! A trick of nature for reproduction's sake?!" I practically spit into her beet-red ear.

"Well, there's also the matter of imitation," she said, abruptly shaking me off. She tugged on her ear and resumed speaking in a normal tone of voice. "There are couples who just look at their parents. They know that this is what their parents did so they will do the same. It's a matter of tradition," Doris asserted, hammering another nail in the coffin of passion.

"Is that connected to the scare tactics that say a woman who doesn't immerse will get all sorts of illnesses?" I asked.

"I'll have you know, I just read a very compelling article about all these illnesses," Doris said, suddenly seething. "Saying it is absolutely forbidden to have intercourse during menstruation, or immediately afterwards, because the mucous membrane, the endometrium, is very sick and gets very irritated when a foreign body enters it."

The discussion of health in connection with sexual relations in impurity always sets the balaniyot aboil.

"But it's not a foreign body. It's my husband. And I'm telling you that even if I didn't go to the mikveh, I wouldn't have sex when I have my period, so what difference does it make to my 'sick' uterine membrane if I did or didn't immerse before I let this so-called 'foreign body' enter my vagina? Anyway, it's not like it comes to pay a sick call when the endometrium is ill!"

"The difference has to do with the impurity," Doris retorted.

"Aha. Once again, we come back to the beginning. Once again, you throw impurity in my face," I protested.

"Yes. But this impurity is not negative. The high priest himself, like us women, was impure at times and could defile things with the impurity of death. He became impure after he slaughtered the ox. He could defile things with the impurity of death. What does this tell us? That impurity has a positive aspect, not a negative one. How can he be purified if there is no impurity? What shall he be purified of? The difference is really that we, the religious, know that, halakhically, intercourse is solely a matter of 'Be fruitful and multiply.' I want to get pregnant and I do it in purity, because in any case there is really no fertility on the fifth day after the period or on the sixth day. The endometrium is very sick. Very sick, and the woman's egg isn't released anyway on those days, and then the sperm is there, but it goes to waste. Wasting seed is absolutely out of the question. It's impure! It absolutely cannot happen, you understand?! And so one doesn't have sexual relations on these barren days. Because there is no sexuality without fertility."

The secular women who immerse, though not believing their fertility to be the primary expression of their femininity and sexuality, seem to do so mostly because they want a "kosher" pregnancy. They all are aware that the time for immersion generally coincides with ovulation and that the odds of conceiving are highest in the days following immersion. Conversely, some use the mikveh as a natural birth-control device, something pious Jews would consider a mortal sin.

"The immersion day is the lucky day. I'm forty and I want to get pregnant. If I don't have sex tonight right after the immersion, I'll miss out on this special day. The day of ovulation. Today and tomorrow is the best time; after that the odds get worse. Last night, my husband was supposed to leave for army reserve duty, but we asked the army to delay his call-up because these are critical days for us," said Orly.

But the immersion day is not always the lucky day.

"I've been married for eight months and still no pregnancy," said Shuli. "I did a blood test and found out that my ovulation days fall within the counting of the clean days. I went to the rabbi, my spiritual guide, and asked permission to move up the immersion by two or three days. He told me: Don't shorten the time. Keep on as you've been doing. On Sukkot* eve, you will come to me with good news."

"If you're not pregnant by then, go to the rabbi and insist that he give you permission to move up your immersion day," said Sima, the Yemenite woman. "For years I couldn't get pregnant. My husband and I went through hell. We consulted every expert. We did fertility tests that showed that both he and I were fine. I was put on medication and nothing helped; no one could figure out the root of the problem. Until an angel was sent to us in the form of a medical intern. A religious fellow, very humble and quiet, who, during rounds one day, was standing next to the senior specialist, listening to him present my case. The intern asked me if I immerse in the mikveh. 'Yes, of course,' I answered. 'Every month without

---

*The Feast of Tabernacles, a holiday that is one of the three Jewish pilgrimage festivals and comes shortly after Yom Kippur, in early autumn.

fail.' And then he said: 'I think that's the problem.' 'How can you say that?' I rebuked him. 'Have you no God?' 'I think your monthly period must be long, and by the time you get to the mikveh, after seven clean days, you've missed your ovulation. You're barren from the halakha.' The astonished senior doctor instructed that I be given an injection that shortened the period of bleeding. That same month, I went to the mikveh on time, and I really did get pregnant afterwards."

"I have two little kids and I don't feel like getting pregnant now. My biological clock is perfectly precise, like a Swiss watch, and for two years I've been delaying my immersion by two days, to naturally avoid pregnancy, without relying on pills or withdrawal," confessed Nurit.

"The mikveh saved me from childlessness," said Claudine. "We were married for five years and I didn't get pregnant. After I underwent comprehensive tests, the gynecologists sadly informed me that my uterus was defective and that I would never be able to conceive. I don't know why, but I suddenly decided to go to the mikveh, like a prayer. You have to understand that I grew up in a small village in Morocco, between a cherry tree and an almond tree, with my grandfather, a farmer who was the head of a tribe of dozens of uncles and aunts, and my grandmother, who was a very dominant personality. I didn't know what Judaism was. I certainly never heard the word 'mikveh.' Ever. There was a *hamam*, a public bath, and people gladly went there all the time to sweat and bathe and pamper themselves. That's all.

"When I got married and we went to Paris to study medicine, all of my friends were assimilated. My uncle, who was my guardian in Paris, took me to a restaurant one time and said to me: 'You see all these women? We Jews must dress like them. You must become a real Parisian.' We were living in the suburbs, and one Sunday, after all the experts had assured me that I would die barren and childless, I told my husband that I'd made up my mind, that I wanted to go to the mikveh. 'What's a mikveh?' he asked. 'It's a Jewish bath-house.' 'Why? Don't we have a bathtub?' he asked. 'Why are you talking about a mikveh all of a sudden?' 'That's what I've decided,' I told him. 'Come and accompany me to the mikveh.' There was only one mikveh in Paris. It was in an old building on Rue Sébastien Froissart. My husband said: 'Why are you coming here? It's disgusting.' 'Wait for me here,' I told him, 'I'm going up.' I was greeted by a scary old woman, everything there was crumbling with age, and there were puddles of water on the floor. After I immersed, I felt like a femininity that was hidden deep inside me had suddenly bloomed. I'd truly grown. I felt what it means to be a woman who wants to give life. On that day I was transformed from a girl, a spoiled medical student, into a woman. Nine months later, I got pregnant."

In the mikveh, the fundamental differences between the worldviews of religious and secular women are blurred. All the women perform rites centered on fertility and sexuality. Fertility is limited to a certain period of life, and thus so is the function of the mikveh. Generally speaking, it is questionable whether a woman's sexuality is determined exclusively by her fertility.[22] However, in the mikveh, femininity, fertility, and sexuality all overlap in perfect harmony.

"Who's next in line for purification?" As Sarah, the bridal counselor on family purity, emerged from the Room 6 corridor, the vestibule was flooded with the fragrance of Chanel No. 5. "Perhaps you, my beauty?" She clutched me by the waist and pressed me to her so tightly that had we been any-where but in the mikveh, I would have taken her for a lesbian.

"No way! I'm not impure," I said, gently but firmly extri-cating myself from her embrace. "I refuse to be called that, and therefore I also refuse to immerse."

"Why? Isn't that a pity? Such a pretty thing like you? Liv-ing in sin." She cupped my face in her manicured hands and took a step back in order to get a better view. "What a horrible shame! May Hashem save us."

"Enough already!" I said impatiently, pulling out of her grasp.

She laced her graceful fingers together pleadingly. "Let me explain it to you. If I don't succeed, no one will, because I am the champion in this. This has been my profession for ten years already, going from house to house, as a volunteer, and persuading women like you to immerse."

"Yes. Dina told me you once nagged someone so much they tossed you down the steps in anger," I said.

"That's a legend," she maintained with a smile. "It is true that it's very hard to convince women who have been married already for ten or twelve years to change their lifestyle. It's better to catch the new brides and start everything off on the right foot, from the very beginning. Then everything flows and it's wonderful. They get used to living with these hardships. I'm not saying it's easy to wait twelve days and to avoid touching, with no hugging and no kissing. Society doesn't encourage discipline and self-restraint. But in the end they thank me, yes? After the wedding they come to the mikveh after every period and keep niddah."

"You're talking about secular brides?"

"Yes. The secular brides are my target audience, because with the ultra-Orthodox bride, the consciousness of impurity and purity, of the sanctity of family purity, is usually in the blood, and it's a given that she, too, like the rest of her community, will piously observe this. The weak link is the secular brides. The ones who receive an hour and a half, or two hours maximum, of instruction from the rabbanit, and come out more confused than when they went in. Because how much can they grasp just like that? These women grew up in—forgive me—a sinful home. Their parents didn't provide them with a good kosher Jewish home. The mother didn't teach the daughter to keep family purity, and so I fear that, at some stage, they'll give up. Anyway, family purity's not an easy thing to keep. Society may ridicule it. There may be troubles between husband and wife, and there's the evil impulse that tries to trip them up. I care so much that I take the time to really sit down and discuss it deeply with them, and explain to them why it's so important. That it's one of the most basic foundations of the Jewish household."

Sarah has developed a method of persuasion in her mission, which she refers to as "holy work recruiting souls for immersion." Her method is based on exploiting the woman's delicate psychological state as she stands on the verge of the most momentous change in her life. Sarah plays on the bride's curiosity, on her fear and faith and her powerful desire for a good, everlastingly happy marriage. In a measured and thoughtful way, Sarah gently presses each button in their psyche and skillfully leads them to do as she wishes.

"How do I really convince them? First of all, I ask them questions. For example, the Torah defines the menstruating woman as impure. What makes her impure? What type of impurity is this? If she is impure, then why is she allowed to enter the synagogue? Why is she allowed to enter the Western Wall plaza? To open a *siddur*?* To open a direct line to the Creator? All of this is permitted to her. But touching a Torah scroll is forbidden to her. Touching the stones of the Western Wall is forbidden to her. Praying to and talking with the Creator is permitted, yet she's forbidden to have any contact with her husband? The Torah prohibited all contact between husband and wife. What's going on here? Is it such a holy thing for them to be together?

"That's how I start with them, with these questions, and then they try to answer me, drawing on the little knowledge they obtained in their counseling session. Usually, they aren't able to answer me very well. Only a few succeed. When I

---

*The Jewish prayerbook.

come to them with questions and they have no answers to give, I spark a desire in them to listen and to know. Then I explain to them what sort of impurity this is. 'You shall not approach a woman in her time of niddah, to uncover her nakedness,' says the Torah, concluding, 'For if anyone commits any of these abominations, they shall be cut off from among their people.' In other words, if a man has intercourse with his wife when she's in niddah, we're talking about *isur karet*—a sin punishable by untimely death and eternal excommunication of the soul from the Jewish people."

This halakhic imperative frightens every Jewish bride on the eve of her wedding. After this stern warning, Sarah immediately takes a step back, knowing that overly aggressive intimidation may backfire.

"I don't linger with them on this, because I don't like to talk much about karet. It's scary. I just touch on it very briefly, to remind them that this threat exists."

Now Sarah switches to terminology the secular bride is more familiar with.

"Why does the Torah define me as impure?" the bride asks.

Sarah readily sides with the bride: "Good question. The first time I heard that a menstruating woman is impure, it really bothered me."

At this point, Sarah starts to explain about impurity and purity, and integrates images from the secular woman's world. "'The granddaddy of impurities is the impurity of the dead—*tum'at hamet,* and we see this with the *kohen.** Do you have *kohanim* in the family?' 'Yes,' some of them say to me. Others mention that at the cemetery there's a separate

---

Kohen (pl. *kohanim*) – a descendant of the Jewish priests who served in the Holy Temple; certain halakhic restrictions apply to such a person. The common Jewish surname Cohen and its variations usually denote someone who is a descendant of the *kohanim*.

road for the kohanim to use. Yet others point out that in the hospital there's also a sign that says 'Entry prohibited for Kohanim,' because they could come in contact with a corpse. These women are familiar with this terminology. So I explain to them why it's forbidden for a kohen to come in contact with the dead, and they listen, and they accept it, because it's something they come across in daily life. Even the secular women, because, after all, we are all Jews, you know. Because, as you know, Israel is partly a state of halakha."

After the talk about hospitals, corpses, and funerals, as the scariness is reaching a peak, Sarah kindly turns to the main subject that interests the young bride this particular evening—romance.

"I get into this subject of what goes on between husband and wife in a very strong way."

"What about husband and wife?"

"Mainly, I talk about the direct connection between immersion in the mikveh and building intimacy that leads to domestic tranquility. Unfortunately, I'm not able to provide the secular women with in-depth counseling on every detail concerning the wedding night, for several reasons. First is the lack of time. Two hours is not enough to convey the whole subject. Second is that these women could actually teach me all about the physical bond between man and woman. Usually they don't stand under the wedding canopy as virgins. Therefore, I focus on the sanctity of the spiritual bond. And you'd be amazed how strongly they respond to this. It really, really speaks to them. I've never had a bride sitting opposite me whose eyes didn't shine with emotion as I spoke of the sanctity of this bond. They always say to me excitedly: 'I never thought about how "Behold, you are betrothed to me"*

---

*In Hebrew, *harei at mekudeshet li*; recited by the groom when placing the ring on the bride's finger during the Jewish wedding ceremony.

has to do with holiness.' Look"—Sarah beamed at her own words—"these secular women are Jews. They have a Jewish soul, and this soul is set afire within their two hours with me. When I talk to them about the bond between the souls, they relate to it immediately without any problem. Apparently, Hakadosh Baruch Hu created a natural human impulse for holiness."

"But he also created the evil impulse," I reminded her.

Just then, the shrill cry of "Kulululululu!" ululated throughout the mikveh, filling the vestibule as a throng of women entered in an array of colors, tongues trilling and right index fingers moving up and down over the puckered lips that protruded from their radiant faces.

"Hallelujah!" shouted one, and a barrage of drumming, on a tambourine and darboukas, answered her. "Here comes the bride!" announced another. "Kulululululu!" answered her companions. Within seconds, they'd formed a circle. "Tonight is the night! Tonight is the night!" sang out an elegant old lady in a black straw hat decorated with three red feathers. With her scrawny hand she led into the center of the circle a young woman, tall and erect as a mannequin. Her feminine curves rounded like the moon at midcycle, her face gleaming like a dazzling spring sky. "Tonight is the night! Tonight is the night! A great joy tonight!" responded the whole tribe to the old lady as the circle of women began to revolve around the pair. "Tonight is the night!" cried the grandmother hoarsely. "A great joy tonight!" responded the circle, clapping in time to the music.

"Mazal tov! Mazal tov!" cried four older women, straining under the weight of baskets overflowing with delicacies.

"May it be an auspicious hour," chorused Sarah and Doris. "Welcome, welcome. Put all the food here on the table. We set up tables for you inside, too, in the celebrations room."

The women sat down and each one opened her basket. Piquant aromas wafted through the mikveh. There were stuffed grape leaves, rice with raisins and walnuts, pigeon in plum and apricot sauce, and marzipan cakes. Each time another bowl was taken out, a new scent filled the air and supplanted its predecessor. Cinnamon and cloves and burnt sugar, coconut and roasted eggs, almonds and rosewater—all the smells came together in wild abandon inside the mikveh.

The circle of dancers had just begun to slow when Sarah, practically floating, plunged into the middle and affectionately embraced the bride: "Ah, my little chickie, how are you?" She clung to the young woman, who was a head taller, stroked her bottom, gripped her by the waist, and yanked her close. "Finally, we've arrived at the most beautiful moment of your life," she exclaimed, pulling the girl's face near and passionately kissing her on both cheeks. "May you be healthy. May you know only good fortune. You deserve it. You deserve it all, my sweetie. Come, come with me." She separated her, almost by force, from the old lady, who was reluctant to let go of her granddaughter.

"What's with her—hugging and kissing my Natalie so much?" fretted the grandmother.

"Don't worry," Doris reassured her. "It's all right. Sarah is just an emotional type who does a lot of touching out of love. But it's not—" She burst out laughing at the sight of the old lady's grimace. "It's not how it looks. She has a husband and six children and everything is fine."

"We've heard about religious lesbians who marry against their will and have children," remarked the bride's mother.

Sarah held Natalie firmly by the waist, and the two disappeared into the brides' room.

"Today, you and your spouse are starting the marvelous process of building a home," said Sarah in her soft, soothing voice. "A Jewish home. Your home is like a temple, a pure place. A place where love dwells. A place built on stable foundations. An eternal alliance. An eternal pact between you and your beloved.

"The only way to build a stable home, a dwelling place of love and peace, is through family purity. The divine formula for preserving love is based on the system of separation. Distance brings you closer. Rabbi Meir, the great Jewish sage, asks: Why does niddah last seven days? Because if the husband grows too accustomed to his wife, he tires of her. Therefore the Torah said: Niddah is seven days, so the wife shall be as desired by her husband as on the day she stood under the wedding canopy.

"You will be his queen. How do you secular put it? He will be your devoted slave. Now come," Sarah said, putting her arm around the young woman's waist. "Let's go out to the big moment. Everyone is outside waiting for you, all excited. You are our queen tonight. Tonight we are all here for you." She relaxed her grip and turned toward the door.

"Kululululululu!" the women greeted the returning pair. Sarah delivered the young woman to her mother, and the whole clan showered the bride with kisses and hugs.

"After me!" Doris proudly marched toward the Room 6 corridor. The mother of the bride marched right behind her, leading her daughter along. After them hurried the mothers-in-law, followed by the grandmother, aunts, sisters, girlfriends, and cousins. All loudly rejoicing in excited anticipation of the bride's immersion ceremony.

6

FEMALE RITUALS, SISTERHOOD, AND FEMALE AUTHORITY

Pur akeyas ventanikas m'aronjan flechas
Si son de amores vengan derechas

From those windows rolling pins are tossed on me
If they come from love they come straight

I heard the voices singing in Ladino before I saw the group of women, seventh- and eighth-generation descendants of the Spanish Marranos, accompanying in slow procession a young bride-to-be clad in a white robe, with a towel around her head and white terrycloth slippers on her feet.

Morena me yaman yo blanca nasi
De pasear galana mi color pedri

Dark one they call me but white was I born
From all my coquettish walks I lost the color of my
skin

The women rave, their voices growing hoarse and blending into a single voice as they form a circle around the young girl.

Morena me yaman los marineros
Si otra ves me yaman me vo con eyos

Dark one the sailors call me
If they call me once more I shall go with them

The singing gets louder as the women circle around. One of them enters the circle, forcefully hugs the bride, lifts her up, and spins around with her in ecstasy. The women circle around the bride faster and faster and, as they do, each one reaches out to touch the bride, brings her hand back to her lips, closes her eyes and kisses her fingertips as if kissing a Torah scroll that has just now, with much rejoicing, been paraded into the synagogue.

The ritual of leading the bride to the immersion, carried out by the women in the mikveh, is a rite of passage conducted under female supervision, and it is just as sacred and important to the participants, perhaps even more so, than the ritual of dedicating a Torah scroll and other rituals that take place in synagogues under male supervision.[1]

The consequence of excluding women from all public religious activity, and of the barring of the woman from sacred pursuits even within the walls of her own home, on the grounds of *kol ba'isha erva* ("a woman's voice is indecent"),[2] is the construction of a "female religion" with a hierarchy, laws, and rituals of its own. These include rites of passage that accompany the biological circle of life and the woman's life-cycle changes, rites connected with birth, adulthood, marriage, and death. Women perform fertility rites, purification rites, and coping rituals that channel anxieties and tensions and get rid of physical and emotional toxins. These rites are performed by women for women.[3] A significant portion of them occur within the mikveh.

The mikveh is a pilgrimage site for women, and in it rituals are performed whose main purpose is to protect the woman's body and soul from evil entities and to connect her with her

Creator, who imprinted in her body the code for the creation of the Jewish genius and the copyright for the creation of life. The Creator elevated the woman and made her his partner in the art of creating life when he instilled in her body an ongoing process of destruction and creation, a process vital to primordial harmony.

Within the "female temple" of the mikveh an entire cultural world is created to which the man has no entry. Here, women fulfill their primal need for renewal by means of the fertility rites that each and every one performs from the time she stands under the wedding canopy until the time she enters menopause and exits the circle of life-creation. These fertility rites are primarily rites of passage.

By definition, rites of passage irreversibly alter the individual's condition or status. The act of circumcision formally ushers the Jewish male child into the Jewish community.[4] The wedding ceremony transforms a single man and a single woman into a married couple and ushers them into a system of duties and privileges that subsequently may only be changed by means of another ceremony—divorce.[5] The bridal immersion ritual, however, although a religious rite of passage composed of three formal stages—cleanliness inspection, immersion, and blessing—does not irreversibly alter the woman's status. It symbolically transforms her from a single, virgin, and immature girl into a mature and fertile woman who is permitted to have intercourse with her husband. However, this status is reversible. It can change in the event that the woman divorces or is widowed.* The same ritual transforms a woman from a state of forbidden impurity to one of permitted purity, but as she is subject to nature's endless cycles of destruction and construction, a woman continually reverts to impurity and must repeatedly repurify herself.

---

*A widow's status is reversed to "unripe" and "not fertile" without the performance of a transformative ritual, as happens with divorce.

Into the formal immersion rituals, additional customs have been faithfully interwoven. These are "rules of tradition," introduced by women, who oversee everything that happens before, during, and after the immersion: the foods, the singing, the dancing, the blessings, and the wishes for good fortune. This is an act of embroidery, the nonhalakhic additive, the feminine adornment that has become an important and integral part of the ritual. These traditions were handed down orally from mother to daughter, from generation to generation, and from place to place. They developed in all corners of the Diaspora and "immigrated" to Israel. Some are performed exactly as they were in their countries of origin, while others have undergone a process of adaptation to modern Israel.

Women's rituals in the mikveh are colorful and fragrant and stimulate all five senses. Anthropologist Victor Turner maintains that it is through the senses that individuals process both the experiential and normative aspects of a ritual.[6] The more senses involved, the more intense the ritual. Measured in terms of Turner's parameters, immersion in the mikveh is an intense and highly concentrated ritual, as all the senses are powerfully involved.

The sense of hearing is invoked through the prayers after every regular immersion, and through songs and celebratory cheers when a bride-to-be immerses. The scrubbing of the body before immersion, the sensation of the water on the body during immersion, and the dancing and hugging and kissing and other physical contact throughout the ritual all engage the sense of touch. Sight plays a role in the meticulous inspection of the body for cleanliness, and in the inspection in the days leading up to immersion for any sign of vaginal secretions. The aromas of the mikveh, of the soap, and the woman's cleansed body, as well as those of the foods that are eaten following the immersion, play to the sense of smell. Finally, taste is invoked through the special foods that, according to various ethnic traditions, should be eaten following immersion in the mikveh (particularly after a bride immerses).

In the mikveh, a sixth sense is added to the mix: an intangible feminine quality that makes the rituals so mysterious and sensuous.

Turner explains that during a ritual it is via one or more of the senses that a message is conveyed to the participants. The experience is both passive and active. For example, the moment the bride's mother pushes the slice of the ring-shaped torte cake into her daughter's mouth, she is transmitting a whole spectrum of sexual and social messages. The pressing of the cake into the bride's mouth may symbolize the penetration of the penis and the tearing of the hymen, signifying society's legitimizing of intercourse between husband and wife. The sweet taste and aroma of the cake recalls the sweetness and pleasure to be had from sexual relations, and the cake itself is a reminder of the purpose of the coupling: consuming the eggs with which it was made promises fertility and the blessings of abundance and success.

But not everyone finds immersion and the sexual intercourse that follows all that wonderful, as I discovered in another conversation at the mikveh with the balaniyot Michaela, Lily, and Doris. "I think that this whole idea of the great pleasure of immersion and sexuality is something you all brought from Morocco," Michaela said, referring to Lily and Doris. "We Ashkenazi* women have a very ambivalent attitude toward immersion. On the one hand it's a blessing, because it cleanses you of impurity, and when you come out of the mikveh you feel like you've shed a hundred tons of filth

---

*Ashkenazi – Jews whose ancestry traces to central and eastern Europe.

from your body and soul. But on the other hand, for many women—though not me, for, like my husband says, I'm an odd one—immersion is a form of punishment. In general, this whole business of sex and the mikveh isn't all that sensuous and joyful and erotic as you Sephardi* women describe.

"Generally speaking—though not for me, like I said—sex is a very difficult obligation for the devout woman. A burden and not a joy. The halakha stresses that the man is obliged to fulfill his conjugal duty toward the woman—in other words, he must have intercourse with her when she is permitted to him—but if it were up to the woman, in many cases her need would be less frequent than his. Lots of times, you see a woman coming to the mikveh looking totally weary. She finishes the immersion and she doesn't rush to get dressed and go home to be with her husband, because her body and soul aren't ready for it at all. She's tired, because while he's sitting in the *kollel,*‡ she's scrambling to support the family. She's stressed because the immersion day is the ovulation day. It's almost certain she'll get pregnant, and that's the last thing she wants. She's weary of giving birth. She already has twelve children at home and she's only thirty-five and has many years of fertility ahead of her and she is forbidden to stop because the spilling of seed in vain is a grave sin punishable by death.

"Only the rabbi can give permission for contraception, and you have to really have one foot in the grave to receive such permission. And even then there's a problem—How does society see you? You're a useless vessel. And one prob-

---

*Sephardi – Jews whose ancestry traces to Spain; in contemporary Hebrew slang, refers here to Jews of North African or Middle Eastern origin (also known as *edot hamizrah*), i.e., Moroccans, Kurds, Iraqis, etc.

‡*kollel* – a yeshiva (Jewish institute of learning, where men study sacred texts, primarily the Talmud) for married men.

lem follows another and they keep piling up until the woman is so weighed down she can hardly move. With you Sephardi women, for some reason, everything having to do with the mikveh—purity, food, sex, sisterhood—all sounds so positive and romantic."

"I know plenty of Ashkenazi women who are interested in nothing but sex," countered Lily. "But as far as the weariness and the social image, there's something to what you're saying."

Whether or not they enjoy the immersion, both Sephardi and Ashkenazi women ascribe magical healing properties to the water. The water's power to purify is inextricably linked to a faith in its curative power. Since impurity is essentially a type of "physical infection," the water may also protect one from actual infections and contagious diseases.[7] Purification in the mikveh waters symbolically marks the body's time to heal from its state of "sickness," the time of niddah when it is vulnerable to germs and diseases, to a "healthy" state, the state of purification.

One woman in the mikveh describes herself as injured when she has her period: "I know that I'm wounded, and no one may touch me while I'm wounded, until I get well. When I immerse the immersion heals me."

When God wishes to demonstrate his power and greatness he performs miracles showing his mastery of the "primeval waters" that filled the universe prior to his creation of the world, and which retained their independence in relation to the Creator of heaven and earth. The story of Creation tells us that, in the beginning, "the earth was unformed and void, and darkness was upon the face of the deep; and the spirit of God hovered over the face of the waters" (Gen. 1:2). God did not command the waters to separate, but he created a firmament in the midst of the waters, which divided "the waters below" from "the waters above" the firmament. Water is the only substance that does not change in the wake of a divine order. Only once in the Creation process do the waters receive an order from God: "Let the waters under the heaven be gathered together unto one place, and let the dry land appear. And it was so" (Gen. 1:9). But this imperative cannot undermine water's independent and ungovernable nature.

God brings on the deluge and splits the Red Sea. When the prophet Jonah tries to escape from God and takes refuge on a ship headed for Tarshish, God stirs up such a great storm at sea that the ship is in danger of sinking and the sailors, having discovered that Jonah is on the run from God, toss him into the water to appease the anger of the God of the Hebrews. With the onslaught of a single wave, God can destroy and drown the world he created. I am the One and Only, who rules the seas, proclaims the Almighty God, and you humans had better obey me. God, according to Jewish tradition, also controls the rainfall. Rain is the reward that God gives the farmer who works the field, and the community as a whole, for obeying his laws and commandments, as it is said: "Then I will give your rains in their season" (Lev. 26:4); and also: "The Lord will open unto thee His good treasure the heaven to give the rain of thy land in its season" (Deut. 28:12). Water is the source of life of the divine creation. The amniotic fluid that surrounds the baby in his mother's womb symbolizes the inseparable bond between God and his earthly partner in the creation of life—woman.

"You won't believe what the mikveh waters really do," Dina, the balanit who, like her mother Leah, has special training in immersing the disabled, tells me. "I see what sorts of miracles happen to my crippled women. No one believes me."

"Try me."

"Shattered women come to me. Some crippled from birth without arms, or legs. Some paralyzed from polio, and some, poor things, that were injured in road accidents, terror attacks, and other disasters, which, unfortunately, we have no shortage of in this country. Their bodies are full of metal and replacement parts and they can barely function. They can't stand up. Not to mention what they look like. Some have ruined faces. Others have holes in their flesh and you can almost see their bones. In short, it's a horror. I immersed one crippled woman who couldn't function at all. She married a fantastic young man. Handsome, healthy, religious, and learned. I think he's even a professor at the university. What do you say to that? He married her. No one could believe it. Even her mother couldn't believe it. And she's not rich, so money didn't play a role. And you can't say that she's an ordinary cripple. She's not easy to handle. The two of us, my mother and I, go in with her and it's not enough. Sometimes Paula or Michaela have to help."

"But what does this have to do with miracles performed by the water? Her husband chose her before the marriage, before she immersed."

"It's true that finding one's match is determined by Hakadosh Baruch Hu, and apparently this young man's purpose is to atone for sins in this world and to ascend straight up"—she pointed to the heavens—"smooth sailing, no stopping. But the miracle has to do with the children. This woman—get this—has four children, and she's pregnant again now."

"Four? Did you say four?"

"You heard right. I don't even know how they do it, you know? She has no legs and no arms and she has a Filipina caretaker who does everything for her. Everything—except for getting pregnant and giving birth. Not one. Not two. Four. And now the fifth is on the way. You don't call that a miracle? Does that seem like an ordinary thing to you? Is that normal?

"Another crippled woman who comes here is just half a

body, no legs. She's a lovely woman and her husband was her teacher at the school for the disabled and fell in love with her. His parents were very upset; they tried to talk him out of it. But he went ahead and married her, a year and a half ago it was, and already they have a child. Baruch Hashem, they are very happy. This was a miracle, too. For a woman like this, against almost all the odds, to get married and then get pregnant so quickly. She herself tells me that every time she immerses she can feel how she's boosting her good fortune. That's a fact."

A woman exiting the mikveh after immersing must not encounter any undesirable entity that symbolizes bad luck. If she crosses paths with an evil entity (*meizik*),* she must go back and immerse again. By contrast, a woman who encounters a righteous person (*tzaddik*) is protected from evil, according to the rules of the female tradition inspired by tales of the Jewish sages.

"She shouldn't come out and see a black cat, heaven forbid, or an Arab. It happens sometimes that an Arab is passing by and then she returns to immerse again," one of the balaniyot, Lily, explains to me. "Why an Arab? Because in Morocco the Jews were a minority amid the Arab population. Here in Israel, too, there's no shortage of Arabs, and here, too, they're dangerous to the woman who emerges purified from the mikveh.

"They say that Rabbi Yohanan Ben-Zakkai‡ was extraordinarily handsome. And he was told that he should sit near the mikveh, at a distance, so that every woman who came out

---

meizik – something harmful or damaging.

‡Lily (and later Dina) most likely meant to refer to Yohanan Bar-Nafha (d. circa 279), who compiled the Jerusalem Talmud and whose extraordinary beauty is written about in the Talmud.

would look at him and then give birth to a tzaddik like him. The biblical Joseph was also very, very handsome. It's all a matter of holiness.

"The encounter with the tzaddik envelops the woman in an aura of holiness and neutralizes any effect of an evil influence," says Lily. "Or maybe it's stimulating," argues Dina, who had joined the discussion. "If I come out of the mikveh and see someone as attractive and pure and holy as Rabbi Yohanan Ben-Zakkai, right away a sexual passion burns in me and I rush home to devour my husband."

The balaniyot take upon themselves the powers of the tzaddik. They appropriate the tzaddik's holiness. This role developed from female beliefs and rituals that were created in the mikveh.

Lily acknowledges that she fulfills the function of the tzaddik: "Over the years, a custom arose, especially with the Sephardi women, that the balanit touches a woman's hand as soon as she comes out of the immersion, and that frees her from the need to do a repeat immersion, if, heaven forbid, she should run into strangers and evil entities on her way out. It's a matter of holiness. What's important is that she comes out of the mikveh and doesn't see anyone until she reaches her husband. That's why, in a lot of mikvehs today, they put up many pictures of great tzaddikim.* When the woman comes out to the vestibule, she looks at the tzaddik. He is the first thing she sees. Here we don't have any pictures of tzaddikim on the walls, so there are women who, after they immerse and recite the blessing, they touch me on the hand. When she touches me, I transfer to her the holiness of the tzaddik, and it's like she's exempt. Then if she goes out and sees someone, she doesn't come back to immerse again. That's all it is."

---

*tzaddikim – the plural form of "tzaddik" (righteous person).

———

Within the bubble of the female world of the mikveh, the balaniyot represent the halakhic male authority. Since men are forbidden to set foot in the women's mikveh,* and the formal rituals that take place there must be done in accordance with the laws of the male-formulated halakha, there is a need for someone to supervise and ensure that these important rituals are performed in accordance with all the laws of the cultural order,[8] someone to bring the rules of the halakha into the mikveh and ensure that they are properly carried out. For this distinguished role the balaniyot were chosen: women who play the male role within this all-female world. They oversee the women to make certain they do not overstep the bounds of what is permitted, and that they perform the ritual immersion as required.

However, the balaniyot are somewhat flexible in their enforcement of the rules. "One mustn't be too stringent with a secular woman who comes to immerse, and scare her away from the mikveh. One should be lenient with the rules and immerse her with a minimum of halakhic offenses. The main thing is that this vital mitzvah, the mitzvah of immersion, be fulfilled," explains Miriam. "The main goal for the balanit is to get the woman to immerse. Before the rabbis give us their advice on these cases, they ask us if the woman is observant or not. 'She's not observant? Immerse her anyway, the important thing is that she immerse,' they say.

"We have one case of an unmarried woman. She has a common-law partner. She has three children from him and she comes to immerse. In principle, it's absolutely forbidden to immerse a woman who isn't consecrated in marriage. A single woman, a divorced woman, or a widow is not sup-

———

*The only exception is the immersion ceremony for a female convert, when the officiating rabbis will stand by the door to the immersion room.

posed to immerse. But if it's possible to partially save her soul, it's a mitzvah for us to do so. 'It's bad enough that she's not married to him and living in sin—she should sin against niddah, too?' say the rabbis. So it's permitted for her to immerse and to cleanse herself of her niddah impurity—at least that way we'll save the souls of her innocent children from the decree of karet. But she's forbidden to recite the blessing over immersion, because she is elevated in purity but not in holiness. Holiness is found only in marriage, which sanctions and consecrates the couple's sexual relations. But immersion is purifying even without a blessing. So in terms of the rules of niddah, she is purified."

"Do all the rabbis agree on this point?" I ask.

"No. The Sephardi rabbis tend toward leniency, and the Ashkenazi rabbis tend toward greater stringency. At first, I asked an Ashkenazi rabbi and he absolutely would not allow the immersion. 'She wants to immerse? Let her get married,' he said laconically. 'But the man isn't willing,' I explained. 'She's constrained by the halakha. She can't force marriage on him.' We wanted to keep her from going to another mikveh and entering under false pretenses. So Doris suggested that we ask the Sephardi rabbi. He was also very against it at first, but in the end, he approved our request and said: 'All right, she may go purify herself from this worm, from this *sheretz*. At least we'll save her and the children from karet.' "

"Ah, what joy," said Sarah, grinning with satisfaction as she sat down behind the table in the vestibule. She was sure she'd won another soul for immersion today. She was confident, from her wealth of experience, that the bride's insecurity about her groom's undying love for her and strong desire to acquire his total love would bring her back to the mikveh month after month, until she got pregnant. She was also confident that after this bride gives birth, she'll continue immersing until her fertile days are over and she has no more blood.

"This is nothing, what you see here now," she said, straightening her elegant new wig. "There are times when three or four come at once. At a peak time, we get as many as five brides in one evening, especially at the end of the counting of the Omer.* You know that, according to the halakha, marriage is forbidden during the Omer. So on Lag ba'Omer‡ and after Shavuot,§ throughout the summer, we get a flood of brides. Four or five families of brides arrive every evening with trays full of food and sweets. They gather in the celebrations room, which was built specially for these parties. You should know that we're the only mikveh in Israel that has such a room," she added proudly.

"Each family puts its traditional foods on the table. Before, and especially after, the bride immerses, all the women dance—old and young, all swaying together to the beat. They bring a tape player and put on Eyal Golan or Sarit Hadad‖ and have an amazing party. Sometimes professional drummers come, too. These women you saw earlier, who were drumming on the darboukas, are professionals, and you see how the rhythm of the drums whips everyone into a state of ecstasy. Sometimes the families mix and then the celebration gets even bigger, until it sweeps up us balaniyot, too. It's the most beautiful thing when you enter this room, when there are several brides, and you hear the music and the singing and the prayers, each in a different language, like at the Western Wall. One's praying in Yemenite, the next in Ashkenazi,

*Omer – the days between the Jewish holidays of Passover and Shavuot, a period of partial mourning in which certain types of celebrations are not held.

‡Lag ba'Omer – the thirty-third day of the Omer, a day on which mourning is suspended and festive celebrations may be held.

§Shavuot – the Feast of Weeks, the second of the three Jewish pilgrimage festivals, falling in late spring or early summer.

‖Eyal Golan and Sarit Hadad – popular Israeli singers in the Oriental style.

another in Moroccan. This ensemble is like the philharmonic —each one in her own language—and Hashem understands each one and knows what she wants and answers her in her own language. And now," she said, breathing deeply with pleasure, "I must run and see how they're managing in the celebrations room."

As Sarah got to her feet, a pale young woman in a wheel-chair appeared in the doorway. Her head was adorned with curls, and a white silk ribbon was tied around her forehead, accentuating the paleness of her complexion. Behind her stood seven women and a little girl of about four.

"Welcome! Come in, come in. What joy!" Sarah ran to them with open arms. "You're a little early. Leah and Dina should be arriving any second, just for you. What is this white ribbon on your forehead?" She placed her hand on the head of the young woman as she led the party toward the center of the vestibule.

"It's a Moroccan custom," answered the mother of the bride, her mature features closely resembling her daughter's. "The groom's family is from Fez, and there they had the custom of the ceremony of the white ribbon and the green ribbon."[9]

"Interesting," Sarah mused. "I've never heard of that. The white ribbon I see. Where is the green ribbon?"

"Exactly a week ago, on the day that Moran, our lovely bride, finished her period, at twilight, she bathed," explained a skinny, stern-faced woman who was part of the entourage, "and her mother tied her hair with a green ribbon she bought with her own money. The green, which is a symbol of fertility, really suited Moran's green eyes. On the same day, I—the mother of Uri, the groom—came to Moran's house and brought a tray filled with homemade sweet cookies, candies, a jar of honey, a bowl of henna powder, a dish of butter, and an egg. I also brought several meters of white ribbon. And in the presence of Moran's mother, Batya, and these fine women"—she gestured toward the three older escorts—"Moran's aunts, we began the ceremony, which is a fertility ceremony to bring blessing upon the bride, that she should have an easy start and a good fate in her new life. Baruch Hashem, I am fortunate to have a good marriage, so I had the privilege of performing this ceremony for my eldest son's bride. Because if, God forbid, I was divorced or widowed, I would have to forgo this honor in favor of another relative who could symbolize 'the good life.' We believe that good fortune chases good fortune and a woman who's been touched by misfortune mustn't touch the bride."

"Not only touch. Even the presence of 'carriers of misfortune' is harmful," Sarah declared, glancing at Moran's spinster cousin Ruthie and her spinster friend. "We recommend to every bride, whatever her background, not to bring with her into the immersion room barren women, spinsters, widows, and divorcees, in the belief that these unfortunates eat away at the good fortune. At this important and delicate time, right before the wedding, the bride has to muster all the positive forces to her side, to keep away the forces of evil."

"It's definitely unhealthy for the bride," confirmed Doris, who had joined the group of women in the vestibule. Doris made no bones about her fundamental objection to unmarried girls participating in the bride's immersion process. "It detracts from the power of the blessing that is given to the bride in her special time in the mikveh. It's no good for someone to take from her a little of her holiness. At this crucial time, the bride is so sensitive"—Doris glanced imploringly at the two spinsters accompanying the bride, who were by this point on the verge of tears—"that she needs all the power of the blessing that the water gives. It's not a time to share. Excuse me, but I do not condone it and I tell all the brides, too, and most of the time they listen."

"And a woman who isn't about to become a bride?" I asked, joining the conversation.

"That we do a lot. Often, a woman enters and after she immerses for herself she makes requests on another woman's behalf. And you wouldn't believe how fast it works. The requests are fulfilled, almost all of them.

"My cosmetician, Tova, a mother of four, has a client of about thirty who's been married for ten years without children. Barren. Every time this client comes to Tova, she lays out her troubles, cries about how Hashem has closed her womb and kept her from having children. One time, she revealed that it was especially important to her to look beautiful that day because it was her immersion day, and she asked Tova to pray for her that it would be her lucky day and she would finally get pregnant. The good-hearted Tova decided to take action. She went to the mivkeh, immersed, and prayed aloud for Hashem to bless her client with at least one child. Three weeks later, Tova discovered that she herself was pregnant. That same day, the client called her, ecstatic. 'I'm pregnant!' she informed her. 'Me, too!' Tova answered. 'I just got the good word!' "

Moran giggled and patted the little girl, her niece, on the head.

"Do men participate in the green ribbon ceremony?" I asked Moran's mother-in-law, bringing the subject back to Moroccan wedding customs.

"Heaven forbid! Only women. We follow the original tradition. Today there are some people who call themselves modern and wreck the tradition by including men. We don't allow the groom to see the bride for forty-eight hours before the wedding. It brings bad luck."

"So what happens with the green ribbon?"

"Well, in the presence of these fine women, I removed the green ribbon from Moran's head. Then I dampened a little henna, added some honey and butter to the bowl with it, mixed it well, and then added a soft-boiled egg, because it's not yet fully cooked." A screech of laughter escaped the mother-in-law's lips as she said this, but she immediately sti-fled it, assuming that Moran, Batya, and the aunts didn't get the traditional joke, which alludes to the groom's "virgin" testicles that have yet to fully mature.

"I put the whole mixture inside a wad of cotton and tied the whole thing to the top of Moran's head with the white ribbon. The white symbolizes purity. I pressed down on the cotton and spread a little of the mixture on her head. We all sang 'Kululululu!' and kissed her and tossed dry henna on her. Then I took a small handful of the mixture, put it in Moran's mouth, and made her swallow it, to ensure that the blessing is absorbed in her body to fertilize her blood. The re-mainder I threw away. Some people give the remainder to the bride's mother, who hides it until the end of the first month of the marriage before throwing it out. But after a few hours, the egg already smells . . ."

"So just imagine how it stinks after four weeks!" exclaimed Moran, crinkling her nose in disgust.

"Since then," continued the mother-in-law, ignoring the interruption, "it's been exactly one week, Moran has worn the white ribbon on her head, and my son, may he live long, has kept the green ribbon tied around his waist—the same green ribbon I took from Moran's head and brought to him. The white ribbon and the green ribbon protect the two of them from demons and other evil entities. Before we came here, we fed Moran an egg white beaten with sugar to boost her purity and protect her from demons. Tomorrow, with Hashem's help, right before the wedding ceremony, my son will take off the green ribbon. And now I have the honor, just before the immersion, of taking the white ribbon off Moran's head.

"May you have much good fortune and blessing and give birth to many children," the stern-faced mother-in-law said as she gently removed the pure white ribbon from Moran's pale brow. Then she bent down and her lips fluttered slightly as she planted a cool kiss on the forehead of the bride, who from this moment on was symbolically detached from her mother's home, and tomorrow, after the wedding, would officially join her mother-in-law's household, her husband's family.[10]

"Kulululululu!" trilled the women joyfully.

"Here they come!" announced Sarah as Leah, Dina, and Paula entered the mikveh for Moran's immersion. Leah, a woman of few words, had been serving disabled women for more than ten years, and her body, slender as a grapevine, had molded itself to this arduous work and seemingly rebuilt itself for the task. The muscles of her arms and legs had thickened greatly from bearing the heavy physical burden of her handicapped charges. Her dark eyes peered out humbly from beneath her droopy eyelids, alertly scanning her surroundings. Generally, she keeps her thoughts to herself.

Dina, Leah's daughter, is her mother's polar opposite, with a body padded with rolls of fat and a mouth that is incessantly taking in food or emitting chatter and giggles. With much patience and love, Leah trained her daughter in the art of immersing disabled women, until Dina became an expert herself. Now Dina is passing this knowledge on to Paula, a newly religious woman of about thirty who avidly drinks in the flood of words that pour from her teacher's mouth. Like Leah, she maintains a studious silence.

"Morani, you're here already? Oh, my sweetheart!" bellowed Dina, rushing over to the young paraplegic. She took the wheelchair by the handles, spun it around, pulled it close, cupped the girl's face in her hands, and pressed it deep against her ample chest. The girl did not resist, but when Dina released her, she saw that Moran's eyes were closed and she appeared to have fainted.

"Bring water! Paula, bring water!" yelled Dina.

"Morani! Morani!" cried the little girl, leaning against her aunt's paralyzed legs.

The women scurried in every direction. "Where's a faucet? Where's a sink? Water! Water! Where is some water?!" they all shouted hysterically.

"Here! Take it!" Paula handed a bottle of mineral water to Dina, who hurriedly emptied it on the paralyzed girl's head. She came to all at once.

"Morani, speak to me," her mother said, shaking her by the shoulders.

"I'm all wet . . . the chair . . ." mumbled Moran.

"It's all right," the women soothed, swarming around her. Her mother stroked her wet hair, one aunt wiped her face, the second smoothed her shirt, and the third wiped the backrest of her wheelchair.

This whole time, the mother-in-law stood apart, stock-still, observing the goings-on as she waited to resume her role in the ceremony.

"Give her some air or she'll faint again," Dina said, dispersing the four women with a sweep of her hand. "Are you okay?" She lifted the girl's dazed face to her.

"She's very emotional?" Paula commented gently from behind Dina's huge back.

"It's natural," said Leah in a soft, deep voice, her eyes offering the bride a comforting caress. "Every bride gets emotional. And you, my dear, have even more reason to be emotional." Her smile dug two deep dimples in the center of her dark brown cheeks.

"*Yalla,** shall we go shower?" boomed Dina, giving Moran a light swat on the back to check that the young woman had completely recovered.

"No need for a shower! She's all ready," cried the escorts. "She prepared herself at home. She only needs to immerse."

"What's this? You already did everything at home?" Dina grimaced in disappointment.

-----

*Yalla – a common Israeli expression meaning "come on!"

"That's how we do it. We Tunisian Jews believe in being as modest as possible with the immersion and getting it done quickly," explained Batya, the bride's mother.

"Okay, but this is the wedding eve! It's not just any regular immersion!" Dina cried, her frustration evident in the veins on her forehead, which swelled symmetrically toward her temples, sank out of sight in the pouches of her cheeks, and reappeared on the sides of her thick neck.

"On the wedding eve in particular, the immersion must be kept hidden. Therefore, we prepare the bride at home," explained Batya. "I remember that I immersed in this very same mikveh when I got married. I was living in the city center then and the mikvehs there were old and decrepit, dark and small, and we heard that a nice new mikveh had opened in another neighborhood, in an out-of-the-way spot. It was very important for us women to know that when we came out of the mikveh, we wouldn't be exposed to the surroundings, for modesty's sake. This building was new and modern then, and the rooms large and well lit. Those were the necessary criteria for a bride's immersion. I remember that there purposely was no big celebration for my immersion. On the contrary, I came with just my mother. When I came out of the mikveh, my mother made the *zrrrrrit* sound for me—what you call kululululu, in Arabic is called *zrrrrrit* in Tunisian. Maybe she gave out a few candies too, to the women who were around. But what I remember most is the balanit who immersed me. She was an Ashkenazi, and there was something authoritative about that. She was very dominant. She was very cordial but also very formal and official. She wasn't affectionate at all. I don't recall her even wishing me mazal tov."

"I wonder who it was," said Leah.

"She was fairly old, she may have passed away since then," said Batya.

"Did she have assistants?" asked Dina, absentmindedly

tugging on two coarse black hairs that protruded from a large mole on the side of her nose.

"No, at the time, there were none. She was the only one. With utter formality she said to me: 'This room is free. You may enter.' She didn't offer any congratulations, of course. Nothing. She was very cold and bossy and we accepted it. In those years, there was this feeling that the Ashkenazim are in charge of everything and, to me, an immigrant from Tunisia, the Ashkenazi balanit was an authority figure, an important person doing an important job. The mikveh is very important in community life, so it was only natural that it be headed by an Ashkenazi woman. She exuded this importance. She gave the orders. She was the complete opposite of you and your mother. You're Moroccans, right?"

"Yes," answered Dina and Leah proudly.

"They say you're not supposed to compliment a person to his face. But how will you know if I don't tell you how wonderful and warm you are? The way you welcomed us the first time, two weeks ago, when you prepared us for the immersion. When you explained things to us, mainly to Moran and reassured her, mostly because of her special condition. You did holy work. May you be blessed . . ." The mother choked up and couldn't continue.

"Kulululu!" wailed one of the aunts. "Today is a very special day. The joy is so great that we decided to deviate from the tradition and to celebrate the immersion all together. Our dear Morani wanted her aunts beside her at this important moment, and you see, honey? We're all here with you."

"You're gorgeous. Beautiful. My darling. Our angel," the four women crowded around the bride, hugged and kissed and caressed her, while her little niece climbed on her knees and clung to her neck.

Only the mother-in-law remained standing stiffly in place, with unsettling quiet.

"Mom, please try to include Uri's mother, too," whispered Moran.

"Okay, okay. Thrilling, isn't it, Mrs. Levy?" Batya turned to the mother-in-law.

"Very," the latter said, raising the corners of her mouth in a semblance of a smile.

"I'm scared," said Moran, nervously twisting her torso around.

"Don't worry. I'm with you," Dina reassured her.

The bell announced that it was time.

"The mikveh is ready," said Paula.

"After me," shouted Dina, and with a confident gait she wheeled the bride toward the Room 6 corridor, leading the group to the immersion room for disabled women.

Only two women entered the room—mother and daughter. The rest of the bride's entourage, the two balaniyot, and the balanit-in-training remained outside.

. "Ring the bell when you're ready," called Dina, reluctant to let them go.

Batya wheeled the metal chair into the room and closed the door behind her, leaving the others outside.

The two women stopped at the edge of the large pool of water set in the center of the room, above which swayed a metal seat attached to a giant handle fixed in the wall.

The mother affectionately hugged her daughter and said, "Come, Morani. Come, my little girl. It's time." Moran raised her arms and the mother lifted her shirt over her head and gently pulled it until her arms exited the sleeves.

"Look, Mom, it's so awful," groaned Moran, skimming her hands over a long, ropy scar that slithered cruelly over her otherwise perfect silky skin from her chest to her belly button.

"God loves you and he gave you your life as a gift," the mother said, hugging her daughter and scattering a bouquet of quick, soft kisses on her head. "This scar is a reminder etched in your body of the miracle. The miracle that happened to us four years ago in the carnage of that bus, when an angel in the form of a young soldier pulled you out of the inferno and lay you down in the row of corpses because he thought you were dead, when suddenly he felt your weak breath and rushed you to the hospital. There in the trauma room, you were saved by the doctors, God's diligent emissaries on earth. And here you are. And I am so privileged. Privileged with the biggest reward in the world—to escort my baby, my youngest child, to the wedding canopy. Not to a funeral, not to a cemetery, but to the wedding canopy. And tomorrow I will hand you over to your wonderful groom, Uri, who loves you with all his heart and appreciates every bit of the soul contained within your beautiful flesh.

"Tomorrow, on your wedding night, Uri will kiss this big scar, a reminder of the knife that cut you in pieces, and he'll give thanks to God for letting the Divine Presence pass through your bisected body that lay on the operating table for an eternity, for bringing you back to life and keeping you far from the world of the dead. God gave you life as a gift and etched in your body a sign that will fade with time but never disappear, a sign of the covenant between you and God. You are a lucky girl, Morani. A lucky girl. God protect you."

"I've dreamt about this moment since I was nine years old, when I came here for Mali's immersion. I remember how excited I was and how proud I was that my big sister was a bride. It was just Mali, us, and the balanit in the room, and when you threw candies on Mali, I prayed to God that I would be a bride like her one day. And now it's here. I don't believe it, but this moment is here." Moran clutched her mother's hands.

"God heard your wish and gave us a little joy after all the horror we went through," Batya said, adjusting a wayward curl that slipped over her daughter's brow.

"I'm ashamed, Mom. I'm embarrassed for Uri's mother to see the scar."

"She won't see it. We've made sure of that. That's why only

I'm here with you. Everyone wanted to come in. Especially your cousin Ruthie and her friend, old maids who wanted to rinse their hands in the mikveh waters after you immerse so some of your good luck will rub off on them. You know, there's a belief that when one bathes in water that a virgin has immersed in, it brings blessing, and they're twenty-five already and nothing, no trace of a man in sight. So Ruthie and her friend wanted to take the opportunity to touch your good fortune, but I said no. I told them that we don't do this. That it's our belief that this weakens the good fortune and strengthens the bad fortune."

"Is that really so?"

"Apparently yes. You don't argue with superstitions. The important thing is that I was able to shut them up."

"Poor things." Moran laughed. "Ruthie's been building up a dowry like crazy. Her closet is stuffed with sets of romantic silk sheets and embroidered towels. She's got everything—except a groom."

"Poor things, poor things—but what can you do? To each his own luck. I spared you from your mother-in-law's clutches the same way." Batya hugged Moran, reluctant to deliver her beloved daughter to the custody of her husband's family. "In the name of tradition and superstition, I prevented her from coming in. With them, only the mother of the groom replaces the green ribbon with the white. With us, only the mother of the bride is present for the immersion."

Among certain Mizrahi* ethnic communities, the most important figure at the immersion ceremony is the groom's mother.[11] Like the balaniyot, the mother-in-law stands in for

---

*Mizrahi – referring to Jews whose families have immigrated to Israel from the Mediterranean lands, and from the Arab lands in particular.

the male side—her son, in this case. She symbolizes the male authority. "On his behalf she enters this female world and inspects the 'goods' from top to bottom," explains Doris. Traditionally, the groom does not see his bride naked until after the wedding. To avoid any misunderstandings on the wedding night, it falls to the mother-in-law to ensure that her son won't be getting something he didn't bargain for. The mother-in-law's role is to examine the bride through a man's eyes, to take a serious and critical male view. She checks whether the bride is suitably attractive and healthy.

First and foremost, she must ascertain that the bride has no physical defects that will hinder the fulfillment of the mitzvah to 'Be fruitful and multiply.' The fact that the mother-in-law has seen the bride naked ensures that, after the marriage, both sides will accept responsibility for any malfunction that arises from her physical condition. "Sometimes the girl had an operation. It happens a lot, right?" Doris tells me. "Then the mother-in-law needs to know what the story is. Let's say she had an operation, and after they're married and everything's fine and then, heaven forbid, the girl doesn't have children—then she has evidence. Proof that the mother-in-law saw that she had an operation before the marriage."

The mother-in-law also sizes up the bride's virtues as a sexual object. Assesses her beauty and her femininity. A bride who is not to the mother-in-law's liking won't be a suitable wife for her son. "Back in Morocco, the mother-in-law would inspect the bride with a magnifying glass to see what her son was getting, to see if she had any defect, any anything. And if she had a beautiful body, she would boast: 'What a beautiful body she has. My son is getting a bride with a beautiful body.' I never would have gotten married if I'd stayed in Morocco. Being skinny and dark with crooked legs and no money—I never would have married. I was lucky we came here," attests Leah.

"That's right," confirms Dina. "In general, in Morocco,

nobody wants their son to marry a dark-skinned woman. What they really liked were the fat white girls." A modern bride who refuses to bow to tradition's dictates and won't allow the mother-in-law to be present at the immersion is taking a big risk. The consequences can be ruinous. "The daughter-in-law of a very good friend of mine didn't want anyone to be present at her immersion," remarked Dina, offering an object lesson. "Because of 'progress,' not, heaven forbid, because she had something against her mother-in-law. 'I am modern. I don't want anyone to see me doing this primitive ritual,' she said. And it was terrible. Just terrible. They divorced after twenty-four hours."

"But Mom, we have to be considerate of their customs, too," protested Moran. "The Moroccans' customs are the opposite of ours. They make everything as showy as possible. For them, the outward impression is the most important thing."

"That's why we gave her the honor of performing the ceremony of the white ribbon and the green ribbon; that's why she bought for you, in keeping with their tradition, the bath towels you'll use to dry yourself after the immersion, and a bathrobe embroidered with gold thread. You'll give her the respect she deserves when you come out of the immersion wearing her embroidered robe and she'll take you by the hand and present you to everyone as if saying that now you are her daughter too. That's what really matters for her. For this honor, she certainly doesn't need to see you naked. Absolutely not." Batya's tone hardened and the veins on her neck stood out.

"It's all right, mother. Calm down. But please, I want little Tlila to come in. Like I came in for Mali's immersion. You think the scar will frighten her?"

"Let's see. If she's frightened, we'll bring her back out," Batya said, pressing the bell affixed to the doorframe.

Moran is ready! announced the ringing bell to the balaniyot, who hurried in. Batya reached out and pulled the little girl into the immersion room, too.

Leah stood facing Moran, who was sitting in her wheelchair as naked as the day she was born, and asked: "Did you inspect your body?"

"I inspected it."

"Did you wash your hair?"

"I washed my hair."

Leah took Moran's hands in hers, bent her head near and studied them for a long time. "You did well to trim your fingernails and remove every trace of polish. Did you know that even clear polish acts as a barrier?"

Leah bent down toward Moran's feet. She held up one foot that was twisted from paralysis, stroked it gently and examined the toenails, then did the same with the other foot. "Trimmed and clean," she declared, satisfied.

"You brushed your teeth? You cleaned deep inside the belly button with a toothpick? You know that's where most of the dirt collects."

"Yes, I did everything."

"You emptied your bladder and your bowels?"

"Yes."

Then Leah got down on her knees in front of Moran. She reached out her hand and passed it over the huge scar that bisected the girl's body. Moran held her breath and her face paled.

"A thick scar," whispered Leah. "But kosher. It's not bleeding and it has no staple or stitch that would constitute a barrier. It is whole and kosher. And you are ready for immersion."

Dina pulled the switch in the wall and the metal arm stirred to life. The gleaming stainless steel chair began to slide slowly out; it descended to the floor of the mikveh then came to a halt right by Moran's feet like a well-trained horse waiting submissively for its mistress to mount and ride it.

"Hug me," Dina knelt by Moran. "Paula, hold the chair," she called to her apprentice.

Moran began to shiver. "Don't be afraid," Leah said as she held her. "This mechanical seat is a very sophisticated and safe device. Nothing will happen to you. We're here to watch over you."

But Moran sat frozen with fear.

"Come." Leah moved Dina aside, bent down to the chair, gathered Moran into her arms, and pressed the girl's chest firmly against hers. She took a deep breath, planted her legs firmly on the floor to support the levers of her arms as they lifted the heavy weight of the crippled Moran out of the wheelchair and pulled her body over the special metal chair. Moran's lifeless right leg dangled from her body. Dina hastened to grab hold of the withered limb while she supported Moran's bottom, and together Leah and Dina carried Moran and sat her down inside the shiny stainless steel chair, which swayed lightly, and secured the safety latch.

"Moran's on the Ferris wheel! Moran's at the amusement park!" giggled little Tlila. "I want to ride, too!" "What a sweetheart," laughed the women, dispelling a drop of the tension that filled the air. "Now, Morani, I'm going to turn on the motor and you will slowly enter the water." Leah pressed another button and, with a screeching lurch, the chair began lifting off the floor.

"Wait!" yelled Moran.

The motor fell silent.

"Mom, where are my nose plugs?"

"Here."

Moran took the tiny, clear plastic clip and put it on her nostrils.

"No, we can't have that," said Leah. "It's a barrier, *hatzitza*. It's forbidden."

"But I can't go under the water without it. I'll get water up my nose."

"We can't have that." Leah's voice was cold as ice. No trace of pleasantness remained. "It disqualifies the immersion."

"So hold your nose with your hand," suggested Batya.

"That's forbidden," declared Leah. "That also creates a barrier. The fingers must be spread out as far as possible so the water enters all the openings."

"But she can't," said Batya testily.

"She can. Hashem gives us powers when we need them. Just watch. You'll see how well she can do it. Hold on," she said, turning to Moran. "I'm turning on the chair. Dina, get undressed and get in the water."

Dina quickly peeled off her clothes. Her long cotton skirt dropped to the floor, revealing a pair of long, thick, dark, sturdy legs. She pulled her linen blouse over her head and stood there in a black Lycra swimsuit that adhered faithfully to every roll of fat. The low scoop neck exposed a colossal pair of breasts and the high cut of the swimsuit bottom flattered her ample thighs. With surprising agility, Dina skipped over to the pool and got in. The chair lurched into motion and began climbing slowly until it was suspended above the pool. When it reached the center, it began slowly descending into the water. Dina pulled the chair and its occupant toward her. "Come, let's get you out of the chair."

"Mommy, I'm scared . . ." whimpered Moran.

"Don't be afraid," said Dina. "I'm holding you. You're on my hands. Get ready."

"No. I'm too heavy. You won't be able to do it."

"You're not heavy. A person is weightless in water. Look, I've got you on one leg—I'm actually holding up the chair with my leg and I don't feel any weight."

"I'm heavy," Moran said, trembling.

"You're not heavy to me. I don't feel you," said Dina in a confident tone. "Come, let's take the chair all the way out . . ." She pulled Moran toward her and held her in both arms.

"Mommy!" cried Moran.

"I won't leave you for a second," said Dina. "Now we're going to drop down under the water. One, two, three." Dina let go of Moran's body so her hands would not constitute a barrier between Moran and the water.

"Morani! Morani! Aunt Batya, Morani fell in the water!" shouted the little girl.

Moments later, Dina grabbed hold of the sinking Moran and lifted her out of the water. "It's okay. See? Here's Morani," Leah reassured the little girl.

Dina hoisted Moran, who was panting and spraying jets of water from her nose.

"And again," said Dina, pulling Moran back down into the water.

"Morani!" yelled the little girl.

"Take the little one out of here, for Pete's sake," said Paula.

"Morani's coming up again!" cried Leah and Batya in unison.

Dina lifted up Moran, who lay atop her outstretched arms, half dazed. "One more time," said Dina, looking at Moran tenderly, like Mary gazing at the dead Christ lying in her arms, and once more she drew her down into the water for a few seconds and lifted her back up. Now she placed Moran back in the metal chair.

"Kululululu!" shouted Batya as tears of joy flowed down her wet cheeks.

"Just a minute. Not yet," Leah ordered.

The metal chair shifted on its track and moved slowly toward the women. Leah took hold of the chair, turned Moran's back to her, and scrutinized it, as if with a magnifying glass, from the nape of the girl's neck down to her tailbone.

"What are you looking for?" Batya said, grimacing.

"I'm checking to make sure that not a single hair fell out and stuck to her back, because that also disqualifies the immersion. It's my job. It's why I'm here. Because it's not sufficient that she goes entirely into the water. One hair could come out by mistake and then the immersion is no good. Most women think that our job is to put a towel on the immersing woman's head and pronounce her 'kosher.' But that's not right. The balanit's involvement in placing the towel and saying 'kosher' isn't binding in terms of the halakha. The woman can put the towel on her head herself and she doesn't need the balanit's blessing. I don't need to say a blessing. She does. I don't even need to say, 'Amen.' The women like it that we say a blessing. They especially like it when we say, 'Kasher! Kasher! Kasher!' at the end, because it adds a flavor of holiness to the ritual. This is just a custom. It's not mandatory." Leah stroked Moran's back.

"Good, excellent. There is no hair," the balanit said at last, picking up a towel, going over to the toilet, closing the lid and covering it: "It is forbidden to utter Hashem's name in the presence of a toilet," she explained to Batya. She took another white towel, placed it on Moran's head, and said: "Repeat after me out loud."

"Blessed art Thou . . . " Leah tightened her grip on the towel.

"Blessed art Thou . . . " repeated Moran, her head lowered.

"Our Lord, King of the Universe . . ."

"Our Lord, King of the Universe . . ." Moran closed her eyes and clasped her hands in supplication. Her torso swayed gently to and fro.

"Who sanctified us with his commandments and commanded us to immerse."

"Who sanctified us with his commandments and commanded us to immerse." Moran's tears flowed and one slid all the way down until it hung like a diamond on her left nipple.

"Amen," said the two of them at once.

"Kasher! Kasher! Kasher!" cried Leah excitedly.

"Kululululu!" shouted Batya again as she rushed to Moran.

"Come, let's get dressed," Dina said, holding Moran, who sat there like a wet and quiet queen. "Now hold onto me tight," Dina leaned toward Moran and gathered the girl's hair behind her ears.

"Wait a minute! What's this??" cried Leah. "What are these orange things in her ears?"

"Earplugs. Moran wears hearing aids and she can't let her ears get wet. She has to put in earplugs."

"This is not good," declared Leah, her expression darkening. "She must be pure in the ears, too."

Leah rang the bell in the doorframe. Within seconds, Miriam appeared. "What's going on? Has the darling girl immersed already?"

"Yes, Baruch Hashem. But only after she immersed did I see that she has earplugs. She needs them. She has hearing aids and she can't get her ears wet."

"This isn't good," said Miriam. "She must be pure in the ears too."

"What do we do?" Batya protectively wrapped Moran in a white towel.

"Does she have a note from the doctor?"

"No, you didn't ask for one," croaked Batya.

Miriam turned and walked out. The air in the room stood still and a dense fog of vapors from the women's tense exhalations added to the uneasy atmosphere. Tlila was suddenly seized with a nagging cough that broke the heavy silence. Each of the women was sunk in thought, as if all alone in the world. The poor bride hunkered under the giant towel that covered her, the gold-embroidered letters of the words 'mazal tov' lying mockingly over her scar. Dina sat her massive body down on a white plastic stool whose four short legs buckled under her weight. "Lean on me," Paula said, putting her calves against Dina's back, "so you won't fall." Batya sat down in her daughter's wheelchair, pulled Tlila onto her lap and patted her lightly on the back to loosen the cough, even though it had already stopped. Leah pressed her hands together in front of her nose, rested her forehead on them in a pose reminiscent of the Indian "Namaste" greeting, and shut her eyes.

"Baruch Hashem, we have a rabbi to ask,' said Dina. "We have a list of rabbis, and it's a good thing. Because in a case like this, I don't know what to do. I know nothing. And we get a lot of these cases. Just this week, this girl came in whose nipples were all full of stitches. She'd done a breast enlargement. I told her I couldn't immerse her with those stitches. They had to come out. The woman said, 'You must be kidding. You can't decide.' I brought Miriam, our rabbanit, and it didn't help. We couldn't convince her. We called the rabbi and he said there was no way we could immerse her with the stitches sticking out and that they had to come out. We told her we could try to take them out, because they were almost all the way out. In the end, she left. Luckily, she came back a week later."

There are times when the balaniyot are not accepted as a halakhic authority by the immersing woman, and only the intervention of the rabbi, the man, and his ruling will convince the woman to heed the balaniyot's demands. The rabbi acts as a support for the balaniyot, especially when a situation arises in which the balaniyot take a strong stand and the woman doesn't wish to accept their ruling. In such a case, the balaniyot turn to the rabbi for assistance. They know that only he, the male halakhic authority, can bring a quick end to the dispute, for you don't argue with the rabbi.

"You remember the bride who came with the piercing?" Paula asked.

"How could I forget? The story was even in the newspaper," Dina replied. "One day, this girl came with her mother and her mother-in-law to immerse. Michaela came to inspect the naked bride before the immersion and what does she find? A piercing, a ring through the bride's belly button. Michaela, very gently, explains to the bride that this is forbidden, that it constitutes a barrier and that the ring must come out, otherwise she can't immerse. The bride refused. The two of them stood there arguing with each other, the bride claiming it was impossible to remove the piercing and Michaela informing her that there could be no immersion and therefore no confirmation of immersion for the presiding rabbi and therefore no wedding. They were arguing and arguing for a long time.

"Meanwhile the mother and mother-in-law were waiting outside with trays full of special foods for the celebration. When they saw the bride wasn't coming out, they sent Paula to check what was happening. She found them arguing, came back and told them, and a big uproar ensued. The two mothers phoned the bride's father and asked him what to do. The father called the chief rabbi and the head of the religious courts in the city, who is known as a rabbi who generally takes a lenient stance. The rabbi backed Michaela. He explained to the father that it was impossible for the woman to immerse with a foreign object stuck in her body. The father persuaded his daughter to remove the ring.

"But then a new problem arose. There was a big fear that the removal of the ring would scratch or wound the bride's flesh, and you can't immerse someone with an open wound, because the blood of a wound [*dam petzi'a*]* acts as a barrier. The wound has to be cleaned with alcohol and you have to wait for the blood to dry up. And it was already late, almost midnight. We sat and talked about what to do. The bride's mother had the idea to call a friend of hers, a jeweler who lived just one street over. We woke the woman and asked for

---

Dam petzi'a is distinct from *dam niddah*, the blood of niddah, and not subject to the same rules.

her help. She came, took a pair of pliers, carefully cut the ring, and removed the piercing. We were all relieved and the bride immersed properly."

The story only added to the oppressive feeling in the room.

"It's all right!" Miriam's voice suddenly sliced through the air and the women heaved a sigh of relief. "The rabbi approved it. He said that even if there's no doctor's note and no assurance that she must keep her ears plugged, we mustn't upset or delay the bride anymore. Especially when she's an invalid."

"Kululululu!" shouted Batya as she tossed candies on Moran, who began to cry, either from all the excitement or in response to Miriam's characterization.

"Don't cry, Morani," Tlila said, embracing her. "You should be happy. You're the bride. Are you going to put on the wedding dress now?"

Dina and Leah toweled off Moran with amazing skill and speed. Within minutes, she was seated in her wheelchair, all dry and clad in a white robe. Her long curly hair fell softly to her waist.

"Tarararaaaam . . . Tarararaaaam . . . Tarararaaaam . . . Ta-ta-ta-taaaaaaa Taaaaaa Ta-ta Tam Tam Tam," the women trumpeted loudly, voicing the classic opening bars of the "Wedding March," a tune that unfailingly gives rise to excitement and goosebumps. They curled their fists, pressed them to their lips, and blew into them forcefully, producing a boisterous fanfare announcing the bride's emergence. As soon as they opened the door they encountered Mrs. Levy, the mother-in-law, who stood facing them erect and stiff as a pillar of salt. The fist trumpets were instantly lowered and the women fell silent. The mother-in-law didn't make a sound either. She just walked to Moran's side, took her hand, and raised it up high.

In the immersion ceremony, the mother-in-law openly demonstrates her approval of and satisfaction with the bride before the entire group of women. Although she wasn't present at the "inspection," Mrs. Levy took Moran's hand proudly and led her out to the assembled crowd of women, to present the happy bride to everyone.

A girl's transition from virgin to wife, from forbidden, unripe, fruit to permitted, ripe and mature, fruit, is symbolized in women's rituals in the mikveh primarily by food. Legitimation for intercourse is given by the community, which participates in the celebration of the bride's fertility by preparing and partaking in the special foods associated with this rite of passage.

"*Mabruk alayki ya 'arusa, mabruk alayki,*"* crooned the velvety voice of the wedding singer emanating from the tape player, accompanying the procession of women as it slowly wended its way down the Room 6 corridor. In front came the bride in her wheelchair, led by the mother-in-law striding proudly alongside her and triumphantly lifting Moran's left hand up high. Next came Batya, one hand pushing the wheelchair and the other holding on to little Tlila, who bounced happily to the sounds of the music. Bringing up the rear, Miriam, Leah, Dina, and Paula marched joyfully along. The procession emerged into the large vestibule, where all were immediately blinded by a dazzling spotlight from the big video camera held by one of Moran's aunts.

"Kululululu!" shouted the three aunts as they tossed candies at the bride and all around. "Kululululu!" answered other women, and from the Room 6 corridor came another procession of women. This bride, in a white robe, was also being led by her mother-in-law. Alongside them hurried the bride's mother, popping honey candies into the women's mouths. "For good fortune and blessing, for fertility and a sweet life," murmured the mother.

---

*Arabic for "Mazal tov, O Bride, mazal tov."

"*Siman tov and mazal tov and mazal tov and siman tov*
. . . *yehey laaanu . . .*" sang another group of women with
pronounced American accents, who carried bottles of juice
and scattered colorful confetti over the head of a woman of
about forty. "May it be an auspicious time," they said, blessing the middle-aged bride, who was wrapped in a light pink
robe.

"Come join our party. We have plenty of food," the Sephardi women called to them as they strode toward the celebrations room bearing their laden trays, like disciplined
worker ants transporting found goods to the colony, entering
with heavy loads and leaving empty-handed to retrieve more,
loading and unloading trays piled high with a variety of pastries and other mouthwatering delicacies.

The Americans happily joined in. "We have a lot of mango
and guava juice. It's really healthy, take some," they told the
Sephardi group. "You ought to try it. It's supposed to be an
excellent aphrodisiac." They all giggled.

"Forget this 'afro' and that 'deesiyac'! Nothing comes close
to our food here on the henna night. We spend weeks cooking huge amounts of food for this feast. The more bountiful
the food, the more bountiful the couple's life will be. The
more sweets we eat here, the sweeter their life will be—like
one long honeymoon. The richer the food, and the more good
ingredients it contains, the more fertile the couple will be.
This is our belief," Moran's three aunts explained giddily.

"The evening of the mikveh is a time for sausages and
shakshouka with eggs,"* Sophie, the Moroccan aunt, the sister of Moran's father, said as a crude pun.

"Shakshouka isn't a festive food," commented Ruthie,
Moran's unmarried cousin.

"Never mind the shakshouka," laughed Moran's pudgy,

---

*shakshouka – a simple Mizrahi dish made from eggs and tomato
sauce; the Hebrew word for eggs (*beitzim*) is also slang for testicles.

vivacious Aunt Sophie. "When your immersion day comes, God willing, I'll serve up fantastic delicacies like you've never tasted in your whole life!"

Aunt Sophie took me aside and told me that she'd always dreamed of opening a catering business that would serve women on the nights of their mikveh visits, providing gourmet meals for modern women who don't have the time to devote to cooking.

"This night has a special festive flavor because of the good meal that the wife cooks for her husband," Sophie gushed. "The mikveh isn't just about going to immerse. The mikveh is also all about the preparations that come before, particularly the special meals that the wife prepares for that night. This cooking prepares the woman emotionally as well as physically. True, it's better if the woman herself does the cooking. But nowadays it's hard for them. Life is so hectic, they don't have the time for these preparations. Really good, gourmet food is equivalent to good sex. Therefore, this is not a quickie night of schnitzel and french fries, which are fast and easy to prepare. This is the night for pigeon stuffed with rice and chickpeas, and quail eggs in a piquant sauce, and oxtail soup with drippings of cow *bzaz*."

"Bzz . . . what?"

"Cow *bzaz*. The fat of cow udders. Also, fig jam, because figs are known to arouse passion and harden the man's penis. Lentils are also good for an erection. Also, water in which chickpeas have been soaked, which I mix in the soup with a little wine, onion, and beef. It's delicious and also improves the quality of the sperm. Whipped egg whites and all kinds of pastries and breads in the shape of lovebirds and fish, a symbol of bounty and blessing. The list is long, Baruch Hashem. The more effort that goes into the cooking, the more pleasurable the sex. You have no idea what gorgeous children are born thanks to my meals."

"You really run such a catering service?"

"Practically speaking, yes. I've been a kind of communal worker for decades now. Everyone in the neighborhood knows me, big and small. I'm like their Western Wall. Any problem or trouble, they come to me. They come for happy occasions and good days too. Naturally, I get the young women who just married and don't know how to cook, and their relationship with the mother-in-law isn't, you know, all that easy, and their mother doesn't have the patience to explain. So what do they do? They come to Aunt Sophie. I teach them, but mostly I cook for them. I know who needs to go to the mikveh and when. I know what each one likes, and especially what their husbands like. I know about the problems at home and which seasonings to put in. This one to heighten desire, that one to neutralize bad odors. I make all sorts of concoctions and they come to me on the afternoon of the immersion day and take home pots filled with delicious food. They're happy because it guarantees the night's festivity, and I'm happy because I feel like I did a mitzvah."

"Immersion is supposed to be kept discreet," I said. "It takes quite a lot of openness on the part of these girls to reveal to you when they go to the mikveh. Do their husbands realize that someone else knows?"

"I'm a bereaved mother. My son was killed in the army five years ago, and now he's an angel who watches over me and guides me in everything that I do. Such a sweetheart of a boy, he's with me all the time. And these girls whom I cook for, they were all friends of his since kindergarten. So they're like my daughters. It's not out of nowhere. But like I told you, my dream is to make a real business out of this for everybody. Do you know what a joy it is for me when I'm invited to a *brit mila** or a *simchat bat*‡ in the synagogue, when they give

---

brit mila – a circumcision ceremony for an eight-day-old Jewish boy.

‡*simchat bat* – a less formal celebration for the birth of a girl.

the name to the boy or girl and I know that this baby was conceived on stomachs filled with my food? What beautiful children! You can see how much sweat went into their creation. Perfectly seasoned. Just like my food."

Aunt Sophie does not own the copyright on the connection between food and sex. The seemingly innocent song sung by the Sephardi woman upon the bride's emergence from her immersion, "Pur Akeyas Ventanikas" ("From those windows, rolling pins were thrown"), is brimming with erotic allusions and symbols taken from the world of cooking. The rolling pin, an implement used to knead and shape dough, symbolizes the erect male phallus. The woman is analogous to the dough, which the phallus flattens and shapes. The song's heroine is originally white, but the sun has cooked and darkened her skin. Only when the white dough is baked well in the heat of the oven does its color turn to brown. The white woman turns dark. She is cooked and is frightened by this cooking, fearing her new status as a married woman who bears responsibility for the family. Therefore, she wants to escape. If the sailors call to her, she will go off with them.

Cooking is the woman's area of expertise and responsibility in the Jewish tradition. There is a universal symbolic parallel between sex and food.[12] From the male point of view, the woman is the provider of food and sex. "A woman who doesn't know how to cook is likened to someone with a defect," declared a prominent rabbi in Israel, spiritual leader of one of the country's ultra-Orthodox political parties. "Why? Tomorrow she'll marry, and what will she give him? Does he want to eat a lot of chatter? She needs to make tasty delicacies for him."[13]

With her body, the woman also becomes a link that joins the internal and the external—she enters into the mikveh, emerges purified, feeds the man, and civilizes the sexual act. Mircea Eliade, the great scholar of religion, claims that eating and sex have a religious value, because they are acts that sanctify the cyclical and eternal act of creation.[14]

"Drinking from a glass" is the refined Talmudic term for sexual relations. The familiar phrase "a man shall not drink from one glass and cast his eyes upon another"[15] reflects the culture's sanctioning of physical pleasure. Man and wife are given permission to drink and to find pleasure in one another's company (the reference is generally to wine or another alcoholic drink that affects the senses), while wantonness is forbidden—in thought as well as deed.

David Biale notes that, according to tenets of the Kabbalah, a type of fusion occurs between the soul and the food that is digested in the body. Digestion reaches its peak in the creation of the sperm, which "is the substance that is most purified of all the body's slag and holds the power not only to create new life, but also to affect the powers of the Divine Presence [*Shekhina*]."[16]

Through their cooking and feeding of the bride, the older women feel that they are contributing to the younger girl's happiness. They are magically able to convey to her some of their experience, abilities, and strength via the delicacies they've cooked, which are taken into the woman's body just as she is undergoing the transformation from a "raw" to a "cooked" state.

Two customs in the mikveh that are related to cooking and food symbolize the bride's transformation from raw to cooked, from nature to culture: the henna ceremony and the ritual of the torte cake.

The henna ceremony is traditionally part of the fertility rituals that take place on the eve of a wedding, either in the mikveh or at the bride's home. The Hebrew word for henna (*hina*) encompasses the essence of the compact between God and the bride that is made on the wedding eve. The letters of the Hebrew word allude to the three commandments in which women are obligated, with the addition of the name of God—het, for challah; yod, for Hakadosh Baruch Hu; nun, for niddah; and heh, for lighting Shabbat candles (*hadlakat nerot*).* If a woman devoutly fulfills the three commandments given to her by God, he will safeguard her from all evil entities, increase the fruit of her womb, and enhance her beauty.

Henna is made from the leaves of the *kofer,* a small shrub or ornamental tree with fragrant flowers that grows primarily in Egypt, India, and North Africa.[17] The dried green henna leaves are ground and soaked in water, which turns them red, and then cooked into a thick paste. The paste is placed in the center of a tray decorated with green leaves and candles. After the bride has immersed, her mother lights the candles, lifts the tray over her own head, and dances a fertility dance to the sound of beating drums. Wiggling her hips, she makes her way to the bride and holds the tray over the bride's head. All the women trill "Kululululu!"

The bride takes the tray from her mother, raises it over her head, and dances with it until she reaches the woman she wishes to bless and holds the tray over her head. The tray lit with candles is passed from hand to hand, above the heads of all the women. The whole time, the women dance to the beat of the drums and are swept into a state of ecstasy. Each time the tray is lifted over the head of the chosen woman, the rest erupt into a joyful "Kululululu!" After all the women have received the blessing, the eldest of the group, the grandmother, dips her finger into the paste and paints a circle on both of the bride's hands. In the center of the circle she places

---

*Alternately, the nun is understood to stand for *nerot* (candles) and heh for *hafrashat challah*: separating a small piece of the challah dough. In the days of the Temple, this was given as an offering to the priests (*kohanim*); nowadays the piece of dough is burned and not used.

a blue candy, to ward off the evil eye. Then the grandmother does the same for all the other women.

The henna leaves a prominent reddish-brown stain imprinted on the skin for many days, preserving the memory of the compact while displaying for all the world a seal of approval for the woman's sexual relations with her husband. All the women who received the mark of the henna are made witnesses to the pact of fertility, love, and loyalty that was sealed in the ritual immersion in the mikveh.

The dry, infertile material symbolizes the virgin girl who is not yet a woman; she is an unripe fruit. Through the moistening and cooking process, the dry, green henna is transformed into moist, red henna, symbolizing the fertile woman brimming with life and vitality. The henna turns red, the color that symbolizes the fertility of Mother Earth—red like the blood that is crucial for the renewal of fertility.

Symbolically, the transformation process undergone by the henna is identical to what happens to the bride's body in the mikveh. She arrives from her mother's home "green" and unripe, and after immersing in the warm water, becomes "red" and ripe. The male side is represented in this "cooking" process by the mother-in-law, who prepares the henna, symbolically strengthening her son's fertility by accelerating the bride's fertility potential.

The henna ceremony also highlights the community's involvement in the bride's physical and symbolic transformation. An important part of the henna ritual is the cooking of festive foods by the women themselves, which enhances the joy derived from the preparations for this traditionally all-female event. Nowadays, the henna ceremony may be a large celebration held at a fancy banquet hall or other venue, with many guests of both genders. This party is usually held about a week before the wedding, and thus is not connected with the bride's immersion.

"The real henna ceremony is when the bride returns from

the mikveh and puts on the henna," Aunt Sophie explained to me. "Then the groom is not around, whether he's Yemenite or Moroccan or Ashkenazi. Not only in the mikveh is the groom forbidden to come near his bride, but also that whole night and the day before the wedding. But these days very few people obey the prohibition against being together. Most ignore the custom, and the bride sees the groom after the henna celebration."

Sophie also tells me about the magical properties of henna. According to the traditional Jewish superstition, demons lie in wait during times of transition, when humans are weak and sensitive. The wedding eve is a perilous time for the couple, who are separated from one another, because the demons, who need humans in order to reproduce, try to mate with each of them. The word "henna" itself is thought to contain a special magical quality that keeps the demons away.

"They used to put this green, magic powder in all the corners of the house, to keep the demons away from the people," Aunt Sophie said excitedly. "The henna fights off the evil spirits."

"Why don't they leave the henna around the house in Israel like they did in Morocco?"

"Because this party they throw today is not a real henna night. It's like a separation party from the family, from the friends and neighbors. The real henna ceremony is when the bride comes back from the mikveh, when they put the henna on her, tie a cloth around it, and her parents lock up the house and sleep there with her, to guard her from the demons. The groom does the same thing in his house. His mother brings a little of the henna from the bride's house, puts it on him, covers it up, and he sleeps there with it the whole night, together with his best man, who's accompanied him for all seven days before the wedding. The two of them share the same bed. That was the custom in our community."

———

The ritual of the round torte cake is another rite of passage enacted in the mikveh. After the bride immerses and emerges from the water, her mother breaks a ring-shaped cake over her head. *Lord, let my daughter be relieved of her virginity on her wedding night, so I may soon hold a grandchild,* she silently wishes, pushing a big hunk of cake into her daughter's mouth and then small pieces into the mouths of the young women who've accompanied her daughter, as a good-luck charm for finding a groom. This fertility ritual is common among women of Kurdish, Syrian, and Sephardi extraction.

The cake is made of flour, from Mother Earth's basic crop; of eggs that symbolize the male genitalia; and of yeast and sugar, which symbolize vitality and sweetness. As the cake's ingredients represent womanhood and manhood that, when combined, are transformed into a new, sweet, and nourishing substance, so the unification of husband and wife shall bear fruit and ensure a sweet marriage. The round hole in the cake's center symbolizes the wholeness of the bride's hymen. The breaking of the cake over the bride's head, the breaking of the hole, symbolizes the breaking of the hymen. Feeding cake to the bride, physically inserting a charm for good fortune into her mouth, is another way of ensuring an auspicious start to her marriage. By chewing and swallowing the cake, the bride's body absorbs its fertility-enhancing and fortune-boosting properties.

Just as unmarried women will dip their hands in the mikveh waters after a bride has immersed, they also wish to eat from the cake that was broken over the bride's head, so the bride's good fortune may rub off on them. Jews from Aleppo also have the custom of boosting the bride's good fortune and the good fortune of other women via the mouth, using candies that the bride sucks on and then transfers from her mouth to the mouths of the other women present.

The interplay between cooking, food, and sexuality is a

constant in a married couple's life, and this interplay begins with the rituals that revolve around the mikveh, where a community of women assists a bride in her transformation from "raw" to "cooked," welcoming her into the sisterhood of fertile, married life.

7

BETWEEN A WOMAN AND GOD

In general, to the women in the mikveh, God is a mighty, all-embracing masculine force that affects the entire world as well as the small individual world of each and every woman.

In those moments when a woman is immersing her naked body in the water, she connects directly to God, as a fetus is connected directly to its mother by the umbilical cord.

"The time of immersion is an auspicious time for prayer. I always dive down, kiss the floor of the mikveh, and pray for the Temple to be rebuilt, for all who are sick to get well, and for all those in need to obtain a good livelihood, because it's such an auspicious time to give blessings and make requests and pray," one woman told me.

"I make wishes for my parents, for the Jewish people. It comes from the heart," explained another. "I feel at the moment of immersion that my heart is pure. Any resentment I have toward others disappears. All the burdens and stress that build up in my daily life just vanish at that moment. I just forget about everything. Look, I haven't been here that many times yet, I've only been married four months, but every time I come out of the mikveh, I feel like something is strengthened inside me, like something has been settled between me and myself, between me and my husband, between me and the whole world."

"Immersion, for me, is the nexus between acceptance of God's authority and the divine blessing," gushed another woman. "God blesses me through the water. When I'm immersing I feel like I'm at the revelation at Sinai. I come out of this place a different person. First of all, I love the water. I feel like I've immersed in primal, ancient waters . . . the actual waters of creation. I feel like this water actually gives me my life back. And the woman who gives me the blessing, the balanit, she feels it, too. I entered the water a barren woman and I strove to emerge from it transformed. To receive something else from this water. And I did receive it. I received three wonderful children."

"I always immerse as many times as possible so I can make more wishes," one woman enthused. "The custom is to immerse either three times or seven times. I don't know what the tradition was in my family, but I do seven. Why seven? Because I have a lot of wishes to make. When I immerse I linger a little in the water because I'm making my wish. I take advantage of it being seven and not three, you understand? The balanit already knows that I like a lot of immersions, so sometimes after I finish the seven she asks me to immerse an eighth time and ask God to grant health and good fortune to a woman I don't even know. I do it happily."

"Each time I immerse I enter completely naked into the substance which the Creator imbued with special properties," another woman reverently explained. "When I merge with this substance, the dirt that is detached from me sinks down and the special qualities that God endowed me with at birth float up to the surface. I see them shining and glittering and I carefully collect them, one at a time, like abandoned, precious, and fragile eggs."

A woman's divine reward for fulfilling the duty of immersion is the privilege of becoming pregnant. Wheelchair-bound Nava immerses and asks God to bless her with children. The withholding and granting of pregnancy are likened to the stopping and coming of the rains, seen as an expression of divine blessing or punishment. The mikveh waters are rainwater. The falling of the rains, the upper waters, and their merger with the lower waters, is compared to the mating of man and woman, as the Midrash explains: "The upper waters [of creation] are male and the lower waters [of creation] are female and the former says to the latter: 'Receive us, you are God's creatures and we are His emissaries.' Right away they receive them, as the female opens up to the male."[1] The womb of a woman unable to give birth is dammed up just as the heavens are dammed up in a state of drought.

The balanit Michaela feels blessed and pampered by God: "I feel like I've allowed myself the greatest luxuries, like I'm allowing the most life to pass through me as possible. Between my third and fourth daughter I didn't get pregnant right away and I wanted so badly to be pregnant again; I was seriously depressed. My husband looked at me and said: 'Where do you get the nerve? You've got some chutzpah to think you deserve to be pregnant and give birth and nurse a baby all the time! It's a great privilege. You need to pray for it.' Hashem grants you the privilege of carrying a child in your body and you have the privilege of bringing him into the world and raising him. I don't need to tell you. If you have children, then you know."

Blood and water are the symbols of female fertility through which a woman communicates with God. The cessation of menstruation signals a cessation of the potential for realization of one's fertility and also the end of the need for immersion in the mikveh. Thus the onset of menopause brings an end to a woman's connection with God through the water and to the sacred bond with her husband. Once she has ceased menstruating a woman may continue to immerse in the mikveh as much as she pleases, but this immersion has no religious meaning. The connection with God is halted with the cessation of immersion as an act of purification. At the same time, the husband's obligation to perform his conjugal duty on the day of his wife's immersion also comes to an end. "She can keep on immersing for the rest of her life, but it's meaningless in terms of the halakha. It doesn't obligate the husband if his wife has immersed today," Miriam tells me.

Immersion in the mikveh is an important central artery connecting the woman to her Creator and her husband. Completely naked in the holy water, the symbol of life, the woman bonds with her Creator and asks him, in this sacred moment, to fulfill her wishes. Upon emerging from the mikveh, she returns home where, naked once again, she bonds with her husband. In Jewish belief, God is a partner in the couple's act of intercourse; God is there between them to oversee the soul's entry into the fetus that is created at the moment of their mating. The upholding of this pure, tripartite connection, man-woman-God, is considered essential for the continued survival of the Jewish people.

"My own belief in God came from Dr. Rivkind, head of the trauma center at Hadassah Hospital in Ein Kerem," provocative young Shuli relates. "He's very famous. You see him all the time on TV saving the lives of people who were badly wounded in terror attacks. They call him the Angel in White. I was brought to him in critical condition after a car accident. I was sixteen and a half. When he saw my mother crying in the emergency room, he brought her outside and said to her: 'Look up to the heavens now, that's where God is, and you thank God, because he brought you your daughter as a gift. I don't believe in God myself, but I feel that he was here just now.' That's what this secular angel told her, and he gave me my personal God as a gift."

Shuli loves the God who protected her from the angel of death's indiscriminate and voracious appetite. But she draws a line between God and religion. "Religion is rules. God is faith. There are certain things in religion that I agree with, like the mikveh, for example. I agree with the mikveh and I immerse. Keeping Shabbat, I agree with that, even though I won't do it. Maintaining a separation between milk and meat, I agree that it's important, but I don't do it. There are certain things that I stick to, in order to strengthen my belief in God."

Shuli feels an unmediated connection with God. "I have a book of Psalms and all kinds of special, miniature-sized books under my pillow. Every night I say 'Shema Yisrael'* and pray. Not out of a prayerbook, I just talk with God, and wish for his blessing."

Shuli's God is an important element in her daily life; he produces small miracles for her and makes the impossible possible: "He fixes my life every day, all day long; he's involved in everything, even the smallest thing. When I go to take a shower and there's no hot water, I say, 'God, please let there be hot water,' and I'm not being cynical, I really mean it. I make it a plea, a request, a prayer. And don't ask me how, but suddenly the cold water turns hot. You'll say it's just coincidence . . . Maybe so . . . But it's a pretty odd coincidence and wiser folks than I have said that there are no coincidences in this world."

Shuli feels that God gives her personal guidance regarding the positive and negative commandments. She immerses in the mikveh because that's what God wants. "I believe that there's a connection. That God wanted me to do this. I have a feeling that whatever I do, I do because God is directing me to do something he wants. If he wanted me to keep Shabbat, he would send me the message and I would do it, but apparently he has no interest in that, as I haven't received any indication from him. You see?"

---

*"Shema Yisrael" – "Hear O Israel" – in this context, a declaration of faith, also the opening line of the prayer recited before going to bed.

"How do you receive an 'indication from him'?" I ask.

"The divine imperative to go to the mikveh I received through my private rabbi, Rabbi Nissim, who is like a messenger from God who fulfills all my wishes and desires and makes the impossible possible. When I was seventeen and a half, I fell in love with a man who was five years older. He wasn't interested in a relationship. He rejected me. Said I was still a baby. The rejection hurt so much I couldn't bear it, so I went and poured my heart out to my aunt. She took me to her rabbi, Rabbi Nissim, to get a blessing. He put his hand on my head, concentrated, closed his eyes, and a few minutes later he opened them and promised me that my beloved would one day be my husband. Three days later, I got a phone call. It was a totally impossible thing that this phone call would come, but it did, from his blessing. Two years later we were married."

"Husband and wife are connected to one another through Hashem," Michaela explains to me. "Hashem is always there between them. Hashem is a part of the couple's relationship, its soul. Performing the mitzvot as an act of holiness, with divine intention, connects earthly mortals with Hashem. Each daily act in our lives, such as eating, drinking, singing, and so on is connected with doing Hashem's will.

"For us, unlike other nations, Hashem's commandments are not just a matter of custom, but require action with intention," she says. I am immediately struck by the similarity between her simple statement and the principles of Eliade's theory on the essence of holiness and the human experience of the sacred. On the more archaic levels of culture, says Eliade, life is perceived by humans as a divine act. Mundane activities such as eating, work, and sex have a religious value and are a part of regular divine worship. Divine worship is man's way of investing his life with meaning by means of connecting with the supernatural powers that rule him. Human experience of the sacred is linked to the idea that the true existential human experience cannot exist within chaos. It requires a concrete awareness of a world that has transcendental meaning, which is intimately and personally connected to the revelation of the holy, the godly, the sacred.[2]

"Napoleon," continues Michaela, "was known for his openness to different cultures. He had soldiers from many different nations and peoples. He decreed that every week a cultural evening would be held. On this evening, a group of soldiers from a particular ethnic group would tell about their culture—the foods, the dances, the songs, the folklore. There was one group of Jewish soldiers of Italian extraction. He said to them: 'Fellows, tonight is your night. Tell us about your culture.' 'In Italy, they eat spaghetti, but we eat gefilte fish,' the Jews said. 'In Italy they eat spaghetti Bolognese with meatballs and Parmesan cheese, but we Jews observe the kashrut laws that prohibit eating meat with milk. The Italians sing serenades that are very charming and we sing *oy oy oy.*' As they were telling this, the Jews thought: 'Wait a minute—is the difference between us only in dress, food, and song? Is that it? That we have one sort of folklore and they have another?' No. They had an epiphany: Judaism is not folklore, and the differences between Jews and others are not merely a matter of customs, but rather essential differences that go beyond cultural differences. 'There's something deeper and more basic here that expresses something else entirely,' thought the Jews who were leading the cultural evening in Napoleon's army. Judaism is more than just tradition and customs. The Jewish people, *'Am Yisrael,* is not just another nation. The word *'am* [people] comes from the word *'amum* [dim]. There are embers that are dim. Each and every Jew is like an ember whose light is dim but quietly yearns for Hashem. The other nations are satisfied with what they have here—the songs, the dances, the foods. The Jew has no interest in the trivial things of this world. All his vitality and appetite for life derive from his longing for Hashem."

Michaela goes on to relate this story to women's immersion in the mikveh. "One might think that Hashem is in heaven and we are on earth and we have no right to involve ourselves in things that are above us, because it confuses us, trips us up. But in reality it is not so. We Jews connect to Hashem. How? By fulfilling the commandments. It's not just once a week on Shabbat, or just at mealtimes, or other specific times, but in each and every action in daily life, and also in the bond between husband and wife."

"Have you no God?! Tell me, how can you talk that way?!" a tall, well-dressed woman scolded a tiny but muscular young woman as they waited in the hall for Sarah, the instructor of brides.

"I don't know if there is or isn't a God," the girl hissed at her mother, who towered over her. She punched the air with a clenched fist sparkling with diamonds. "And you know what, Mother? I don't care, either. Got it?"

"You must do this, Na'ama. So come on and let's get it over with nicely," her mother said with quiet authority.

"How could anything nice happen in this disgusting place?" whined the daughter. "Don't you see how completely revolting it is? The whole thing grosses me out. And all this coercion really disgusts me. This whole obligation to immerse in the mikveh or else I won't get the lousy permit to marry—it disgusts me. I don't understand why you wouldn't agree to bribe the rabbanit. Everyone does it. You give her a hundred shekels and you get a note for the rabbi. And the rabbi doesn't even ask for this note anyway—it's just to scare you. All my friends got out of going to the mikveh; I'm the only one who has to go through this nightmare. And it's all your fault," she added, jabbing her mother's thick arm with her jewel-bedecked fist. "You're so full of it! You eat pork and all kinds of *treif** and then suddenly you go all religious on me. 'It's our tradition,'" she said, contorting her face and derisively mimicking her mother. "'You'll do what your grandmother did and what I did before I married your father. You're not just a bride. You're my daughter and you're a Jew. A Jewish bride must be pure when she comes to the wedding canopy.' Yeah, I'm going to be really pure when I come out of this filth. Why don't *you* go immerse if it's so important to you? Why does my body have to suffer from all your bullshit? Who knows what sort of diseases I'm going to catch here?!" She was yelling now. "You know what this is?! This is a brutal mental and physical rape! The kind of rape that deserves several life sentences!"

"Calm down!" ordered Miriam, and it was apparent that this wasn't the first time the balanit had encountered a hysterical secular bride in revolt against the rabbinate's rigid rules.

The girl froze.

"First, I ask that you respect this place. Outside, you may say whatever you like. Here, you are subject to the rules of the mikveh. Second, you have to immerse anyway, so come on and let's do this in a civilized manner."

"I don't want to immerse," the young woman responded, her voice weakening a bit. "It's coercion. What will I get out of it?"

"You'll get kosher, talented, and successful children. This is the secret of the difference between us and non-Jews. Immersion in the mikveh is the secret of the Jewish genius—the secret of the Jews' brilliance and excellence, which is the envy of the whole world."

"What nonsense! Do you have any scientific proof of this? Where do you get such gibberish?"

---

*treif – everything that is nonkosher.

"Those are the words of the living God!" Miriam exclaimed.

"It's sheer arrogance," the young woman sneered. "It's baseless vanity. It's total rubbish that any civilized and enlightened person with half a brain would toss right in the trash."

"It's the essence and the chief purpose of immersion in the mikveh. It's from Hashem, not from man," Miriam replied with unruffled certainty.

"Yeah, well, then it's beyond primitive."

As numerous as the women who immerse are the definitions, interpretations, and meanings of immersion as an expression of their connection with God. Broadly speaking, one can distinguish between the religious women, for whom immersion in the mikveh is first and foremost the fulfillment of a divine imperative, plain and simple; and the women who define themselves as secular, for whom immersion embodies an emotional connection to God out of faith in his ability to affect their lives. Then there are secular women who may believe in a higher power but still reject the Jewish characterization of God, feel they're being forced into immersing against their will (prior to marriage), and swear they will never again set foot in a mikveh.

The differences between the various approaches to God illustrate the limitations of the term "religion," as described by Eliade: There is no more precise word in the lexicon than "religion" to describe the experience of the sacred. The term "religion" has a long history and is applied indiscriminately in the context of different cultures. It need not always refer to faith in God, but may relate to the experience of the sacred, for which the starting point is one's relation to the notions of being, meaning, and truth, concepts vital to human existence. Through the experience of the sacred, the human mind is able to comprehend the distinction between the true, powerful force that is full of meaning, and dangerous chaos that is devoid of meaning.[3]

Describing the experience of women during immersion in the mikveh as "a human experience of the sacred" is more accurate than simply calling immersion a religious ritual. The women believe that God sees every act of humankind and deems each worthy of either reward or punishment. They believe that they, as individuals, have the ability to create a direct connection with God without need for mediators, and that they must strive to realize this potential in their daily contact with God. For them, God is an entity with whom one can negotiate. A woman who fulfills the three main duties imposed upon her by divine command stands a good chance of receiving a blessing from God. This blessing will protect her and her family's health: "There are three things that bring good fortune: niddah, lighting Shabbat candles, and separating challah [*hafrashat challah*]. These are the three things that are incumbent upon a woman. If she separates challah, she will have very easy births," says Miriam.

The relationship between the woman and God inside the mikveh is described as an intimate symbiosis. The moment of immersion is a woman's private moment of communion with herself, with her body, with her soul, and with the spark of the divine that resides within her.

God's word is what infuses human sexual relations with emotional content, and herein lies the difference between human and animal mating. Tamar, the American, for example, believes that the divine commandment to maintain family purity is akin to "magic angel dust that dispels the boredom and bestiality of the act of love. When a young lady doesn't go to the mikveh, it's like there's no difference between her and an animal. With animals, sex happens wherever and however and whenever they feel like doing it, and it's not beautiful. There is no magic, no special quality, and no beauty of intimacy: things religion is trying to preserve. Observing the rules of niddah extends the courtship period. I've been with my husband for three years already and it's like we're still in the courtship stage, as if we just met an hour ago. That's exactly what's so wonderful about it."

"I'm not a religious person," admits Moran, the paraplegic bride. Yet it is important to her, at this decisive moment in her life, to uphold God's will and to be married in full accordance with Jewish religious precepts. She defines immersion in the mikveh as an act that binds her to family, to tradition, to God, and to holiness. At the rational level, Moran tells herself, "This is not for me," but on the emotional level, the connection to the religious experience thrills her so much she gets chills. "To tell you the truth, there's a kind of holiness in this ritual. Even though I'm totally secular, I have an affinity for the tradition. The family is what preserves tradition. Our family observes special traditions for the Jewish holidays, for bar mitzvah and bat mitzvah ceremonies, for weddings and for circumcision [*brit mila*] and redemption of the first-born son [*pidyon haben*] ceremonies." By immersing in the mikveh, Moran is pleasing her relatives and, above all, pleasing God in the hope that she will receive a happy life and a successful marriage in return.

Along with all the positive feelings connected with romance, courtship, and marriage, etched in the hearts of women who immerse is a deep fear of God's wrath over failure to observe the mitzvah of immersion. The decree of karet—the eternal excommunication of the souls of children born to a woman who does not immerse—is the most frightening of all. This potential punishment acts as a negative psychological catalyst that motivates women to immerse. One drop of information about karet is enough to terrify the young and emotional bride on the eve of her wedding, and that information is ingrained in her consciousness as a dark, terrible threat to her family life.

"I read to them an explicit verse from the Torah that is also read on Yom Kippur during the afternoon service [*mincha*]," Sarah tells me. "'And you shall not approach a woman during the separation period of her uncleanness, to uncover her nakedness' [Lev. 18:19]. The Torah concludes: 'For whoever does any of these abominations, the souls that do them shall be uprooted from the midst of their people' [Lev. 18:29]. In other words, if a man lies with his wife in a state of niddah, we're talking about the punishment of karet. I don't linger with them on this point, because I don't like to go into the topic of karet, it's very scary," explains Sarah, knowing that a single comment on the subject is enough to strike terror into the hearts of the religious women and some of the secular women, too.

Orly, the childless marathon runner, comes regularly to the mikveh because her fondest wish is to have a healthy child. For Orly, God, immersion, and fertility are all closely connected, and so she is obsessive about using the mikveh. Orly describes herself to me as a nonreligious woman who attended a religious school as a child and, like every Jewish woman in Israel, received instruction from the rabbanit prior to her wedding. But she also read about the decree of karet in a book on family purity that she borrowed from her sister "out of intellectual curiosity." Since then, she has consistently immersed in the mikveh for fear of God's wrath. Her connection with God is not a religious one, but rather an emotional-psychological one: "I wasn't sure I would keep it up. But I get scared. Sometimes I think I won't go, and then this fear hits me and I tell myself that if I got pregnant and something went wrong, my conscience wouldn't be clear. I'd always feel like maybe it was because I didn't immerse that this thing happened to me. So I don't take any chances. It's psychological. For me, the mikveh has nothing to do with religion. It's in the soul. It's stuck inside my head by now. I don't fight it anymore. I immerse and it soothes my conscience and fills me with hope that my wish for a child will come true."

Orly describes her relationship with God via observance of the commandment to immerse in the mikveh as a give-and-take relationship of reward and punishment. There is an apparent inconsistency here. The fear of God and of punishment for not fulfilling the divine imperative seems to contradict the perception of purification in the mikveh as an emotional act unconnected to God's commandment. Perhaps this indicates an identification of God with the soul. For Orly, God is something that touches the soul, and keeping God's laws is equated with adherence to the dictates of her soul and conscience. She feels good when she's doing what's needed in order to prevent disasters, and in this way she neutralizes the profound fear in her heart. "If I don't immerse and something happens to me, this could be the reason, so to avoid that possibility, it's just better to come here," she says.

Yet another patron of the mikveh, Juliet, a pediatrician, places both hands over her heart to indicate where the soul resides: "It's a real deep feeling, from here, that connects me to God." She feels that she receives a blessing and life from God. She receives God's blessing in the mikveh and he grants her life anew each morning. "You receive life every day. Every morning you receive life. You come out of sleep and suddenly you're alive again. You know what that means? It's constantly renewing itself, like a flowing stream. The ability to create life is a kind of partnership with God, and when I was able to give life I felt like I was in a 'cooperative' with God. I'm giving life now; I've moved up a level."

Nurit, who's majoring in Hebrew literature, immerses in the mikveh for herself and for God. She believes that God sees her actions. "I come out of here and I feel pure, because it's all linked. We also do it for him," she says, gazing upward, "for the Creator. I know that when I immerse in the mikveh, things will go well for me that month. There were times when I didn't immerse. I didn't make it here a couple of times, and those months were rough for me. My husband and I fought a lot and things weren't so good at home. I felt that it was because I hadn't come to the mikveh that something happened." Despite this, she claims she does not feel a close, direct connection with God. She limits and tempers her communication with him. But she does feel that God raises her up higher. "They say that when you do a mitzvah, you go up a level," she says. "I don't do it for anyone else. I do it for myself, because I want to, because I want things to go well for me and I feel that if I do this, then that's what will happen."

Nava, who is disabled, describes the connection with God via immersion in the mikveh as a conscious, unique, and intimate bond between him and her. Both she and God know if she has truly immersed and this truth belongs exclusively to the two of them. "Every woman who comes to the mikveh, it's her private right. It's her account alone with the Creator. It's just between her and him. She could tell people that she immersed when she didn't. It's her private business." Nava views the mikveh primarily as a place where the truth is exposed, where "one stands naked before God." She puts a negative aspect of the female image—the capacity for dishonesty and deception—up against God's exalted capacity to see into the innermost, secret part of a person's heart and mind. Immersion is "between the woman and the Creator, because between her and her husband she could also play games, but to the Creator she cannot lie. He is above all of us." It takes an especially arduous effort for Nava to immerse in the mikveh, but she believes that the extra hardship is reflected in the return: "My exertion is great, but the reward is even greater." Nava connects with God through wholehearted prayer. In the mikveh, she performs a ritual of confession and absolution before God. She reveals to him her wrongdoings and feels that he washes them away with the water and forgives her. She communicates with God through prayer, noting that when one is in a state of physical purification, one's spiritual purification is heightened.

"You bet it's heightened," says Michaela. "Because the number seven is equal to the universe. The mikveh is equal to the number eight, the number of Hashem. And so when you're in the mikveh, you connect to him directly. It's like you're entering the womb with Hashem, blessed be he."

8

BETWEEN MAN
AND WIFE

"I read in the newspaper that British scientists have discovered that at a woman's most fertile time of the month, nature makes her look more attractive without [her] trying at all,"[1] Shuli told Shlomit, the breast-feeding instructor, as they sat waiting for an immersion room to become available. "Tell me—Don't I look prettier today? Isn't my skin more radiant and smooth? My lips more tempting? You think my blockhead of a husband is going to be all hot for me because this is the sexiest day of the month?" She leaned into Shlomit.

"Quit teasing." Shlomit playfully pushed her off and went to speak with Doris.

"When will Miriam be here?" she asked.

"Miriam is sitting shiva,"* said Doris.

"Oh no! Who for?"

"Her youngest daughter, Ruhama."

"Was she caught in the terror attack the other day? How old was she?"

"Twenty-five."

"When was the funeral?"

---

*shiva – the seven-day mourning period in Judaism; the family of the deceased "sits shiva."

"There was no funeral," sighed Doris.

"What do you mean? My God!—there was nothing left to bury?!"

"There is no body." Doris's head shook from side to side, carrying her body along so that both swayed like a pendulum. "It's the worst that could possibly happen. No body. No funeral. No grave."

"How did it happen, Doris?" Shlomit grimaced in dread.

"It's just a disaster! Such a terrible disaster that has befallen Miriam. And she doesn't deserve it, such a righteous woman. No, no, she doesn't deserve it," lamented Doris.

Shuli and some of the other women who heard Doris's keening came and clustered around the balaniyot's table.

"Tell us already," they implored her, anxious to hear what in the world could have happened to the strongest woman in the mikveh.

"Ruhama left her husband and her three young children and went off to live with another man, may Hashem protect us, in another city."

"But how did Ruhama die?"

"That's how she died. A whore like her is considered as good as dead. The family has ripped their garments [*kar'u keri'a*]* and is sitting shiva. There's no way back from something like this."

"For God's sake, Doris, you'll be the death of me! You had me thinking . . . I thought she really died . . ." Shuli exhaled angrily and sighed with relief.

"The modesty patrols, which are like the ultra-Orthodox police, located the criminal," Doris reported. " 'You have placed a terrible stain for all generations on all members of your family!' they rebuked her. 'Now no one will want to marry into your accursed family!' They warned that if she didn't return to her husband right then and there she would

---

*keri'a – tearing one's garment as a sign of mourning.

be dooming her entire family to karet. They gave the man a vicious beating. 'One more day with her and you're dead, so it's better we take her and return her, or what's left of her, to her husband's household,' they said, and they grabbed and pulled Ruhama, tried to drag her to the car that was waiting outside. She wriggled out of their grasp and defied them. Tough as nails, she is. Stubborn. Unyielding. 'I have a right to my life! You won't tell me what to do! Get out of here!' She shooed them away like they were pesky flies landing on her open wound to lick her blood. 'Go tell my father and mother that I am not coming back to that disgusting man they forced me to marry. Period.' She spoke to them brazenly like a whore. The young men said she even hugged and kissed and fondled the secular devil right in front of their eyes just to show that she meant it. What can I tell you? There's no greater curse for a mother than to have to sit shiva for a daughter who's gone bad. She went out into an evil culture and now it's as if she's dead. *Ribono shel olam,*"* she wailed, lifting her hands toward the ceiling, "How did poor Miriam sin that you would do this to her?"

"Come on, that's just too much! How can anyone sit shiva over a living person? It's forbidden!" railed Yehudit, the Ethiopian woman, who had just come out of the Room 6 corridor, her hair wet after immersion.

"And it doesn't sound to me like that's the end of the story, either," muttered Shlomit cynically. "You never know—she might come back from the dead one of these days."

"Of course, these things can change," said young Shuli.

"We've all heard about women who fell head over heels and left home, only to come crawling back with their tails between their legs a couple of months later," Lily added, trying to hearten Doris.

"As far as the family and the ultra-Orthodox community

Ribono shel olam – "Dear God!" (lit. "Master of the World").

are concerned, she's dead," declared Doris. "I just don't understand how such a thing could happen."

"It could happen to anyone. Falling in love is a part of nature," said Shuli.

"What's happened here goes against nature!" Doris cried despairingly. "It goes against all the laws of nature between a man and a woman."

"What are you talking about? It's completely natural to go where love takes you," the other women responded, nearly unanimously.

"If Ruhama were a man, then it would be natural," Doris agreed with them, "because that's how the male constitution is built. But for such a thing to happen to a woman, and an ultra-Orthodox woman from a pious and pure family? That goes against all the laws of nature."

"What male constitution? What are you talking about?" asked Shuli.

Doris stood up, planted her feet, opened her mouth, and with all the passion of an angry prophet began preaching her gospel to the secular women gathered around her.

"The male brain is built entirely differently from the female brain." Her face, dimmed with sorrow up to now, suddenly lit up with the splendor of her message. Her voice was quiet and authoritative. "The man's brain is built to see nothing but his own needs in a woman. And Baruch Hashem that this is so. Otherwise, he would never approach the woman." Instinctively, her hand shot up and adjusted the collar of her shirt, as if she wished to ensure herself worthy of a man's gaze. "Women aren't built the same way, not at all, Baruch Hashem. A woman can see a man and not have any desire . . ." She took a deep breath and glanced at her audience, expecting a reaction. The women stood there listening attentively, mute. Their body language signaled curiosity, an eagerness to hear more about the world order dictated by the Creator.

"And at the same time that he has this kind of brain,

the man also has a certain sense inside his head. A sense of smell."

"What smell?" asked Yehudit.

"The smell of love," Doris replied, unconsciously twisting her wedding ring, which was sunk into the flesh of her right index finger. "Because what is love, really? Love is just a smell that's spread between a man and a woman. Otherwise, there's nothing," she said, now addressing me, looking me firmly, calmly, and confidently in the eye. "Understand?" she asked before turning back to the others. "So it's only natural for a simpleminded man, captive to his inferior impulse, to run after a woman's smell. But could a woman ever grow tired of her husband's smell, which is perfumed by the sanctity of marriage, and become entranced by the filthy, impure smell of another man? And the smell of a secular man at that?"

Perhaps commanded by a sixth sense, Doris's audience of secular women respectively kept their mouths shut—except for Shuli, who raised her hand and bounced up and down like an overeager schoolchild. "British researchers say that men prefer a woman's natural smell when she's at the height of her fertility," she said excitedly, repeating the news she'd given Shlomit.

"Quit fooling around," the other women chided. Doris's theory sounded utterly ludicrous and alien to their secular reality. But these women loved their balanit, who purified their bodies and often relieved their emotional burdens too, and they didn't wish to argue with her and add to her pain, so they bit their tongues and lowered their heads, privately acknowledging that all that interested them at this moment was the function of ritual immersion in their emotional lives and their marriages, nothing more.

Ultra-Orthodox women readily accept the premise that there is an essential physiological and mental difference between men and women. In fact, they celebrate it.

"There's a difference between a man and a woman," Miriam had instructed me in one of our early talks. "And the difference is in the way they are born. A man can never become pregnant and give birth. Emotionally, too, a man will not be a woman and a woman will not be a man. This difference is not random. It was deliberately designed by Hashem at the time of creation, like everything else on earth, and it is the foundation of the family order that reflects the order and harmony of this world."

The difference between the sexes dictates a clear division of roles within the frameworks of society and the family. Spiritual authority belongs to the man, the figure of culture and intellect. The "administrative" branch in the religious family is the woman. She is Mother Earth, who represents nature, gives birth to the children, and practically and actively implements the spiritual imperative.

"In Judaism, the woman is called 'the housewife' [*akeret habayit*], as the commentator Rashi explains, because she is the essential part, the *ikar,* of the home, the *bayit.* What this means is that she, more than the father, is the one who educates the children," Miriam asserts. "The father, of course, does his part in the spiritual sense of transmitting the tradition and Judaism, but the mother is the one who really puts it into practice."

This interpretation of the term *ikar habayit* is closely tied to the notion in Psalms that "the entire glory of the king's daughter is within" (Psalms 45:14), the verse that is often cited by the rabbis to tout the ideal of women's modesty in Judaism. Both reflect, in the view of many scholars, the division between man and woman in patriarchal society, the confinement of the woman to the walls of her house and her exclusion from public life. Professor Rachel Elior maintains that this sentence, and a host of others, such as "A woman is like an unfinished vessel until she forms a covenant with the one [her husband] who makes her a finished vessel" (Babylonian

Talmud, Tractate Sanhedrin 22b), are expressions that reflect control, the enforcement of authority, ownership, separation, enslavement, exclusion, and isolation between the sexes.[2] Historian Yael Azmon notes that the exclusion of women from being counted in a prayer quorum is also due to modesty.[3] The male sages felt that women possessed an insatiable impulse and therefore had to be kept away, since women are identified with materialism and constitute a threat to male spirituality.

"Be fruitful and multiply and fill the land," commanded God, granting permission to every Jewish husband and wife to satisfy the sexual impulse with which he imprinted them—on condition that not one bit of sperm is spilled in vain and that all conjugal energies be directed at pregnancy. The rabbinic leadership welcomed the sexual physicality that produces pregnancy within the framework of the family, and warned against fruitless passion that derives from the devil and poses a danger to the mental balance of the individual and to the social balance of the community as a whole.

"Woman is clearly perceived of as a vessel and object meant to serve the purpose of fertility and continuity of the generations," writes Elior.[4] "The normative rabbinic image of marital intimacy ascribes higher status to the husband," states Daniel Boyarin, who has researched the treatment of sex in Talmudic culture. "The woman is entitled to be sexually satisfied, but she occupies a marginal position in the relationship."[5] In Boyarin's view, the Talmudic tradition is not misogynistic; rather, it is andocentric—clearly placing men at the center. Talmudic tradition takes a favorable but unequal view of women, Boyarin claims. Men, for example, are permitted to indulge in sexual fantasies about the beautiful, seductive female demons who populate the sexual impulse,[6] but sex with their spouses must be directed solely at procreation. Women are absolutely forbidden to indulge in sexual fantasies. During intercourse, they must concentrate on opening their wombs and on lovingly and devotedly taking in the Divine Presence, so that conception may occur inside them.[7]

However, none of these learned theories appears to correspond with women's actual attitudes. Most of the women who immerse in the mikveh, religious and secular alike, say that the woman's sexuality is a vital, key component in the relationship between husband and wife, even if the fundamental purpose is the fulfillment of the commandment to be fruitful and multiply. The way they see it, the bolstering of a woman's sexual awareness only fuels the man's passion and desire and helps to build a healthy sexual relationship that provides a strong base for family life as a whole. Immersing women believe, as did the Jewish sages, that passion provides the glue that binds a couple together, and that sexual pleasure is a vital incentive in family life—as long as both members of the couple know their place and their role within the broader family framework, of course. Miriam argues that the division of roles between the sexes fosters partnership, not separation, creating order and balance in the family and preventing chaos. "Judaism doesn't make a separation. It's a mistake to think so. The separation is solely in accord with the woman's biological condition, because she was created one way and he was created another way, and each needs to fulfill his or her role and not switch roles. The confusion of roles is what brings destruction upon the world. No good can come of it. The Creator created the world exactly as it needs to function, but what happened? People thought they were smarter than that, and messed everything up. When a woman wants to be like a man, and he tries to be like a woman, it will never work."

Religious women believe that the essential difference between men and women—that is, women's ability to give birth—places the man in a subservient state. The "barren" man, who is incapable of producing life in his body and is driven primarily by the force of his sexual impulse, is considered to be an emotionally, spiritually, and physically inferior creature.

It's obvious to the women in the mikveh that a woman's dignity is intricately linked to the upholding of clear boundaries between husband and wife. But contrary to the male perception, which sees the woman as temptress and instigator, as the one who induces the man to throw off all restraint and surrender completely to his sexual appetite, they contend that the man's biological inferiority is what drives his ungovernable sexual impulse and what compels them, the women, to take responsibility for keeping it under control.[8]

One Orthodox woman who comes to the mikveh tells me, in the voice of a liberated, independent feminist: "It is written that the woman was given an extra portion of wisdom [*bina yetera*]. She is more sensitive; there are many things that she understands much better than a man does. The ability to give birth is truly a great privilege for her, because the continuity of the Jewish people can come only through the woman and not through the man. But at the same time," she continues, abruptly changing her tone to that of a submissive wife, "remember what Hashem said to Eve: 'Your craving shall be for your husband and he shall rule over you'" (Genesis 3:16). She recites the justification for the husband's control over his wife, a mantra on which she'd been raised since childhood, thereby restoring to every man, and her husband in particular, his unquestionable authority and dignity.

Seeking to reconcile the apparent contradiction in her mind-set, she states: "There are lots of things in this world that are beyond the comprehension of our very limited intelligence. It's written that the authority in the household is supposed to be in his hand, and we follow the halakha that divides up the management of the household, and says what belongs to the husband and what belongs to the wife."

God provided two halakhic tools to act as weapons in restraining the male impulse: the first is Torah study, which serves as "an antidote against the evil impulse."

Miriam offers further illumination: "It is written: 'I created the evil impulse, I created an antidote.' What is the antidote to the evil impulse? Torah study. It is written: 'If the wicked one—the evil impulse—meets you, drag him to the study house where he will relent.' It's also written that the woman is closer to the Creator than the man, therefore the man must study Torah all the time," she tells me, employing the rationale originated by men that has been adopted by ultra-Orthodox women to legitimize their exclusion from studying the Torah and the other sacred texts that are a basic element of Jewish identity.[9]

Miriam and her cohorts have developed a special flexibility, a talent for seeing the glass as half full when it comes to the male laws that discriminate against them. The origin of this mental pliancy may lie in the archaic philosophy described by Carol Ochs and Mircea Eliade, which holds that, in a matriarchal system, reality is changeable, fluid. Woman is identified with the seasons and fertility and man with the desert, which stands in opposition to cyclicality.

The barren essence of the "masculine" desert contradicts the concept of divine abundance: the withholding God versus the giving God. The arid desert rejects fertility for barrenness; it embodies stasis and stability rather than change and mobility. In a patriarchal system, reality is not changeable; it is permanent and unchanging. Patriarchal religion and philosophy, which focus on the permanent, reject and deny women's mysterious transformative capacity by rejecting a world in which things are impermanent. Their eyes are focused on the perfect, the incorruptible, the unchanging, on the spiritual parallel to the concrete, material nature of the desert. The permanent and unchanging is the basic divinity. That being the case, the permanent and unchanging male world is the spiritual embodiment of the divine. The difference between fertility and barrenness, farmland and wasteland, settler and nomad, lies in the conception of a stable world as a supreme value, as opposed to the ephemeral nature of the world of women. Consequently, a man's moral perceptions are utterly different than a woman's, says researcher Carol Gilligan:[10] Men perceive morality as universal principles of justice and equality. Women perceive ethics in terms of helping and pleasing others; men define morality as obeying rules, even if this requires the ending of an interpersonal relationship. Women are prepared to alter rules in order to preserve an interpersonal relationship. Good men deal with rules; good women deal with relationships.

To illustrate her theory, Gilligan cites examples from the Bible: Abraham was prepared to sacrifice his only son, Isaac, in order to prove his complete faith in God. In contrast, in the case before King Solomon, the mother was prepared to forgo the justice to which she was entitled in order to save her son's life.[11]

Miriam's words echo Gilligan's theory and embody a positive and original female explanation for the exclusion of women from Torah study: women have no need for such "an antidote against the evil impulse," because they are already close to God by virtue of their emotional makeup and thus devoid of the evil impulse to begin with.

The second tool for restraining male impulsivity, so the women believe, is immersion in the mikveh.

In Jewish tradition, there are two female figures in the life of Adam: Lilith and Eve. Lilith, created like Adam, from the earth, fled from him and descended into the waters of the Red Sea, the dwelling place of the demons. She refused to return to Adam and was punished by God, who sentenced one hundred of her demon offspring to death, day after day. Lilith symbolizes Eros, the impulsive, sexual, seductive side of woman. Lilith is identified as "the black woman," possessing an intrinsic sexuality and the capacity to attract and seduce. She also contains forces of destruction, since she is not bound to preserve the cultural tradition. Eve, on the other hand, who was created from Adam's rib and designated to be a helpmeet to him, is submissive to his desires, gives birth to his children, and symbolizes maternal love, loyalty, and family harmony. Eve is identified as the wise and beloved "white woman," whose primary role is to preserve the family unit and traditional-cultural continuity.[12]

Immersion in the mikveh conflates the figure of the "white woman" with the "black woman"; it merges the traditional, modest housewife in charge of maintaining the family and with whom intercourse is taken for granted, with the attractive, seductive woman possessed of unique feminine qualities. Immersion gives legitimacy to the idea of these two opposite faces of femininity coexisting harmoniously within the marital relationship.

Immersion in the mikveh is simultaneously a way of exerting control over the evil impulse and an ingenious device for fanning a married couple's sexual appetite. Maintaining passion in married life is exceedingly difficult, explains Dr. Nahum (Norman) Lamm in his book, *Suga Bashoshanim* (*A Hedge of Roses*).[13] One of the greatest threats to a marriage is the routine that takes over a couple's sex life once the newness of marriage has worn off. It's relatively easy to get married, but preserving the marriage bond is another matter entirely. The Talmud likens this task to the splitting of the Red Sea. The most incredible aspect of the miracle wasn't the splitting of the sea, but rather the way the waters remained standing to either side, in defiance of the pull of gravity, for as long as needed. Marriage may be viewed in a similar light. Sexual attraction brings a couple closer and strengthens their bond in the first years of marriage. But when the initial force of this attraction has faded, that bond is in danger of slow deterioration and requires regular renewal for the couple to retain a semblance of their early passion.

"Immersion in the mikveh is better than any ninety-nine pieces of advice on how to make him want it, on how to rouse him from his slumber," proclaims Dina.

"The secular women have to send their men to the sex clinic, but for us the mikveh is the solution," says Lily.

"I read in the paper," Michaela adds, blushing with excitement, "that in the past three years, the number of people seeking treatment for sexual problems has doubled. Women mostly complain about men's lack of sex drive and problems with impotence, when he can't, you know . . ." She stifled a giggle.

"There's no lack of such cases, that's for sure," Doris says, nodding her head. "As soon as she comes in here, you can see it—from her sadness, the speed with which she goes through the motions, her behavior. All of a sudden, she breaks into tears and then starts telling . . ."

"What does she tell?"

"What doesn't she tell? All the woes in the world, and then some . . . the pain of rejection, the scars of psychological abuse. We had this gorgeous one, this sexy young woman, like a supermodel she was. She married this man, he seemed perfectly fine, every part of his body in good working order. Only the structure of his brain was skewed, and his soul was crippled. And she couldn't notice this handicap before the wedding because she married as a virgin. He rejects her. He doesn't want to make love to her. Month after month he has no desire. And not, heaven forbid, because he wants another woman. No, not at all. The Internet interests him, the computer interests him, the television interests him, food interests him. But her? Not in the least. And still, each month she immerses. With sorrowful eyes and an aching heart she enters the water with a desperate prayer: maybe this time. Maybe this time this criminal husband of hers will touch her."

An oppressive silence prevails in the mikveh. The women furtively size each other up. No one wants to be the one in this criminal's bed. *It's not me!* announces their body language. *I'm not the one enduring such torment. I'm wanted. I'm desired. I'm blessed.*

"That's a very rare case," Leah says, breaking the silence. "Normally, immersion encourages good habits, helps to create beautiful customs in a couple's sex life, and ensures that the husband doesn't take his wife for granted."

"Not only that," Miriam reminds her, "but it also creates a gentle transition to menopause, when the woman no longer menstruates [is *mesuleket damim*] and there are no more restrictions on when the couple may have relations."

"That's true," confirms Michaela. "Take me, for example. I'm so used to immersing and like it so much that, even though I haven't menstruated in a few years, I still count the days and immerse and keep apart from my husband as if I was still getting my period. The truth is that, in the beginning, when my period disappeared, I was panicked. I was afraid to tell my husband. I was afraid he would stop treating me like a woman and I kept on going to immerse as if I still had my period. I didn't tell him and he didn't notice the difference. But the hot flashes got worse and so did my pangs of conscience, until I finally broke down and told him. I'll never forget how I cried, but he was an angel. He comforted me and told me he loves me even more, because now I'm like him, unable to give birth and pure all the time. And we agreed that we'd continue to keep the clean days in order to preserve our custom."

Immersion confers the balance and control that "civilize" nature, that build and perpetuate a regular rhythm of physical and emotional needs and habits.

Keeping the permitted and forbidden days primarily preserves the wife's honor in her husband's eyes. The fact that the man cannot quench his sexual appetites whenever he feels like it elevates the woman's value and standing. "With you secular, everything is free and open, all the time, with no limits," confides Miriam in a moment of intimacy. "With us, the moment everything is released . . . it's like a tightly wound spring, you know, that you stretch . . . and stretch . . . and when it's finally released, the pleasure is just incredible." She was caught up in this reverie for a moment before hastily composing herself and assuming her official facade. "A woman's encounter with her husband right after immersion is completely different from what it's like for a woman who doesn't have this restriction, who's basically available to him anytime, what we call *hefker*, so he takes her for granted."

By means of immersion, the woman exercises control over the man's sexual impulse. She prevents a lustful husband from taking advantage of her and treating her like a mere vessel for the satisfaction of his sexual appetites. She obligates a lazy husband who's lacking in passion to have intercourse with her once a month at least. Observing the mitzvah of immersion is the glue that binds a marriage together and keeps it from falling apart. Control over the proper frequency of sexual relations is an important element in the couple's life, which leads to esteem for the woman in her husband's eyes and in her own eyes.

Honor holds a central place in the life of the Jewish community and the Jewish family. Honor is synonymous with a good name, a good reputation. The rabbis say that a woman's sexuality is liable to imperil a person's good name. A man who loses control over his wife's behavior—or over his own behavior because of a woman—loses his honor, loses his masculinity. In Mediterranean cultures, one of the most crucial determinants of honor or shame is the man's ability to exercise control over the virtue of the women of his household, or alternatively, to impinge upon the virtue of women from another family. The preservation of family honor is equated with the preservation of masculinity.

I couldn't help but wonder: does the husband of a secular woman have to consent to his wife's observance of the mitzvah of ritual immersion? I asked some of my acquaintances in the mikveh.

"I didn't ask and he isn't willing to accept this lifestyle," Juliet, the pediatrician, told me. "After five days, he's going out of his mind and tells me that he's going to go out with other women. I tell him I have no objection. He can go out with all the women he wants. I'm keeping myself pure."

"First of all, I asked my husband how he felt about it. It's not something you do by your decision alone," countered the young Shuli.

"I'm the one who dictated this lifestyle," admitted the Frenchwoman, Claudine, "and my husband took it very hard. Our sex life changed and he has never come to terms with it in all these years, not even now. It's tough, very tough. It's tough for him to understand. My husband can understand anything as long as it's rational. He could learn Chinese if he had to. Chinese is rational. The mikveh isn't. I'm just beating my head against a brick wall with him. He always says, 'I just don't get it. What's it all about, really? What's the point of this immersion?' Even when I finally got pregnant after years of infertility he refused to connect it with the mikveh."

According to rabbinical authorities, the commandment to be fruitful and multiply actually applies to the man and not the woman. The man is obligated to fulfill this commandment and is rewarded for it. The woman is neither obligated nor rewarded; she merely serves as a helpmeet to the man, as a means to the fulfillment of the commandment by her husband.[14] A paradox exists between the halakhic view, which regards the imperative to be fruitful and multiply as a commandment incumbent upon men, and the fact that physiologically, this commandment is dependent upon the woman.

The women in the mikveh do not see themselves as vessels or as means to the fulfillment of a male commandment. Nor do they perceive the appropriation of the privilege of

204 *The House of Secrets*

this commandment as a halakhic injustice. In their view, this ostensible negation of their part in the vital imperative to be fruitful and multiply is precisely what grants them control over men. The mikveh essentially places control over the fulfillment of one of Judaism's most important commandments in women's hands.

"The Creator gave us an 'atom bomb.' We mustn't use it because it's not a conventional weapon. It's nuclear and very effective as a threat," Miriam tells me, revealing a glimpse of the intimate balance of power between her and her husband. "The woman's duty to maintain family purity is also the source of her power."

According to this viewpoint, immersion in the mikveh is far from a symbol of the humiliation, exclusion, and subordination of women; instead, it is a tremendous source of power. "It's the man's duty according to the halakha to have sexual relations with his wife on her immersion day in order to satisfy her conjugal rights on her days of ovulation, when the chance that his sperm will trigger conception is at its highest," explains Miriam. "No one but he can give her what she is entitled to, for she is forbidden to all the rest of the world. If he doesn't, he's committed a sin. Satisfying his wife's conjugal rights is a sacred duty, just as sacred as his duty to lay on phylacteries [*tefillin*]. There are two times when a man is obligated to have relations with his wife: on the day of her immersion in the mikveh and on Friday night. All other days are permitted in accordance with desire.

"It's the woman's right to prevent her husband from coming near her if he doesn't treat her nicely," Miriam continues. "A husband is forbidden to have sexual relations with his wife against her will. It has to be on the condition that she desires it wholeheartedly, otherwise, the halakha calls it rape. He cannot come to her if she is not mentally, personally willing. We, the women who come to immerse in the mikveh, are conscious of the incredible power that has been given to us. Hashem, who authorized the man to be the ruler of the household, to be the one who fulfills his instructions, learns Torah, and runs the household in the spiritual sense, is the very same Hashem who put this weapon in our hands."

"By virtue of this weapon, the husband cannot put his wife in his pocket and think she belongs to him and he can do with her as he pleases," Michaela adds. "He is under a constant threat, which seriously reins in his pretensions to exclusive control and authority in the home."

"The woman cannot play with his feelings," caution the balaniyot Sarah and Lily. "We were taught not to turn this whole business of going to the mikveh into imposing conditions on the husband, heaven forbid. If he does something against his wife's will or if she gets mad for some reason, to threaten that she won't go to immerse—it's forbidden. Halakhically, it's her duty. When her time comes, she is required to immerse, otherwise she's called a 'rebellious wife' [*isha moredet*] and her divine punishment is death. On the other hand, the halakha obligates him to make sure that she'll want to go to immerse on time. He knows that if he upsets her and she decides, by her own thinking, that she's not going to immerse this time, she loses all the clean days that she counted. She has to start counting all over again. Every Torah-observant Jewish man knows that there is such a danger, and he'll make sure that at least during the time that she's counting and until she has to immerse, she won't get to a situation in which she has to do the calculation all over again. It's all calculated, right up to the limit, for the sake of maintaining the wholeness of the family."

"This 'atomic weapon' must not be used as a tool for material blackmail. That just turns the woman's body into merchandise for the trader," Doris warns. But the existence of the threat preserves the balance of power in the family. This balance of powers ensures that domestic tranquility (*shalom bayit*) is maintained. The halakhic significance of the power

held by women is their ability to prevent the man from fulfilling his duty to be fruitful and multiply, which, theoretically,
could lead to the extinction of the Jewish people. But in fact
the real power of this weapon is in preventing the man from
satisfying his sexual appetite. "The fundamental difference
in the emotional makeup of the man and the woman in regard to having sexual relations," argues Miriam, "works to
the man's disadvantage and gives an advantage and power
to the woman, whose chief weapon against the man is her
sexuality. When the man is hungry to have sex, he's dependent on the woman's good graces. If she doesn't immerse in
the mikveh, he can't come near her. Then he knows that for
a whole month he's got to, as they say, keep from exploding.
To only look at her and no more."

"And she doesn't explode?" I questioned.

"When a woman is really angry she doesn't want her husband. A man, on the other hand, can—as they say—fight like
crazy with his wife in the morning and at night lay with her
in bed. It doesn't bother them. That's their nature. That's the
way it is, that's men. But a woman, when she's hurting, she
doesn't want him. Period."

Mindful of the enormous power she holds, the woman
must demonstrate self-control and emotional maturity. She
mustn't toy with the man's feelings or use the mikveh as a
bargaining tool in everyday affairs. Only when all patience
has been exhausted and the man's conduct is truly horrible,
shall the woman choose, having no other choice, to use this
"atomic weapon" that the halakha placed in her hands, as the
only means of imposing her will on the wayward tyrant and
reining him in.

Three times in the course of history have Jewish women em-
ulated Lysistrata* and united in a "sexual rebellion" against

---

*The title character of Aristophanes's play, she rallied the other
women to withhold sex from their husbands until the men halted their
bloody battles.

the men. The first rebellion was the "immersion rebellion" in Egypt. At the end of the twelfth century, Jewish women in Egypt refused to immerse in the mikveh.[15] According to the writings of Maimonides, the rebellion had two underlying causes: the physical discomfort the women experienced in using the mikveh, and the influence of Karaite* women, who followed a different custom of simply pouring water on the body. This rebellion lasted several years, rendering the men distraught. In an effort to end the crisis, Maimonides and his colleagues resorted to issuing radical decrees: they threatened that the women could lose their *ketubah*‡ and compelled them to swear that they had immersed in the mikveh before they were entitled to receive their *ketubah* money.[16] The two other rebellions occurred in the thirteenth century, one in Byzantium and the other among the Ashkenazic communities. In Byzantium, Jewish women were immersing in nonkosher mikvehs that were not filled with "living water" (*mayim hayim*)—that is, rainwater untouched by human hands, as commanded by the Torah.§ Many women revolted against their husbands; refused to have marital relations, and requested divorces.[17]

These three events attest to the women's freedom of movement, to their self-awareness and their capacity for social cohesion. "Between the lines echoes the voice of powerful women, very different from the ideal of the submissive and shy figure depicted by thinkers during the Middle Ages and the early modern period," says historian Avraham Grossman,[18] reinforcing the testimony of the religious women in the mikveh, who recognize their power and ability to fight for

---

*The Karaite movement of Judaism opposes rabbinical interpretation and strives to adhere to the *pshat* (the plain meaning) of the biblical text.

‡The Jewish marriage contract; it stipulates how much the man must pay the woman in the event of divorce.

§This is discussed further in chapter 1.

their rights within the family and community and to obtain recognition as independent human beings with desires and needs that must be respected and accepted. Jewish sisterhood is a critical tool in the war between the sexes and enhances the strength of each and every woman who immerses.

The continuity of the Jewish people depends on the imperative of immersion. Despite its being a male halakhic imperative, immersion is perceived by the women as a female imperative that passes from generation to generation and bridges the worlds of the secular and religious women. The women in the mikveh feel themselves a part of a chain of powerful women, who set an example of independence within the male world: "We belong," say the immersing women, "to an exclusive club of strong and impressive women who have influenced the history of the Jewish people. We are perpetuating the chain of Jewish women that began with Eve, the first woman, and continued through the four Matriarchs: Sarah, Rebecca, Rachel, and Leah."

The modern woman turns the mikveh into a source of spiritual power. This is how she proudly links herself to the chain of powerful women throughout the generations. This source of power has been discovered by secular women, too. Young women whose mothers never immersed feel intricately tied to the female Jewish tradition. Through immersion, they are linked to a strong, proud, and glorious chain of Jewish women.

Religious and secular women alike, despite fundamental differences in their outlooks and ways of life, express their independence through immersion in the mikveh—they feel that it is they who hold control over the fate of their marriage and the power to decide and act upon their desires within their family life.

Immersion in the mikveh truly encapsulates the Jewish female experience as it has crystallized over the generations. In the mikveh, women open up about their troubles and voice their dearest wishes and deepest hurts before other immersing women and the balaniyot, who listen closely and gently and discreetly steer them toward assistance. Requests and pleas to God are whispered inside the immersion pool, when tears mix with the primal waters. Voices of song, blessings, and rejoicing are heard in the henna ceremonies, and the sounds of laughter and friendly chatter fill the mikveh vestibule before and after immersions.

Like the whistling of the ignorant child in the Hasidic folktale, whose inchoate but heartfelt Yom Kippur prayer is welcomed by God above all others, so, at the moment of immersion, does the woman's voice, coming from the bottom rung of the ladder in the view of the halakha, open up the gates of heaven—the gates of mercy—and redeem the entire community. She is rewarded with her ability to ensure the continuity of the Jewish people.

Paula tells a story that epitomizes this profound faith in immersion as the ultimate act of Jewish female identity:

"A Jewish woman who was on her final journey on the Nazi death train instructed her seven-year-old daughter to keep the mitzvah of immersion: 'My precious little girl, you know nothing, you don't understand what I'm talking about. But I beg you, if you want us to go on being mother and daughter, to perpetuate the generations of our family and the generations of the Jewish people and to remain Jews—you must keep the mitzvah of immersion. You don't know what it means yet, but when the time comes, seek to immerse and make sure to keep this mitzvah well. Then God will never leave you.' "

Epilogue

The saying "Don't judge a book by its cover" could have been coined with my old mikveh in mind. The square, decrepit building, with its sooty walls devoid of any shred of charm or beauty, is analogous in my mind to the clever detective who conceals his brilliance beneath an ordinary exterior, remaining unobtrusive and so catching unseeing fools off-guard. A random passerby gazing up at the lone house at the top of the street would have no inkling of the rich world inside. The life sagas witnessed by the mikveh walls could fill myriad books and serve as inspiration to writers of the sort of dramas and melodramas that satisfy the emotional cravings of millions of people. Love, sex, hope, disappointment; the joy of childbirth and the pain of bereavement; wounds inflicted by male cruelty; old wives' tales; the scars of emotional and physical trauma; coping with physical handicaps; fear, greed, hatred; jealousy and sisterly encouragement; demons, spirits; the tantalizing smells of festive foods; the sounds of song; prayer and weeping; ringing bells and beating darbouka drums—all merge into a powerful feminine bouquet that curls up through the mikveh chimney and ascends to the heavens to connect with the Divine Presence (*Shekhina*). Above the women in the mikveh, the Divine Presence has not gone away. Their temple, the mikveh, remains steadfast and stable and serves them three hundred and sixty-three days of the year.

Afterword

Two pioneering Jewish women—one in Israel and the other in the Diaspora in the United States—who didn't know of one another, are reinventing the traditional mikveh. They removed their temple, the mikveh, from the custody of men. They built it themselves in keeping with a vision born of the impulse to reshape the immersion experience, to reflect the needs of the societies in which they live, and to provide an alternative to the Orthodox conception of purification based solely on halakhic authority. The Israeli is attorney Shimrit Beinhorn-Klein, from Petah Tikva. The American is Anita Diamant, of Boston, Massachusetts, author of the best-selling book *The Red Tent*.

In 2004 Beinhorn-Klein entered a mikveh to immerse on the eve of her wedding and walked out with a dream. Dissatisfied with everything about her immersion experience—the wait in line for immersion, the impersonal and intrusive treatment she received, the decrepitude of the place and its lack of aesthetics—she dreamed of a different kind of mikveh. She shared this dream with a close friend, who put her in touch with her mother, Ester Hemli, a religious woman from the El-kana settlement and a successful entrepreneur with a proven track record. From that moment, Hemli set about turning Beinhorn-Klein's dream into reality. After three years of hard work, the two women opened a new mikveh, utterly distinct in concept and design from its counterparts in Israel. This mikveh, in Givat Shmuel, near Tel Aviv, is built with private money instead of public funds, is independent of the religious establishment and yet thoroughly kosher, sanctioned by both the local council and the National Center for Family Purity. Rabbi Landau, the chief rabbi of Bnei Brak, gave it a Chabad* seal of approval. The private initiative by these two women received the rabbinate's blessing.

Following Hemli's vision, the women called their mikveh *Ivria* (Hebrew Israelite Woman), a name that perfectly encompasses their original concept. They describe the place in the terms of a boutique spa. Its four floors offer women ritual immersion in addition to massage services, hair styling, beauty treatments, reflexology, henna ceremonies, yoga classes, meditation, parenting workshops, Reiki, bat mitzvah celebrations, bridal showers, makeup, jewelry, belly dancing, marriage coaching, bachelorette parties, birthday parties, books, art, and more.

The walls of this women's temple, alternating between glass and stone, convey a feeling of airiness and transparency, eliciting feelings of tranquility, harmony, and inner peace. Here the woman receives everything she needs, beginning with a plush white robe and slippers. The idea is to create a place that is embracing and pampering, that imparts feelings of purity, well-being, relaxation, and joy.

The intention is to celebrate within the mikveh the stations in the Ivria woman's life cycle from bat mitzvah up until age 120. Instead of the standard prayers that are affixed to the walls of the traditional mikveh, printed on the doors of the new mikveh are texts by Hebrew women poets throughout the generations. Words and images related to the natural world are scattered about the walls: grass, butterflies, flowers, sky, blessings, fragrance, rain, clouds, air.

Each immersion room is thematically linked to a heroine from the Diaspora and designed in the spirit of her land of origin. One room, for example, is dedicated to Yukiko Sugihara, wife of Chiune Sugihara, the "Japanese Schindler"

---

*Chabad – another name for the Lubavitch Hasidic movement.

who saved many Jews during World War II. Next door is a Moroccan-themed room, dedicated to Solika, the beautiful, virtuous, and God-fearing heroine of legend who chose to die a martyr's death rather than convert to Islam and marry a Moroccan prince.

To the traditional halakhic function of the mikveh—the purification of the woman from her niddah impurity—a wide range of other functions have been added, in response to popular demand. To the traditional rites of passage—immersion and fertility—a variety of other rites have been added, invented by the proprietors of the mikveh, such as those specifically tailored to the individual woman's age and life situation, to the nature of the "transition," to the purpose of the celebration.

At Ivria, Reshit Nashit is the name given to the bat mitzvah girl's first celebration of her femininity, a dedication ceremony in the mikveh. Accompanied by a circle of her close friends, the girl attends a workshop on the subjects of purification and friendship. The girls are introduced to the facility, where they will later come to clean and purify themselves on the eve of their wedding. In the course of the ceremony they go from one Ivria station to the next. At the salon, their hair is done into little braids, and in the cosmetics room, designs are drawn on their hands. Sometimes questions come up about lice—a common scourge in Israel—so there is also some discussion of hair care, skin care, and hygiene.

"The bat mitzvah celebration in the mikveh," explains Ester Hemli, "is a rite of passage for a girl who is maturing but not yet a woman. She is going from the state of being a child to that of being a teenage girl and here in the mikveh we introduce her to femininity.

"We invented the rituals here. They are not written in any halakha and, of course, are not binding in any way. When my first granddaughter was born I wanted to hold a ceremony to welcome her into the family dynasty. I brought all the grandmothers and aunts and girl cousins and we gave her a very meaningful reception. From the great-grandmother, she was passed from hand to hand to hand, and each one of the women blessed her. I see a beauty in this that stimulates a feeling of bonding and closeness. You can add things without going against the halakha. The intention isn't to invent another Torah but rather to flow with the halakha—to do everything within the framework, but to be creative.

"A birthday party for an eighty-eight-year-old grandmother might be held here alongside a childbirth-preparation course. Beauty treatments alongside a guided-imagery workshop for teenage girls, giving them tools for coping with pressures and tensions. Bridal counseling alongside a quick, concentrated head-and-neck massage for the busy Ivria woman."

Here in this women's temple, the women continue the immersion tradition while adding a new dimension to it, appropriating for themselves the role traditionally held by men. They turned the mikveh into a business—a business run by women for women. Instead of restricting themselves to a small sign announcing Ritual Bath for Women (*mikveh tahara le-nashim*), there is an artfully designed Web site. Instead of a head balanit, there is a director. Instead of a balaniyot's table, a busy administrative office. Behind the modern reception desk sits an attractive and friendly receptionist. The simple tin can has been replaced by a complex accounting system. The modest fees for immersion have grown to include a whole package of workshops and beauty treatments. The solitary mirror of the traditional mikveh has been replaced by a beauty and hair salon. The toweling off and embrace of the balanit are replaced by the ministrations of a team of masseuses. The celebrations room has been augmented with a lecture room and a library housing a photo gallery of the founders' families.

Here they've preserved the principles of the halakha while adding many of their own. They've stretched the canvas of female rituals from age 12 to age 120. The principle of modesty is maintained, yet extended into a broader interpretation. Hidden behind a plain wooden fence, from the outside the mikveh looks like a nondescript office building. The fact that other activities besides immersion take place here actually enhances a woman's privacy, says Ester Hemli, because no one can be sure whether a woman has come to immerse in order to reunite sexually with her husband or for some other purpose. Maybe she is at Ivria simply to get a massage.

The guestbook that lies on an ornate table in the lobby is filled with expressions of gratitude that illustrate how great the need for such a place was for women from the whole spectrum of Israeli society. This mikveh is a place where the mitzvah of immersion can be fulfilled in comfort. It's a place that identifies with them as Ivria women and not necessarily religious Jewish women.

The famous Hebrew poet Alexander Penn, embodied in the texts of his poems printed on a white curtain in one of the bathrooms, is the sole male presence in the mikveh. This is a place in which men are not permitted to set foot, says Hemli. Nor are gentile women.

The mikveh envisioned by Anita Diamant welcomes both men and women for immersions, and invites non-Jews to study and learn about mikveh as well. It is a pluralistic mikveh that serves women and men alike. Bat mitzvahs and bar mitzvahs; non-Jews who wish to convert; those who may have been turned away from a more traditional mikveh—homosexuals, divorcees, widows, and unmarried women—are welcome here.

Here there is no spa. Instead, there is an education center devoted to progressive Judaic studies, with lecture halls and an art gallery. Conferences are held on topics related to Judaism and art exhibitions on Jewish topics are presented. Here men, women, and children immerse. Here the most important thing is the intention, the *kavanna*.

Diamant's vision sprang from a personal experience she had as a result of the immersion of a man—her husband. He underwent an immersion ceremony for conversion in a traditional Orthodox mikveh.* The ritual had just concluded and the couple found themselves celebrating this deeply significant transformative moment in a parking lot. But it wasn't until years later, while Diamant was working on a book about conversion to Judaism and watched as dozens of men, women, and children waited under the beating sun one day to enter the mikveh to become Jews, that the recognition fully dawned that the Orthodox mikveh was not for her.

She dreamed of a different kind of mikveh. Her mikveh would be a place for contemplation and celebration, for meditation and song. Each convert would have a personal, moving, spiritual ceremony, in keeping with the sanctity of the conversion event. In her mikveh, converts would find themselves surrounded by family and friends. Together they, like the brides and the grooms and the bat mitzvah girls and bar mitzvah boys, would celebrate with the entire community in spacious, warmly inviting surroundings. This would be a place where celebrants could rejoice, but also a place that would comfort the grieving, commemorate recovery from illness, and give strength to the faltering; a mikveh that would serve the entire Jewish community without regard for family status, age, or gender; a mikveh that would accord each and every person all due respect.

Diamant recruited her good friends, engaged the help of people with expertise, and secured the necessary funding

---

*According to various customs, Jewish men use the mikveh to attain ritual purity on certain occasions, such as before Shabbat or a Jewish holiday; a bridegroom before his wedding; a kohen before reciting the priestly blessing. A convert to Judaism also immerses in the mikveh. In Orthodoxy, there are separate mikveh facilities for men and women.

to build her dream mikveh. In May 2004 she inaugurated her dream in the Boston suburb of Newton, and she called it Mayyim Hayyim—Living Waters Community Mikveh and Education Center.

Mayyim Hayyim is an alternative mikveh, built in accordance with the principles of halakha but connected more to the spiritual than halakhic aspect of Judaism. It answers a need felt by many in twenty-first-century American Jewish society—people who consider themselves spiritual believers, secular or religious, but who are not mitzvah-observant. Mayyim Hayyim embraces the Jewish community as a whole in an inviting way, and strengthens Jews' bonds with their ancestral roots.

At Mayyim Hayyim, the concept of modesty (*tzni'ut*) is interpreted and applied in a completely different way than it is in Orthodoxy. On the one hand, the mikveh actively promotes itself. It is housed in a lovely nineteenth-century building with two wings branching off from its sunlit reception area—one containing a study center, art gallery, and celebration room and one containing the mikvehs and preparation rooms. A bride and groom may immerse at the same time in the two separate mikveh pools. But each may also be present (while dressed) at the other's immersion ceremony.

On the other hand, individual privacy is maintained. Mayyim Hayyim has women-only hours every evening for those who immerse in observance of niddah or for any other purpose. In conversion ceremonies, the presiding rabbi will stand on the other side of the door and, through an open window high over his or her head, will hear the convert recite the blessing under the guidance of the male or female mikveh guide. The mikveh guide will check for loose hairs, considered a barrier between the person and the water, solely with the consent of the person who wishes to immerse.

Mayyim Hayyim is quenching the thirst of many in the Jewish community who yearn to sip from the wisdom of

Judaism without coercion, and is educating a generation of young people from bar mitvah and bat mitzvah age to adopt Jewish values. Values such as Intention; Love; Acceptance; Spirituality; Openness; Tolerance.

Mayyim Hayyim welcomes non-Jews seeking to learn about Judaism. However, entry into the mikveh waters is permitted only to those non-Jews who are in the process of conversion. Would Madonna be allowed to immerse at Mayyim Hayyim? "Only if she were converting to Judaism. Non-Jews seeking a spiritual immersion will not be permitted to immerse at Mayyim Hayyim. This is the boundary. We have our own boundary and this is it," says executive director Aliza Kline. "Not because the waters would become 'contaminated,' since living waters do not become impure, but because boundaries must be demarcated in order for a certain character to be retained." Delineating boundaries is the essence of Judaism. This is where Mayyim Hayyim draws the line.

The insistence on boundaries means that the staff of Mayyim Hayyim has to deal daily with issues dictated by the reality of Jewish minority life in the Diaspora. They search for answers to tough questions, such as whether it is permissible to immerse a born Jew who belongs to the Christian organization Jews for Jesus. According to the halakha, he is a Jew. According to his faith, he is not.

Or what happens when an interfaith couple in which the wife is not Jewish brings their baby to the mikveh for conversion? Can the mother enter the mikveh with the baby? Is it proper for a mother who belongs to a different religion to enter the mikveh waters to immerse her child for the sake of conversion?

"Each rabbi decides in his or her own way," says Aliza Kline. The answers may be as numerous and varied as the different strands of Judaism.

Teams of volunteers, including rabbis, cantors, Jewish educators, psychologists, academics, and artists from various denominations and backgrounds have developed the values, rules, and blessings used at Mayyim Hayyim.

There is a guiding set of principles at Mayyim Hayyim, which, like the halakha, sets certain boundaries and limits. And there are seven intentions (*kavannot*) that are essentially a modern interpretation of the traditional preparation of the body for immersion, with the addition of a preparatory meditation.

The first is: "*Hineini*—Here I Am." The individual is asked to take a moment to reflect upon the reason she or he is about to immerse. Following this declaration, the person is to concentrate upon the six additional preparatory meditations, each accompanied by a specific instruction as to how to prepare body and soul for immersion. Rather than "We shall do and we shall listen" (*na'aseh venishma*), as in the traditional mikveh, here the mantra is "We shall listen and we shall do"; first comes the spiritual explanation, followed by the practical instruction.

At Mayyim Hayyim, there is a different understanding of purity and impurity. There is ritual readiness and ritual unreadiness. This is the essence of the change that occurs in the people who immerse. They enter the immersion after an extended preparation process that takes them from unreadiness to readiness. They declare "Here I am," and the immersion symbolically completes the transformation.

A bar mitzvah boy or bat mitzvah girl who comes to immerse in the mikveh first goes through a process of mental preparation, and only immerses when he or she feels ready to take on the burden of adult responsibility in life. A bride will immerse only when she feels ready to take on the responsibility inherent in the act of marriage, responsibility for building a home and family and all that entails.

The need to declare "I am ready" with full intention can also help facilitate the grieving process. For example, a bereaved person who is returning to society after sitting shiva (the traditional seven-day mourning period) or observing a month or year of mourning, during which time the individual existed on life's fringes, is helped by the immersion ceremony that, together with the declaration "I am ready," marks a return to the circle of life.

"When you are not ready, the mikveh helps you to become ready. It gives you the respect to take the time for yourself. Because only you, the individual, know when you are ready and when you are not. And when you come to that recognition, we will give you all the strength and support in the world to put this readiness into actual practice," says Aliza Kline.

"Where is God in all of this?" I asked her.

"God is everywhere in the mikveh. Some of our visitors are seeking a closeness to God; others are not. The language of the divinity here is male and female."

Like its Israeli counterpart, Mayyim Hayyim has taken the rites of passage in the mikveh and stretched them far beyond the boundaries of purity and impurity between man and woman, to all facets of life.

At Mayyim Hayyim, immersion ceremonies are held for men and women in accordance with suggested readings and *kavannot*, focusing primarily on conversion, niddah, and life transitions. Each area encompasses dozens of types of rituals, and each ritual is tailored according to need. They include, for example, rites of passage for recovery from serious illness; for the onset of menopause; for divorce; for the adoption of children; for receiving a doctorate; for retirement; for the last child leaving the nest; for a woman who has lost weight; for coping with loss, as after a miscarriage; and for coming out of the seven-day mourning period.

Ritual immersion is perceived in a different light from the traditional view. A woman or girl may immerse at any point during her monthly cycle. Mayyim Hayyim says that, according to Jewish law, the mikveh waters cannot become impure, and so it is not a problem for women to immerse while menstruating.

Niddah is a subject of some mystery to many Jewish women in the Diaspora. Unlike Israeli Jewish women, these women are not obliged to provide confirmation of a proper halakhic immersion in order to get married, and a majority of them are thoroughly unfamiliar with the concept of niddah. Even the word "mikveh" is foreign to many of them. Mayyim Hayyim dispels the mystery and provides instruction on all the rules of niddah and its sources.

At Mayyim Hayyim there is no balanit or balan. There are female mikveh guides and male mikveh guides who are carefully selected and given special training. All are spiritually inclined. They are not necessarily mitzvah-observant.

The desire for a new perspective on the mikveh is not confined to these two new centers. The Israeli pioneers say they are being implored by women to fill the country from north to south with more such temples. Diamant and her team are already consulting with other communities in Los Angeles and San Diego planning to build their own community mikvehs and education centers, modeled after Mayyim Hayyim. Centers of this kind have also been sprouting up in Europe.

What will happen to the traditional mikveh? Are we witnessing a transformation of the mikveh and its removal from male control to the control of women, who will dictate the rules according to their needs and outlook, who will design these new mikvehs according to the shifting needs of place and time? Will such a "female religion," centered on compassion and coercion-free acceptance, that demonstrates flexibility as needed, supplant the halakha? By gathering Jewish women into the mikveh and heightening the feeling of Jewish sisterhood, will women realize the destiny imprinted in them from creation to produce, educate, and protect the generations to come? Are we witnessing the rise of a process of female empowerment that is perpetuating and strengthening the chain of Jewish generations, extending from the matriarch Sarah through the women of the Second Temple period, who devoutly preserved their tradition of immersion, to the millions of Jewish women in Israel and the Diaspora today, to the women of succeeding generations?

Time will tell.

Acknowledgments

To the wonderful women who opened their hearts to me and shared their secrets and desires with me and permitted me to record their emotions and observe their rituals and allowed me into the most intimate recesses of their souls.

To the faculty of the Department of Jewish and Comparative Folklore at the Hebrew University in Jerusalem, and most especially to the advisor for my master's thesis, upon which this book is based, Dr. Hagar Salamon, who taught me so much and instilled in me confidence in my ability as a researcher and preserver of folklore.

To the eminent Professor Dov Noy, who found my master's thesis worthy of receiving the distinguished prize named for him and the late Dr. Tamar Noy.

To my dear friend Professor Edwin Seroussi, for his sage advice during the writing of this book.

To Roni Modan, who gently and with care took me under the wing of Modan Press.

To Shula Modan, who helped me separate the wheat from the chaff.

To Myra Barak, who turned every painful sacrifice into a winning choice and edited my words with wisdom and sensitivity.

To Anne Hartstein Pace, who gracefully and insightfully transformed each Hebrew word and sentiment into English.

To my first-class agent, Deborah Harris, for believing in me and in the angels.

To the staff of Modan for their dedicated and professional care.

To Amy Caldwell and the staff at Beacon Press for their personal and professional treatment.

To Janine Lazar, who took me by the hand and showed me the way.

To my father, Yitzhak Alayof, who taught me all about Jewish prayer.

To my mother, Behira Alayof, who was always there to offer help and support in tough times.

To my man, my love, who made me believe that this book was destined for greatness.

To my dear eldest child, Rafael Polak of blessed memory, who filled me with his *neshama yetera*.

Thank you.

I couldn't have created this work without you.

Notes

PROLOGUE

1. A complete list of the rules concerning menstruation is in Mordechai Eliahu, *Darkhei Tahara* [*Paths of Purity*] (Jerusalem: Sukkat David Press, 1986), pp. 63–87. Henceforth: Eliahu.

2. The Torah says that during the time of her monthly menstruation every woman is *teme'ah* (impure or unclean) and *metam'ah* (defiling), and is to be "banished" from society. "You shall not approach a woman in her time of unclean separation," in her time of *niddah*, according to Lev. 18:19. In the name of God's law, the great Jewish sages throughout the generations permitted themselves to pry deep into the woman's body, to intrude on her privacy down to the most minute detail, to pile on ever more intricate and esoteric halakhot: there are laws governing which blood is pure and which is impure, laws about stains from vaginal discharges originating in the menstrual blood that are larger than a *gris* (the Talmudic measure of a grain of wheat) and smaller than a *gris*. Halakhot discuss at length and categorize the types of vaginal discharges according to color (those that are unclean and those that are not unclean). They discuss the rules pertaining to menstrual bleeding and the rules pertaining to a bride; the rules about childbirth and the rules about miscarriage; the rules governing purification from niddah and the rules pertaining to coitus and postcoitus; and countless more. Over the years, the sages formulated the laws and passed them down as the Oral Torah, until they were sealed and fixed in the Mishna and the Talmud and the primary halakhic treatises, and to this day, from east to west, from one side of the world to the other, with varying degrees of stringency, rabbinic authorities continue to tirelessly debate and amend the laws concerning a woman's state of uncleanness, as if the Creator, through the engine of evolution, continues to refine a woman's reproductive system, thus requiring modification of the rules concerning her purity and impurity for every generation.

3. For more regarding the color of stains, see Eliahu, pp. 29–32.

4. For more on the rules concerning feces as a barrier, see Eliahu, p. 165.

[1] THE PLACE

1. Aryeh Kaplan, *Memei Gan Eden: Hamistorin shel Hamikveh* [*Waters of Eden: The Mystery of the Mikveh*] (Jerusalem: National Center for Family Purity in Israel, 1983), p. 11. Henceforth: Kaplan.

2. Pinhas Kehati, ed., *Mishnayot Mevoarot.* Vol. 2, *Seder Taharot* [*Kehati Commentary on the Mishna*]. (Jerusalem: Mishnayot Kehati Press–Heichal Shlomo, 1996), pp. 221–22. Henceforth: Kehati.

3. See Nissan Rubin, *Reshit Hehayim: Tiksei Leda, Mila Upidyon Haben Bimkorot Hazal* [*The Beginning of Life: Rites of Birth, Circumcision, and Redemption of the First-born in the Talmud and Midrash*] (Tel Aviv: Hakibbutz Hameuchad Press, 1995), pp. 13–17. Henceforth: Rubin.

[2] THE BALANIYOT

1. For more on the characteristic structure of tales of holiness from Islamic lands, see Heda Jason, "Ha'askola Haformalistit Bemehkar Hasifrut Ha'amamit," *Hasifrut: Quarterly for the Study of Hebrew Literature,* Benjamin Hrushovski, ed. (Tel Aviv) 9 (1970), pp. 53–83.

2. Another, quite different, arena where something similar occurs is in the ritual washing of the dead in preparation for burial (*tahara*); only Jewish women may perform the *tahara* on the body of a Jewish woman.

[3] A DOSE OF IMPURITY

1. Kaplan, pp. 50–53.

2. Ibid.

3. Isaac Halevy Herzog, preface to *Ish Ve'isha Shezakhu: Hayei Hamishpaha Hayehudit Mehebet Refu'i Upsikhologi,* Sheindel Weinstein, ed. (Jerusalem: National Center for Family Purity in Israel, 1988), pp. 6–8.

4. Rahamim Ben-Amara, *Sefer Hadrakha Lamishpaha Hayehudit Begashmiyut Uberuhaniyut* [*Guidebook for the Jewish Family in Material and Spiritual Matters*] (Jerusalem: Torah Vehesed Press, 1996), pp. 127–28. The quotes from this source have been translated from the Hebrew.

5. Paulo Coelho, *Warrior of the Light: A Manual* (New York: HarperCollins, 2003).

6. Yehuda Berg, *Dialing God: Daily Connection Book; Technology for the Soul* (Los Angeles, CA: The Kabbalah Centre International, 2003).

[4] BLOOD AND BANISHMENT

1. This is evidently the source of the obligation for a married woman to cover her hair.

2. The Torah permits a man to have two wives.

3. For a broad discussion of this issue, see Amira Eran, "Hatzela Hashniya: Hatfisa Hara'ayonit shel Ha'isha Behagut Yemei Habeinayim," in *Hatzela Hashlishit: Hayahas el Ha'isha Bamishna, Behagut Yemei Habeinayim Ubeshirat Nashim Bat Zmanenu,* edited by Amira Eran, Einat Ramon, and Tlalit Shavit (Tel Aviv: Mofet Institute, 2001), pp. 29–87. Henceforth: Eran.

4. Avraham Even-Shoshan, *Milon Hadash: Menukad Umetzuyar* (Jerusalem: Kiryat Sefer Press, 1947), p. 966. Henceforth: Even-Shoshan.

5. Rubin, p. 15. See also Claude Lévi-Strauss, *The Raw and the Cooked,* trans. John and Doreen Weightman (New York: Harper & Row, 1969).

6. For more on the principle surrounding bodily secretions, see Howard Eilberg-Schwartz, *The Savage in Judaism: An Anthropology of Israelite Religion and Ancient Judaism* (Bloomington: Indiana University Press, 1990), pp. 180–87.

7. See Rubin, pp. 15–16.

8. After childbirth, a woman is in an interim state—a liminal state between holiness and impurity. She is allowed to be within the realm of the profane, but forbidden to enter the realm of holiness. The term "liminal state" was first coined by Arnold van Gennep in *The Rites of Passage* (Chicago: University of Chicago Press, 1961; originally published in French, 1908), and later expanded upon by Victor W. Turner in *The Forest of Symbols: Aspects of Ndembu Ritual* (Ithaca, NY: Cornell University Press, 1967), pp. 93–111. Henceforth: Turner. For more on this subject, see Rubin, pp. 19–21.

9. See Rubin, pp. 18–19.

10. Raphael Patai, *Hamayim: Mehkar Liyedi'at Haaretz Ulefolklor Eretzyisraeli Bitkufot Hamikra Vehamishna* [*The Water: A Study in Palestinology and Palestinian Folklore in the Biblical and Mishnaic Periods*] (Tel Aviv: Dvir Press, 1936), pp. 12–13. Henceforth: Patai.

11. Eliahu, pp. 11–12.

12. See Thomas Buckley and Alma Gottlieb, eds., *Blood Magic: The Anthropology of Menstruation* (Berkeley: University of California Press, 1988), p. 16. Henceforth: Buckley and Gottlieb.

13. Ibid., pp. 16–18.

14. See Eliahu, pp. 38–57, and Tehila Abramov, *Sod Hanashiyut Hayehudit: Hebetim ʿal Taharat Hamishpaha* [*The Secret of Jewish Femininity*] (Jerusalem: Feldheim Publishers, 1990), pp. 70–74. Henceforth: Abramov.

15. More allowances may be made when it is the ailing husband who requires his wife's help than when the situation is reversed.

[5] PURITY AND SEXUALITY

1. Carol Ochs, "Nomad and Settler in Patriarchal Religion," *Feminist Studies* 3, nos. 3–4 (1976), pp. 56–61. Henceforth: Ochs.

2. Midrash Vayikra Rabbah 14:9, p. 317.

3. Erich Neumann, *The Great Mother: An Analysis of the Archetype,* translated by Ralph Manheim. 2nd ed. (New York: Bollingen Foundation, 1963), p. 55.

4. Babylonian Talmud, Tractate Niddah 9a.

5. Ephraim Talmage, *Sefer Habrit: Vikuhei Radak ʿim Hanatzrut* [*The Book of the Covenant and Other Writings*] (Jerusalem: Bialik Institute Press, 1974), pp. 86–87.

6. Ochs, p. 57.

7. Babylonian Talmud, Tractate Niddah 31a. See also Rubin, p. 43.

8. In the past, a thick tablecloth would be placed over the windows to keep out all light from outside; today, the windows are covered with heavy curtains.

9. Benny Nahmias, *Hamsa: Kemi'ot, Emunot, Minhagim Urefuah ʿAmamit Ba'ir Ha'atika Yerushalayim* (Tel Aviv: Modan Press, 1996), p. 99.

10. If he has just the one room and no book cupboard, the books should be covered with two layers of tablecloths; if the mezuzah is inside the room, it must also be covered.

11. Mishna, Horayot 3:7.

12. Tractate Yoma 66b.

13. Sota 3:4.

14. Tractate Sota 3:4–5.

15. Babylonian Talmud, Tractate Kiddushin 70a.

16. For more on women's status as reflected in patriarchal terminology, see Rachel Elior, "Nokhehot Nifkadot," "Teva Domem," and "Alma Yafa She'en La Enayim" ["Present but Absent," "Still Life," and "A Pretty Maiden Who Has No Eyes"], *Alpayim* 20 (2000), pp. 214–70. Henceforth: Elior.

17. For more on the motifs discussed here, see Buckley and Gottlieb.

18. Meir Shalev, *Fontanella* (Tel Aviv: Am Oved, 2002).

19. Nitza Abarbanell, *Hava VeLilit* [*Eve and Lilith*] (Ramat Gan: Bar-Ilan University Press, 1994), p. 33. Henceforth: Abarbanell.

20. The observance of family purity is a central component of Jewish identity that differentiates Jewish society from non-Jewish society in the Diaspora. One striking example of the struggle to shape and preserve the character of a Jewish minority amid a Christian society via close adherence and scrupulous fulfillment of the rules of niddah may be seen among the Beta Israel Jews, who lived as a minority in Ethiopia. In a society in which blood holds utmost significance, menstrual blood became a central issue in the cultural negotiation between the Jewish minority and the Christian population that surrounded them in the villages. The Jews devoutly maintained family purity as required by the divine commandment in the Torah. The woman's removal to the blood house was such a prominent sign that the existence of blood houses became a key symbol of the existence of Jewish life in a village. By making a public display of the niddah rituals, the Jewish community underscored its separation and distinction from the surrounding society. See Hagar Salamon, *The Hyena People: Ethiopian Jews in Christian Ethiopia* (Berkeley: University of California Press, 1999), pp. 97–100.

21. Hagar Salamon, "Dam Etzel Beita-Yisrael Ushekhenehem Hanotzrim Be'Ithiyopiya" ["Blood between the Beta Israel and Their Christian Neighbors in Ethiopia: Key Symbols in an Inter-Group Context"], *Mehkarei Yerushalayim Befolklor Yehudi* [Jerusalem Studies in Jewish Folklore] 15, ed. Tamar Alexander and Galit Hasan-Rokem (1993), pp. 117–34; and Yael Kahana, *Ahim Shehorim: Hayim Bekerev Hafalashim* [*Among Long-Lost Brothers, A Young Israeli Woman Discovers the Falashas*] (Tel Aviv: Am Oved Press, 1977).

22. Susan Starr-Sered observes that elderly women define their postfertility femininity by their ability to preserve the family's spirituality. See Starr-Sered, "Ruhaniyut Nashim Bekontekst Yehudi" ["Women's Spirituality in a Jewish Context"], in Azmon, ed., *Eshnav Lehayehen shel Nashim Behevrot Yehudiyot* [*A View into the Lives of Women in Jewish Societies: Collected Essays*] (Jerusalem: Zalman Shazar Center for Jewish History, 1995), pp. 245–57. Henceforth: Azmon, *Eshnav*.

[6] FEMALE RITUALS, SISTERHOOD, AND FEMALE AUTHORITY

1. The definition of the term "ritual" is a matter of controversy in the anthropological and sociological literature. In the narrow definition, the term is confined to the realm of religious conduct and is

viewed as a formal behavior that is repetitive, stylized, accompanied by recitation or song, sometimes accompanied by specific body movements and sacred objects. All of this activity is directed toward the divinity or some supernatural entity. In the broader definition, the term extends beyond the religious realm and refers also to secular rituals, which draw their power from ideologies and values of earthly origin. In this broader outlook, a ritual is the act of an individual, or individuals, the chief component of which is the symbolic content contained in the action, such as the placing of the wedding ring on the bride's finger. The act of putting on the ring is not an act of gift giving from the groom to the bride, but rather an act symbolizing belonging. See Rubin, p. 13.

2. Babylonian Talmud, Tractate Berachot 24a.

3. See Rubin, pp. 26–31.

4. Like other rituals in Judaism, this rite of passage involves *hasara* (removal); for more on this, see Samuel Cooper, "On the Rules of Mixture: Toward an Anthropology of Halacha," in *Judaism Viewed From Within and From Without: Anthropological Studies,* ed. Harvey E. Goldberg. Albany, NY: State University of New York Press, 1987.

5. See Rubin, pp. 13–14.

6. See Turner.

7. See Patai, p. 32.

8. From a cosmological standpoint, the female lack of stability, manifested in women's continually changing biological cycles, places women in the gray areas of the cosmic system, where they fall outside the defined cultural order and are more closely identified with the world of demons, spirits, and evil entities (See Rubin, pp. 52–61). The fact that women are not a permanent part of the realm of culture, but instead continually enter and leave it, puts them closer to the magical realm, as may be seen in the female rituals in the mikveh.

9. Also described in Rahel Wasserfall, "Poriyut Vekehilah: Tekes Haseret Halavan Vehaseret Hayarok Bemoshav shel Yotzei Maroko" ["Fertility and Community: The White Ribbon and the Green Ribbon Ceremony among Moshav Residents of Moroccan Descent"], in Azmon, ed., *Lehayehen shel Nashim Behevrot Yehudiyot,* pp. 259–71.

10. For more on this ceremony, see ibid.

11. For more on the mother-in-law's role, see ibid. and Rachel Rosen, "Tfisat Hanashiyut Bekerev Yotzot Maroko Bemoshav Be'Yisrael" ["The Perception of Femininity Among Women of Moroccan Descent on a Moshav in Israel"], MA thesis, Hebrew University of Jerusalem, 1981.

12. See Julian Pitt-Rivers, "Women and Sanctuary in the Mediterranean," in *The Fate of Shechem; or, The Politics of Sex: Essays in the Anthropology of the Mediterranean,* ed. Julian Pitt-Rivers (Cambridge: University of Cambridge, 1977), pp. 113–25.

13. Quoted by Zvi Aloush in *Yedioth Ahronoth,* October 24, 2004, p. 24.

14. See Mircea Eliade, "Cosmogonic Myth and 'Sacred History,' " in Mircea Eliade, *The Quest: History and Meaning in Religion* (Chicago: University of Chicago Press, 1969), pp. 72–87. Henceforth: Eliade.

15. Babylonian Talmud, Tractate Nedarim 20b.

16. David Biale, *Eros Vehayehudim* [*Eros and the Jews*] (Tel Aviv: Am Oved Press, 1994). Henceforth: Biale.

17. Even-Shoshan, p. 797.

[7] BETWEEN A WOMAN AND GOD

1. Quoted in Patai, p. 145.

2. See Eliade, pp. 72–87.

3. Ibid.

[8] BETWEEN MAN AND WIFE

1. *Yedioth Ahronoth,* April 25, 2004.

2. Elior, pp. 218–19.

3. Yael Azmon, "Hayahadut Vehahadara shel Nashim min Hazira Hatziburit" ["Introduction: Judaism and the Distancing of Women from Public Activity"], in Azmon, *Eshnav,* pp. 13–43. Henceforth: Azmon, "Hayahadut."

4. Elior, p. 225.

5. Daniel Boyarin, *Carnal Israel: Reading Sex in Talmudic Culture* (Berkeley: University of California Press, 1993).

6. Descriptions of men being tempted with sexual fantasies by beautiful female demons who use the men's sperm to conceive and give birth to demons appear in Jewish literature throughout the generations. For the story of a demon named Na'ama, who is compared to Lilith, see Abarbanell, pp. 27–29. For examples of medieval Hebrew stories about marriages between beautiful demons and human beings, see Eli Yassif and Haim Pesah, eds., *Ha'abir Hashed Vehabetula: Mivhar Sipurim 'Ivriyim Miyemei Habeinayim* [*The Knight, the Demon, and the Virgin: An Anthology of Hebrew Stories from the Middle Ages*] (Jerusalem: Keter Publishing House, 1998), pp. 25–27, 155–73. For a discussion of the features of the genre, see Tamar Alexander, "Ha'itzuv Hajanari shel Sipurei Shedim: Nisu'im bein Gever Lesheda" ["Design

of the Demon Story Genre: Marriages between a Man and a Demon"],
in Azmon, *Eshnav*, pp. 291–307.

7. Yael Azmon points out that uninhibited sexual behavior attributed to a woman has negative ramifications in human history. The expulsion from the Garden of Eden is understood to be a consequence of women's unbridled sexual behavior. The lesson of the story of the expulsion from the Garden of Eden is that women should never again be allowed to influence human history. See Azmon, "Hayahadut."

8. Avraham Grossman discusses the subject of women's modesty in medieval Europe and the question of whether greater stringency in the chivalric code regarding women's modesty stems from women's wanton nature or from men's unrestrained lust. See Grossman, *Hasidot Umordot: Nashim Yehudiyot Be'eropa Biyemei Habeinayim* [*Pious and Rebellious: Jewish Women in Europe in the Middle Ages*] (Jerusalem: Zalman Shazar Center for Jewish History, 2001), p. 187. Henceforth: Grossman; David Biale provides an extensive discussion of male impulsivity, noting that all that is known about women's sexuality is reflected through the male point of view. In the Talmudic writings, we have an exclusively male perspective, which is inherently different from the female perspective. Women's voices in Judaism were not preserved. See Biale, pp. 7–20, 65–68.

9. On the centrality of the text in consolidating Jewish identity and the prohibition against women studying Torah, a prohibition that stands as a powerful example of the exclusion of women from activities related to the core of Jewish identity, see Azmon, "Hayahadut," pp. 24–25.

10. Carol Gilligan, *In a Different Voice: Psychological Theory and Women's Development* (Cambridge, MA: Harvard University Press, 1982).

11. Ibid.

12. See Abarbanell, pp. 23–53.

13. Nahum Lamm, *Suga Bashoshanim*, part 1 (Jerusalem: National Center for Family Purity in Israel, 1998), p. 246.

14. On male appropriation of the commandment to be fruitful and multiply, see Eran. See also Maya Leibovich, "Pri Urvi Umil'i et Haaretz," in *Baruch She'asani Isha?* eds. David Ariel-Joel, Maya Leibovich, and Yoram Mazor (Tel Aviv: Yedioth Ahronoth Press, 1999), pp. 129–37.

15. See Grossman, pp. 185–215.

16. Grossman speculates that the revolt, which lasted a number of years and involved many women, must have had women leaders, but

their names have not been preserved. Women's ability to organize such a large-scale revolt indicates, in Grossman's view, that the women were not confined to their homes and that they were in close contact outside the home. He notes that the usual meeting places for women were apparently the synagogues, the mikvehs (prior to the revolt), and perhaps also the public baths (*hamam*). Grossman also asserts that only those with high self-regard and a firmly established social position could withstand for years the considerable pressure exerted by Maimonides and his peers. Grossman, p. 214.

17. "The high rate of divorce frightened the Sages, led by Rabbi Meir of Rothenburg (the Maharam), the premier Ashkenazi Sage of the time, and they sought to quell the phenomenon in unconventional ways, by waging war on women's power. The terms used at the time by the Askhenazi Sages to describe the women ('arrogant,' 'wanton,' and so on) are indicative of women's power and of the big gap between the reality and the submissive image ascribed to them." Grossman, pp. 215, 443–50.

18. See Grossman, pp. 215–16.

Hebrew Bibliography

Abarbanell, Nitza. *Hava VeLilit [Eve and Lilith]*. (Ramat Gan: Bar-Ilan University Press, 1994).

Abramov, Tehila. *Sod Hanashiyut Hayehudit: Hebetim 'al Taharat Hamishpaha [The Secret of Jewish Femininity]*. (Jerusalem: Feldheim Publishers, 1990).

Alexander, Tamar. "Ha'itzuv Hajanari shel Sipurei Shedim: Nisu'im bein Gever Lesheda" ["Design of the Demon Story Genre: Marriages between a Man and a Demon"]. In Azmon, ed., *Eshnav Lehayehen shel Nashim Behevrot Yehudiyot*, pp. 291–307.

Azmon, Yael. "Hayahadut Vehahadara shel Nashim min Hazira Hatziborit" ["Introduction: Judaism and the Distancing of Women from Public Activity"]. In Azmon, ed., *Eshnav Lehayehen shel Nashim Behevrot Yehudiyot*, pp. 9–43.

Azmon, Yael, ed. *Eshnav Lehayehen shel Nashim Behevrot Yehudiyot [A View into the Lives of Women in Jewish Societies: Collected Essays]*. (Jerusalem: Zalman Shazar Center for Jewish History, 1995).

Bar'am-Ben Yossef, Noam. *Bo'i Kala: Minhagei Erusin Vehatuna shel Yehudei Kurdistan [Brides and Betrothals: Jewish Wedding Rituals in Afghanistan]*. (Jerusalem: Israel Museum Press, 1997).

Ben-Amara, Rahamim. *Sefer Hadrakha Lamishpaha Hayehudit Begashmiyut Uberuhaniyut [Guidebook for the Jewish Family in Material and Spiritual Matters]*. (Jerusalem: Torah Vehesed Press, 1996).

Bereshit Raba [Midrash Raba on the Book of Genesis]. Theodore-Albeck, Ed. (Jerusalem: Wahrman Books, 1965).

Biale, David. *Eros Vehayehudim [Eros and the Jews]*. (Tel Aviv: Am Oved Press, 1994).

Eliahu, Mordechai. *Darkhei Tahara [Paths of Purity]*. (Jerusalem: Sukkat David Press, 1986).

Elior, Rachel. "Nokhehot Nifkadot," "Teva Domem," and "Alma Yafa She'en La Enayim" ["Present but Absent," "Still Life," and "A Pretty Maiden Who Has No Eyes"]. *Alpayim* 20 (2000), pp. 214–70.

Eran, Amira. "Hatzela Hashniya: Hatfisa Hara'ayonit shel Ha'isha Behagut Yemei Habeinayim." ["The Second Rib: The Perception of Women in Medieval Thought"]. In *Hatzela Hashlishit: Hayahas el Ha'isha Bamishna, Behagut Yemei Habeinayim Ubeshirat Nashim Bat Zmanenu [The Third Rib: The Attitude Toward*

Women in the Mishna, in Medieval Thought and in Contemporary Women's Poetry]. Amira Eran, Einat Ramon, and Tlalit Shavit, eds. (Tel Aviv: Mofet Institute, 2001), pp. 29–87.

Even-Shoshan, Avraham. *Milon Hadash: Menukad Umetzuyar* [*New Dictionary of the Hebrew Language: Annotated and Illustrated*]. (Jerusalem: Kiryat Sefer Press, 1947).

Geertz, Clifford. *Parshanut shel Tarbuyot* [*The Interpretation of Cultures*]. (Jerusalem: Keter Publishing House, 1990).

Gov, Anat. *Lysistrata 2000: Komedia Yevanit 'al pi Aristophanes* [*Lysistrata 2000 (After Aristophanes)*]. (Tel Aviv: Hakibbutz Hameuchad Press, 2001).

Grossman, Avraham. *Hasidot Umordot: Nashim Yehudiyot Be'eropa Biyemei Habeinayim* [*Pious and Rebellious: Jewish Women in Europe in the Middle Ages*]. (Jerusalem: Zalman Shazar Center for Jewish History, 2001).

Hasan-Rokem, Galit. "Hakol Kol Ahoti: Dmuyot Nashim Usmalim Nashiyim Bemidrash Eicha Raba" ["The Voice Is the Voice of My Sister: Feminine Images and Feminine Symbols in Lamentations Rabba"]. In Azmon, ed., *Eshnav Lehayehen shel Nashim Behevrot Yehudiyot*, pp. 95–111.

Jason, Heda. "Ha'askola Haformalistit Bemehkar Hasifrut Ha'amamit" ["The Formalist School in the Study of Popular Literature"], *Hasifrut: Quarterly for the Study of Hebrew Literature*, edited by Benjamin Hrushovski (Tel Aviv) 9 (1970), pp. 53–83.

Jerusalem Talmud, Tractate Sota. (Bnei Brak: 1994).

Kahana, Yael. *Ahim Shehorim: Hayim Bekerev Hafalashim* [*Among Long-Lost Brothers, A Young Israeli Woman Discovers the Falashas*]. (Tel Aviv: Am Oved Press, 1977).

Kaplan, Aryeh. *Memei Gan Eden: Hamistorin shel Hamikveh* [*Waters of Eden: The Mystery of the Mikveh*]. (Jerusalem: National Center for Family Purity in Israel, 1983).

Kehati, Pinhas, ed. *Mishnayot Mevoarot*. Vol. 2, *Seder Taharot* [*Kehati Commentary on the Mishna*]. (Jerusalem: Mishnayot Kehati Press, 1996).

Lamm, Nahum. *Suga Bashoshanim*. Part 1. (Jerusalem: National Center for Family Purity in Israel, 1998). (English translation published 1966; see English bibliography.)

Leibovich, Maya. "Pri Urvi Umil'i et Haaretz" ["Be Fruitful and Multiply and Fill the Land"]. In *Baruch She'asani Isha?* David Ariel-Joel, Maya Leibovich, and Yoram Mazor, eds. (Tel Aviv: Yedioth Ahronoth Press, 1999), pp. 129–37.

Mishna: Seder Taharot. (Jerusalem: Horev Press, 1994).

Nahmias, Benny. *Hamsa: Kemi'ot, Emunot, Minhagim Urefuah 'Amamit Ba'ir Ha'atika Yerushalayim* [*Hamsa: Amulets, Beliefs, Customs and Folk Medicine in the Old City of Jerusalem*]. (Tel Aviv: Modan Press, 1996) pp. 245–57.

Patai, Raphael. *Hamayim: Mehkar Liyedi'at Haaaretz Ulefolklor Eretzyisraeli Bitkufot Hamikra Vehamishna* [*The Water: A Study in Palestinology and Palestinian Folklore in the Biblical and Mishnaic Periods*]. (Tel Aviv: Dvir Press, 1936).

Rosen, Rachel, "Tfisat Hanashiyut Bekerev Yotzot Maroko Bemoshav Be'Yisrael" ["The Perception of Femininity among Women of Moroccan Descent on a Moshav in Israel"], MA thesis, Hebrew University of Jerusalem, 1981.

Rubin, Nissan. *Reshit Hehayim: Tiksei Leda, Mila Upidyon Haben Bimkorot Hazal* [*The Beginning of Life: Rites of Birth, Circumcision, and Redemption of the First-born in the Talmud and Midrash*]. (Tel Aviv: Hakibbutz Hameuchad Press, 1995).

Salamon, Hagar. "Dam Etzel Beita-Yisrael Ushekhenehem Hanotzrim Be'Ithiyopiya" ["Blood between the Beta Israel and Their Christian Neighbors in Ethiopia: Key Symbols in an Inter-Group Context"]. *Mehkarei Yerushalayim Befolklor Yehudi* [*Jerusalem Studies in Jewish Folklore*] 15. Tamar Alexander and Galit Hasan-Rokem, eds. (1993), pp. 117–34.

Starr-Sered, Susan. "Ruhaniyut Nashim Bekontekst Yehudi" ["Women's Spirituality in a Jewish Context"]. In Azmon, ed., *Eshnav Lehayehen shel Nashim Behevrot Yehudiyot*, pp. 245–57.

Talmage, Ephraim. *Sefer Habrit: Vikuhei Radak 'im Hanatzrut* [*The Book of the Covenant and Other Writings*]. (Jerusalem: Bialik Institute Press, 1974).

Wasserfall, Rahel. "Poriyut Vekehilah: Tekes Haseret Halavan Vehaseret Hayarok Bemoshav shel Yotzei Maroko" ["Fertility and Community: The White Ribbon and the Green Ribbon Ceremony among Moshav Residents of Moroccan Descent"]. In Azmon, ed., *Eshnav Lehayehen shel Nashim Behevrot Yehudiyot*, pp. 259–71.

Weinroth, Avi. *Feminism Veyahadut* [*Feminism and Judaism*]. (Tel Aviv: Yedioth Ahronoth Press, 2001).

Weinstein, Sheindel, ed. *Ish Ve'isha Shezakhu: Hayei Hamishpaha Hayehudit Mehebet Refu'i Upsikhologi* [*Man and Wife That Merited: Jewish Family Life from a Medical and Psychological Perspective*]. (Jerusalem: National Center for Family Purity in Israel, 1988).

Yassif, Eli, and Haim Pesah, eds. *Ha'abir Hashed Vehabetula: Mivhar Sipurim 'Ivriyim Miyemei Habeinayim* [*The Knight, the Demon, and the Virgin: An Anthology of Hebrew Stories from the Middle Ages*]. (Jerusalem: Keter Publishing House, 1998).

English Bibliography

Boyarin, Daniel. *Carnal Israel: Reading Sex in Talmudic Culture.*
Berkeley: University of California Press, 1993.

Buckley, Thomas, and Alma Gottlieb, eds. *Blood Magic: The Anthropology of Menstruation.* Berkeley: University of California Press,
1988.

Cooper, Samuel. "On the Rules of Mixture: Toward an Anthropology
of Halacha." In Harvey E. Goldberg, ed., *Judaism Viewed From
Within and From Without: Anthropological Studies.* Albany: State
University of New York Press, 1987, pp. 55–74.

Eilberg-Schwartz, Howard. *The Savage in Judaism: An Anthropology
of Israelite Religion and Ancient Judaism.* Bloomington: Indiana
University Press, 1990.

Eliade, Mircea. "Cosmogonic Myth and 'Sacred History.'" In Mircea
Eliade, *The Quest: History and Meaning in Religion.* Chicago:
University of Chicago Press, 1969, pp. 72–87.

Gennep, Arnold van. *The Rites of Passage.* Translated by Monika B.
Vizedom and Gabrielle L. Caffee. Chicago: University of Chicago
Press, 1961.

Giddens, Anthony. *Modernity and Self-Identity: Self and Society in
the Late Modern Age.* Stanford, CA: Stanford University Press,
1991.

Gilligan, Carol. *In a Different Voice: Psychological Theory and
Women's Development.* Cambridge, MA: Harvard University
Press, 1982.

Grossman, Avraham. *Pious and Rebellious: Jewish Women in
Europe in the Middle Ages.* Hanover, NH: University Press of
New England, 2003.

Lamm, Norman (Nahum). *A Hedge of Roses: Jewish Insights into
Marriage and Married Life.* New York: P. Feldheim, 1966.

Lévi-Strauss, Claude. *The Origin of Table Manners.* Translated by
John and Doreen Weightman. New York: Harper & Row, 1978.

Lévi-Strauss, Claude. *The Raw and the Cooked.* Translated by John
and Doreen Weightman. New York: Harper & Row, 1969.

Neumann, Erich. *The Great Mother: An Analysis of the Archetype.*
Translated by Ralph Manheim. 2nd ed. New York: Bollingen
Foundation, 1963.

Ochs, Carol. "Nomad and Settler in Patriarchal Religion." *Feminist
Studies* 3, nos. 3–4 (1976), pp. 56–61.

Pitt-Rivers, Julian. "Women and Sanctuary in the Mediterranean."
    In Pitt-Rivers, ed., *The Fate of Shechem; or, The Politics of Sex:
    Essays in the Anthropology of the Mediterranean.* Cambridge,
    England: Cambridge University Press, 1977, pp. 113–25.
Salamon, Hagar. *The Hyena People: Ethiopian Jews in Christian
    Ethiopia.* Berkeley: University of California Press, 1999.
Starr-Sered, Susan. "Ritual, Morality and Gender: The Religious
    Lives of Oriental Jewish Women in Jerusalem." *Israel Social Sci-
    ence Research* 5, (1987), pp. 87–96.
Turner, Victor W. *The Forest of Symbols: Aspects of Ndembu Ritual.*
    Ithaca, NY: Cornell University Press, 1967.
Van Gennep, Arnold. *The Rites of Passage.* Chicago: University of
    Chicago Press, 1961.
Wasserfall, Rahel R., ed. *Women and Water: Menstruation in Jewish
    Life and Law.* Hanover, NH: University Press of New England,
    1999.

Index

husbands' rejection or discomfort with niddah, 100–101, 105, 108–9, 203; permissiveness of sexual relations of, 77, 78, 201–2
secular Jewish women: and abstaining from sex during menstruation, 112; and gender/sex differences, 191–92; as impure and defiling, xxiii–xxiv, 35–41, 43; independence of, 110–11; and "kosher" pregnancy, 114–17; negative attitudes of, toward mikveh, 179–80; and physical grooming, 109–10; reasons of, for immersion in mikveh, 4–6, 11–17, 92–124, 183; relationships between God and, 181–83; and search for spiritual and emotional satisfaction, 55–56
secular sex education, 78–80
semen/sperm, 61, 74, 75, 78, 85, 86, 101, 114, 194
Sephardim: attitude of, toward Ashkenazi women, xxii, 10; attitude of, toward immersion, 130, 131; definition of, 130*n*; and immersion of unmarried women, 137; men's prayer for success in sexual intercourse, 81; negative attitudes of women toward mikveh, xxii
sex education, 78–80. *See also* bride instruction
sex roles. *See* gender/sex roles
sexual intercourse in marriage: "drinking from a glass" as Talmudic term for, 166; God as partner of, 175; halakha on first act of sexual intercourse, 76–89; man's obligation of conjugal duty, 130, 204; after mikveh, 4, 12–17, 111–12, 135, 202, 204; and mitzvah to be fruitful and multiply, 19, 38, 41, 91, 92, 112–13, 150, 194–95, 203–6; pregnancy as goal of, 194–95; and preservation of sexual attraction, 199–200; and prohibition against wasted seed, 61–62, 78, 114, 194; prohibition of, during niddah, 37, 40, 61–62, 68–71, 119–20, 184; prohibition of, on Yom Kippur and Ninth of Av, 1; prohibitions pertaining to men on, 87–88, 130, 166, 204–5; and spiritual bond, 121–22; and weariness of women, 130–31; and wife's honor, 201–3; woman's focus during, 194–95; and women's power,

204–7; women's satisfaction in, 87, 92, 92*n*, 194. *See also* sexuality
sexuality: connection between food and, 129, 164–66, 170–71; connections between fertility, femininity and, 72–76, 91, 92, 110, 114, 117; as distinct from fertility, 109, 117; of Lilith, 198–99; male sexuality, 81–83, 191–92, 194–96, 200, 202, 206. *See also* sexual intercourse in marriage
sexual organs. *See beit hastarim* (house of secrets, women's private parts); uterus; vagina
sexual problems, 200–201
Shabbat, 70, 70*n*, 98, 103, 111, 111*n*, 176, 182
Shabbat candles, 103, 111, 167, 182
shakshouka, 162, 162*n*
Shalev, Meir, 101–2
shalom bayit (domestic tranquility), 68, 101, 121, 205
Shavuot, 138, 138*n*
Shekhina (Divine Presence), 166, 210
Shema Yisrael (Hear O Israel), 47, 47*n*, 176, 176*n*
sheretz, 137
shidduch (arranged match), 76
shiksa (non-Jewish woman), 51, 51*n*
shiva (seven-day mourning period), 188–91, 188*n*, 219–20
Shlomit, 73, 188–90
Shuli, 100, 105, 108, 111, 175–77, 188–92, 203
siddur (Jewish prayerbook), 119, 119*n*
Sima, 96, 97, 101–5, 109
simchat bat (celebration for girl's birth), 164–65, 164*n*
siyagim (boundaries), 63
Solika, 213
Solomon, King, 198
Song of Songs, 113
Sophie, Aunt, 162–65, 169
sperm. *See* semen/sperm
Stephens, William, 67
Suga Bashoshanim (A Hedge of Roses) (Lamm), 199
suga bashoshanim (hedge of roses), 68
Sugihara, Chiune, 212–13
Sugihara, Yukiko, 212–13
Sukkot, 115, 115*n*